Christian Spirituality and Ethical Life

Christian Spirituality and Ethical Life
Calvin's View on the Spirit in Ecumenical Context

PAUL S. CHUNG

With a foreword by Veli-Matti Kärkkäinen

⁌PICKWICK *Publications* · Eugene, Oregon

CHRISTIAN SPIRITUALITY AND ETHICAL LIFE
Calvin's View on the Spirit in Ecumenical Context

Copyright © 2010 Paul S. Chung. All rights reserved. Except for brief quotations in critical publications or reviews, no part of this book may be reproduced in any manner without prior written permission from the publisher. Write: Permissions, Wipf and Stock Publishers, 199 W. 8th Ave., Suite 3, Eugene, OR 97401.

Pickwick Publications
An Imprint of Wipf and Stock Publishers
199 W. 8th Ave., Suite 3
Eugene, OR 97401

www.wipfandstock.com

ISBN 13: 978-1-55635-790-9

Cataloging-in-Publication data:

Chung, Paul S., 1958–

Christian spirituality and ethical life : Calvin's view on the spirit in ecumenical context / Paul S. Chung ; with a foreword by Veli-Matti Kärkkäinen.

xiv + 164 p. ; 23 cm.

ISBN 13: 978-1-55635-790-9

1. Calvin, Jean, 1509–1564. 2. Holy Spirit. 3. Christian ethics—Reformed authors. I. Kärkkäinen, Veli-Matti. II. Title.

BT121.2 .C471 2010

Manufactured in the U.S.A.

Contents

Foreword by Veli-Matti Kärkkäinen • *vii*

Acknowledgments • *xi*

Abbreviations • *xiii*

Introduction: Calvin's Theology of the Spirit in the Context of Christian Life • 1

1 The Spirit in Cosmic Dimension • 15

2 The Spirit in the Trinity • 32

3 The Spirit as Communicator of Christ for the Christian Life • 46

4 The Spirit and the Law • 81

5 The Spirit and the Church • 109

Excursus: Christian Politics in Confession and Resistance • 127

Conclusion • 135

Afterword: The Ecumenical Legacy of John Calvin in Reformed and Neo-Pentecostal Dialogue • 148

Index • 161

Foreword

QUITE SURPRISINGLY, AT THE beginning of the third millennium, we find ourselves living in the midst of a renaissance of the Holy Spirit. Pneumatology, the doctrine and spirituality of the third person of the Trinity, has risen to the center of theological reflection at the international and ecumenical level. Books, studies, monographs, conferences, and events dealing with various aspects of the doctrine of the Spirit abound, that not only at the academic level, but first and foremost in the pews and marketplaces where spirituality, the work of the Spirit, is lived out at the grassroots level.

The current discourse on the Spirit, while building creatively and critically on the biblical and historical foundations of the Christian tradition, is not content to repeat or even rephrase what the church has believed during the first two millennia. New questions, new challenges, new proposals are arising: What is the relationship between the works of Spirit in the church and in the world, in creation, the economy, arts, human relationships, and so on? How does the Spirit help Christians to flesh out and embody spirituality that is relevant to all aspects of life, not only to sanctification and the Christian walk? How do we discern the Spirit from and in relation to (other) spirits?

In order for theological reflection on the Spirit to respond to these and related challenges, two foundational perspectives have to be acknowledged. First, pneumatological discourse can only be meaningful insofar as it takes into account the diverse and rich variety of approaches to the experience of the Spirit ecumenically. No church can claim a monopoly on the Spirit, and no tradition is a specifically "spirited" one. In other words, only by carefully listening to and learning from the various, often even conflicting testimonies concerning the Spirit, can we proceed in pneumatological discourse. Second, talk about the Spirit must always be contextual and, therefore, culture-specific. The Spirit of God is no general

Foreword

spirit hovering above the cosmos but a person of the triune God who indwells believers and creation in specific and tangible ways.

The author of the present work, Dr. Paul Chung of Korea, in a recent article on pneumatology, clearly brought to light this changed situation in theology:

Feeling uncomfortable with the traditional relationship between divine revelation and the human experience of the Holy Spirit, a number of scholars are now seeking to construct a new paradigm in pneumatology. The attempt generally stands as a challenge to neo-orthodox theology, especially with respect to the theological Christocentrism of Karl Barth. The theological necessity for a new pneumatology is reflective of the current ecumenical climate arising from dialogues between the mainstream Protestant and Catholic traditions, the Orthodox churches, and the Pentecostal (Charismatic) movement.[1]

Chung went on to note that this new ecumenical and social context in which we find ourselves has "brought to the discussion a universal affirmation of pneumatology from a trinitarian perspective," through which we seek "a new paradigm by focusing on the human experience of the Holy Spirit. In this new outlook, spirituality in a personal sense is connected with and extended to the social experience of God within the context of a trinitarian pneumatology."[2]

Paul Chung presents us with a powerful and engaging proposal to that effect, delving into the theology of the Holy Spirit of one of the most significant shapers of Christian theology, namely Jean Calvin of Geneva. The choice of the theologian may be quite unexpected for many. While no student of the father of the Reformed tradition would be ready to dismiss his interest in the Spirit, very few would go as far as B. B. Warfield, who claimed Calvin to be "the theologian of the Holy Spirit." In popular estimation, Calvin is depicted as the theologian of the First Article rather than the Third.

Chung's meticulous and detailed inquiry into the pneumatology of Calvin—originally written as a post-doctoral advanced dissertation in connection with scholars at the University of Basel, Switzerland (such as Prof. Dr. Martin A. Schmidt) and at the Graduate Theological Union (such as Prof. Dr. Timothy Lull and Prof. William Bouwsma), Berkeley,

1. Paul Chung, "Calvin and the Holy Spirit: A Reconsideration in Light of Spirituality and Social Ethics," *Pneuma* 24 (2002) 40.

2. Ibid.

Foreword

California, and now finally revised again—brings to light an exciting, largely unknown facet of the Reformed theologian, namely a holistic, socially-oriented doctrine of the Spirit and spirituality. Chung's study is a masterful blend of historical Reformation studies, dialogue with the most recent systematic theologies, especially views of Barth and Moltmann, systematic analysis, and creative constructive proposals.

The author argues convincingly that not only is Calvin a first-rate theologian of the Holy Spirit, but furthermore, that his theology of the third person of the Trinity is strongly oriented to social, even political aspects of life. The integral relationship between the Spirit, spirituality, and social ethics in Calvin's thought is set in proper perspective in this book. As such, the book is also a major study in the relationship between pneumatology and ethics, an area rarely studied outside the Catholic circles but growing rapidly in ecumenical scholarship, for example, in the work of the World Council of Churches.

According to Chung, the primary locus of the Spirit for Calvin was the cosmic and universal dimension, the Spirit as the agent and continuing force in creation. Out of this cosmic orientation arises Calvin's ecological concern, a major motif in the most recent theologies of the Holy Spirit as represented by Moltmann, Pannenberg, "Green theologians," eco-Feminists, and many others. Here Calvin's theology of the Spirit and spirituality also links to social concern, justice, and peace, since taking care of both nature and society are included with the noble task given to men and women: participating in God's gracious and loving administration of the cosmos, to God's glory and honor. Anticipating much of what current pneumatology stresses, namely, the integral relationship of the work of the Spirit in creation, human life, the individual Christian, the church, and finally the eschaton—it is the same Spirit of God who gives birth both to life in general and new life in Christ—Calvin's spirituality aimed at a holistic vision. This vision, unfortunately, was lost too often in Protestant theology in general and pneumatology in particular, until it began to be recovered towards the end of the second millennium.

Apart from the main thesis, the book is filled with exciting, engaging, and alert contributions and observations. In a detailed analysis, Dr. Chung examines critically the much-discussed problem of Calvin's view of government and politics and its relation to the church. Furthermore, the author also dares to revisit such main themes of Calvin studies as the doctrine of election.

Foreword

In addition to presenting fresh, sometimes challenging interpretations of major issues in Calvin studies, the book also offers an ecumenical feast for all interested parties. Lutheran readers will find an intriguing analysis of the similarities—rather than differences, so often presented—between their own and Calvinist traditions with regard to the doctrine of salvation and the Eucharist, among other topics. Eastern Orthodox students will be fascinated by Chung's creative correlation between Calvin's pneumatological doctrine of salvation that focuses on the idea of union and the ancient doctrine of *theosis*. This also echoes several motifs that the New Perspective on Luther studies, especially in Scandinavia, has brought to light in their insistence on the idea of deification and union being one of the key themes of Luther's own doctrine of salvation. Catholic readers will be helped by a detailed study of several themes in Reformation/Counter-Reformation theology. Pentecostal-Charismatic readers will find an interesting appendix in the book, namely, an assessment of the recent ecumenical report from the International Dialogue between the World Alliance of Reformed Churches and Pentecostals. In that dialogue, which began in 1996 and still continues, pneumatology has been the focus: the role of the Spirit has been studied in relation to creation, church, and individual Christian life.

Dr. Chung brings to the study of theology in general and Calvin's pneumatology in particular a unique set of qualities. As an Asian theologian, he was trained in the Mecca of Reformed studies, the University of Basel. Not only did he study Reformed theology widely, but he has also distinguished himself as an interpreter of Lutheran studies, and we wait eagerly the release of his monograph on the relevance of Luther's theology to the Asian context. Having finished his doctorate in Europe and making post-doctoral research in Berkeley, he began to teach at one of the leading American consortiums of theological studies in Berkeley, California. His current placement at Luther Seminary, St. Paul, MN—a seminary known for global mission and interfaith interests—as well as his continuing travelling to Asia and elsewhere gives Dr. Chung a unique opportunity to continue promising and exciting scholarship.

Veli-Matti Kärkkäinen
Professor of Systematic Theology, Fuller Theological Seminary,
Pasadena, CA
Docent of Ecumenics, University of Helsinki, Finland

Acknowledgments

THIS POST-DOCTORAL DISSERTATION WAS written (comparable to a *Habilitationsschrift*) under personal consultation with Professor Martin Anton Schmidt at the University of Basel, Switzerland. I give special thanks to American scholars, Professor William J. Bouwsma at the University of California in Berkeley and President and Professor Timothy Lull of the Graduate Theological Union and Pacific Lutheran Theological Seminary, Berkeley, CA. Since graduating from the *Theologische Fakultät* of the University of Basel with a doctoral dissertation on *Karl Barth und Die Hegelsche Linke* (Peter Lang, 1992), I have been interested in the theology of Martin Luther and John Calvin in regard to their reception in the East Asian context. This concern led me to do academic research on Reformation theology at the University of California, Berkeley and the Graduate Theological Union from 1992 to 1995.

I also thank Professor Martin A. Schmitt, to whom this book is much indebted. His *Gutachten* is a great academic honor for my Calvin study. Professor Lukas Vischer gave me useful academic insights into Calvin's theology of the Spirit. For the revised edition, I would like to thank University Press of America for the reversion of rights and Wipf and Stock for reprinting the revised edition. Beth Chung should also be mentioned with gratitude for her editorial work on the revised edition. In this revised edition, my attention is given to a study of Calvin in a wider ecumenical spectrum. Finally, I am grateful to my family and soul friends in the religious community whose affection and care helped me to realize that there is more to life than becoming a well-known scholar.

I appreciate the following for permission in using selected texts: Calvin, *Institutes of the Christian Religion* (Library of Christian Classics), edited by John T. McNeil. Used by permission of Westminster John Knox and T. & T. Clark. *The Commentaries of John Calvin*, 46 vols. Calvin Translation Society, 1843–55. Reprint, 22 vols. Used by permission of Baker Book House. Wilhelm Niesel, *The Theology of Calvin*. Used by per-

Acknowledgments

mission of Baker Book House. Paul Chung, "Korean Reformed Response to The Final Report, 'Word and Spirit, Church and World—The Final Report of the International Dialogue Between Representatives of the World Alliance of Reformed Churches and some Classical Pentecostal Churches and Leaders—1996–2000,'" *Pneuma* 23 (2001) 54–60. Used by permission of *Pneuma: The Journal of the Society for Pentecostal Studies*.

Abbreviations

BC   *The Book of Concord: The Confessions of the Evangelical Lutheran Church*. Translated and edited by Robert Kolb and Timothy J. Wengert. Minneapolis: Fortress, 2000.

CD   Karl Barth, *Church Dogmatics*. 13 vols. Edited by G. W. Bromiley and T. F. Torrance. London: T. & T. Clark, 1936–61.

CR   *Iohannis Calvini Opera quae supersunt omnia (Opera)*. 59 vols. Corpus Reformatorium (CR). Edited by W. Baum, E. Cunitz, and E. Ruetz. Brunswick: C. A. Schewtschke, 1863–1900.

OS   *Iohannis Calvini Opera Selecta*. 5 vols. Edited by P. Barth and W. Niesel. Munich: Kaiser, 1926–1962.

Comm.   *The Commentaries of John Calvin*. 46 vols. Calvin Translation Society, 1843–1855. Reprint, 22 vols. Grand Rapids: Baker, 1979.

LW   *Luther's Works*. American edition. Vols. 1–30. Edited by Jaroslav Pelikan. St. Louis: Concordia, 1955–1967. Vols. 31–55. Edited by Helmut T Lehman. Philadelphia: Fortress, 1967–1976.

WA   *D. Martin Luthers Werke. Kritische Gesamtausgabe*. 61 vols. Weimar: Hermann Böhlhaus Nachfolger, 1883–1983.

Introduction

Calvin's Theology of the Spirit in the Context of Christian Life

In the study of the theology of the third article of the Creed—the Holy Spirit—there is a tendency among scholars to feel uncomfortable with the traditional relationship between divine revelation and the human experience of the Holy Spirit. To overcome the dichotomy of the Spirit and human experience, a number of scholars are now seeking to construct a new paradigm in the study of the Holy Spirit.[1] These attempts as a rule stand as challenges to neo-orthodox theology, especially with respect to the Christocentrism of Karl Barth.

The theological necessity for a new pneumatology is reflective of the current ecumenical climate arising from the encounter of and the dialogue between the mainstream Protestant and Catholic traditions, the Orthodox church and the Pentecostal (Charismatic) movement. For instance, if the Orthodox church becomes an ecumenical partner with the Western mainstream churches, the question of the fallacy of the Nicene Creed of 381 and the consequence for trinitarian theology need to be carefully dealt with. Moreover, the substantial growth of the Pentecostal church and its understanding of the Holy Spirit stand as another serious challenge to all mainstream churches.

Aware of this ecumenical task, Jürgen Moltmann has brought to the discussion a universal affirmation of pneumatology from a trinitarian perspective, through which he deals with the human experience of the Holy Spirit in seeking a new paradigm. Here spirituality in a personal sense is connected to the social experience of God within the context of a trinitarian pneumatology.

---

1. For a discussion of the parameters of the debate, see Jürgen Moltmann, *The Spirit of Life: A Universal Affirmation*, trans. Margaret Kohl (Minneapolis: Fortress, 1992) 1–14.

First of all, Moltmann's concern in projecting a trinitarian formulation of pneumatology is related critically to the "relationship between the Trinity and the kingdom of God, *trinitas* and *monarchia*." He is aware of the danger, unresolved since the councils of the early church, of a monarchial, subordinationist pneumatology.[2] Therefore, he makes a concerted effort to overcome such a monarchial pneumatology in favor of a social trinitarian formulation. Emphasizing the independence of the Holy Spirit as a distinct person in relation to the Father and the Son, he brings to the fore "the direct working of the Holy Spirit, the inspiration, feelings, visions and dreams of the Spirit."[3] As long as the unity of the triune God is secured, the unique fellowship, or communion of the triune God, is stressed and developed rather than the one homogeneous substance.

Moltmann focuses on how to overcome the false alternative between revelation and the human experience of God. If the Spirit is experienced by the human being, human experience becomes the foundation of theology, where the qualitative difference between God and human beings would disappear. However, if the Spirit is not experienced by human beings, the foundation of theology becomes God's revelation of Godself, in which the qualitative difference between God and human beings prevents human beings from having any immediate relation to God.

According to Moltmann, representatives of Reformed pneumatology, such as Hendrikus Berkhof and Alasdairi Heron, find it difficult to solve this dilemma, which Moltmann sees as the main problem in the study of the Holy Spirit today. In his view, God's revelation does not contrast with the human experience of God. Even though Barth saved the continuity of the Spirit with the human spirit (in his 1929 lecture "The Holy Spirit and Christian Life"), Moltmann argues that Barth's eschatology was still not directed toward the future of the new creation of all things.

Be that as it may, eschatology, which means the doctrine of the last things, plays a significant role in Barth's theology of the Spirit. The time between the era of the Christian church and the parousia of Christ is filled with the power of the Holy Spirit inspiring the church in expectation and hope of God's promise and future, which is fully revealed in Christ. This promise denotes the redemption or consummation of the world which retains significance for humanity as well as for the whole universe. The

---

2. Jürgen Moltmann, *History and the Triune God: Contributions to Trinitarian Theology*, trans. John Bowden (New York: Crossroads, 1992) 57–58.

3. Ibid., 58.

INTRODUCTION: *Calvin's Theology of the Spirit*

work of the Spirit between "already" and "not-yet" leads the church toward God's future as well as brings the unbelievers to life and faith. God had elected humanity in Christ from eternity and in time is reconciled to the world, so that the unbeliever is positively appreciated in light of divine grace and in the promise of the Spirit (CD IV/3.2 §73).

Moltmann's approach to eschatology, within a pneumatological-trinitarian framework, encompasses the historical experience of the Spirit. In Moltmann's view, juxtaposing revelation and experience leads to revelation without experience, or experience without revelation.[4] Thus, in relation to the understanding of the Spirit, spirituality is taken to mean a "living relationship with God's Spirit."[5] Moltmann attacks the separation of body and soul, prevalent in Western Christian thought since Augustine. Augustine downplayed the body and nature in favor of an inward, direct experience with God. Augustine's concentration on "God and the soul" resulted, according to Moltmann, in a despising of the experience of society and nature.[6] But from a pneumatological perspective, Moltmann's concern becomes clear: to relate spirituality to vitality of life, (i.e., love of life).[7] Therefore, spirituality, understood as the correspondence of the spirit and creation, should encompass the "liberation of the body from the repressions imposed by the soul, and the suppressions of morality, and the humiliations caused by self-hate."[8]

Interestingly enough, Moltmann, in his project of trinitarian pneumatology, sees John Calvin in a positive light. In accordance with Werner Krusche, Moltmann writes:

> Jean Calvin at first answered the question in the negative: the image of God has a spiritual nature, since God is Spirit...Here Calvin was only repeating the tradition of Augustine...Following biblical tradition, he distinguished between the image of God in creation and in redemption: human beings are...redeemed in the image of the "incarnate God"...Therefore in the process of redemption and

---

4. Moltmann, *Spirit of Life*, 7.

5. Ibid., 81.

6. Unlike Moltmann, Santmire suggests that Augustine, in his theological maturity, would contemplate "the whole of reality as a universal, richly endowed history, guided and blessed by God throughout." H. Paul Santmire, *The Travail of Nature: The Ambiguous Ecological Promise of Christian Theology* (Minneapolis: Fortress, 1985) 58.

7. Moltmann, *Spirit of Life*, 86.

8. Ibid., 95.

consummation, believers become the image of God *tam in corpore quam in anima*.[9]

With respect to Moltmann's approach and emphasis on pneumatology, it is of importance to retrieve John Calvin's theology of the Spirit as a paradigmatic example of the proper attention being given to the relationship between spirituality and social ethics.

An understanding and appreciation for Christian spirituality is essential if one is concerned with the experience of God as revealed in Jesus Christ through the gift of the Holy Spirit. Pneumatology has often remained dogmatic and categorical, even as it seeks to reflect on the human experience of God. In a discussion of pneumatology, therefore, it is necessary to recognize and to investigate spiritual experience, not only in terms of the individual, religious dimension—the so-called interior life—but also in terms of its integration with the historical, social and cultural realms of human life—outward life. Thus, the question of spirituality should be treated in relation to personal and social activity. A dogmatic approach to pneumatology of this sort must then come into dialogue with spiritual experience and its socio-ethical implications.

So why reconsider Calvin in a discussion of pneumatology in connection with spirituality and social ethics? Is it appropriate to take Calvin as a model in constructing a new paradigm for understanding the Holy Spirit, especially in regard to the relationship between spirituality and socio-ethical reflection? Was he not too old-fashioned, too preoccupied with the glory and absolute sovereignty of God, thus putting aside human experience and responsibility? Is predestination not the hallmark for Calvin's whole theology, threatening human spirituality and freedom?

With regard to Calvin's theology of the Spirit, in *Calvin and Augustine* Benjamin Warfield characterizes John Calvin as preeminently "the theologian of the Holy Spirit."[10] Two other European scholars, Simon van der Linde and Werner Krusche, have also examined Calvin's pneumatology in detail. Van der Linde focuses on the general and special operations of the Holy Spirit,[11] while Krusche describes Calvin's theology of the Spirit

---

9. Moltmann, *History and the Triune God*, 62.

10. Benjamin Warfield, "John Calvin the Theologian," in *Calvin and Augustine*, ed. Samuel G. Craig (Philadelphia: P. & R., 1956) 484–85.

11. Simon van der Linde, *De Leer van den Heiligen Geest bij Calvijn, Bijdrage tot de Kennis der Reformatorische Theologie* (Wageningen: Veenman & Zonen, 1943).

INTRODUCTION: *Calvin's Theology of the Spirit*

on the trinitarian basis of its relationship and interaction with creation, anthropology, and ecclesiology.[12]

However, describing Calvin as a preeminent theologian of the Holy Spirit may be in contradiction with his more popular descriptions of the sovereignty of God or predestination. Wilhelm Niesel has addressed the difficulty of arriving at "any conspectus of Calvin's theology as a whole" with regard to Calvin studies.[13] While some have described pneumatology as dominating Calvin's overall theology, a historical view of Calvin studies shows a general lack of academic interest in Calvin's spirituality and social ethics from a pneumatological point of view. This study seeks to address this shortcoming and to promote Calvin's theology of the Spirit in discussion of Christian spirituality and social ethics.[14]

There have been many enduring caricatures and misunderstandings of Calvin, especially in regard to later Calvinism and Puritanism, often generated by stressing Calvinist doctrinal rigidity. Leaving aside many important ideas relating to spiritual experience and social justice in Calvin, later Calvinistic churches went a different way than Calvin himself. Accordingly, an adequate understanding of Calvin's pneumatology within the context of spirituality and social ethics is generally incompatible with the traditional Calvinist views, such as those found in the Confessions of Dort or Westminster. Consider, for instance, Total Depravity, Limited Atonement, Unconditional Election, and Irresistible Grace—these popular Calvinistic doctrines may express to some extent Calvin's theological thought, but they mostly ignore what Calvin himself actually wrote in order to improve human life, especially in the social, political and economic realms.

What is central to Calvin's teaching of the Holy Spirit? Did Calvin take seriously the spiritual aspect of human experience with God in Jesus Christ within the context of pneumatology? What place does spirituality hold for Calvin's theology of the Spirit? What is the theological relationship between the Holy Spirit and human spirituality? These questions lead

12. Werner Krusche, *Das Wirken des Heiligen Geistes nach Calvin* (Göttingen: Vandenhoeck & Ruprecht, 1957).

13. Wilhelm Niesel, *The Theology of Calvin*, trans. Harold Knight (Grand Rapids: Baker, 1980) 9–21, 251–54.

14. Ibid. See also E. Saxer, "Hauptprobleme der Calvinforshung-Forschungsbericht 1974–1982," in *Calvinus Ecclesiae Genevensis Custos*, ed. Wilhelm H. Neuser (Bern: Lang, 1982) 93–112.

me to first consider how Calvin elaborated and integrated his teaching of the Holy Spirit in relation to his other theological emphases.

As a theologian and a reformer, Calvin's genuine concern for the Spirit and spirituality is manifested in the practical motivation of his *Institutes of the Christian Religion*. Considering "the end to which the Holy Spirit calls him [a person]" the *Institutes* was designed primarily "to help simple folk, . . . to guide them and help them to find the sum of what God meant to teach us in his Word."[15] Theologically, his *Institutes* underlines the dynamic function of the Holy Spirit in admonishing and illuminating the human being in light of the word of God. This pneumatological function is linked to his whole dogmatic framework and gives dynamism to it. In addition, basic instruction in the Christian religion is necessary for "the whole sum of godliness (*pietatis*) and all that needs to be known in the doctrine of salvation: a work very well worth reading for all Christians with a zeal for godliness."[16]

As for the person and work of the Holy Spirit, Calvin conceptualizes the Spirit as the bond of the Father and the Son within the Trinity (*Inst.* I.xiii.19.23). The Holy Spirit as the Spirit of the Father and the Son functions to mediate the dynamic being of the triune God in an immanent as well as in an economic way. In regard to the immanent, the Spirit is involved in the dynamic being of hypostatic union and office in the one person of Jesus Christ. In the context of economic trinity, Calvin's teaching of the Holy Spirit contains implications for social ethics. It has also been said that Calvin stresses the work of Christ only in relation to that of the Holy Spirit, and vice versa: "A true, adequate knowledge of divine things is possible only via God's self-revelation in Christ and self-authentication via the Holy Spirit."[17] Furthermore, in a Christological context, the *munus triplex* of Christ (prophetic, kingly, priestly), which is linked to the work of the Spirit, retains its ethical bearing on Christian life—as God's love is revealed to us by Christ, so it is the Holy Spirit who makes Christ present to us.

---

15. John Calvin, *Institutes of the Christian Religion*, preface to the final French edition of 1560, ed. John T. McNeil (Philadelphia: Westminster, 1960) 6.

16. John Calvin, Preface to 1536 edition of the *Institutes*. Cf. Lucien Joseph Richard, *The Spirituality of John Calvin* (Atlanta: John Knox, 1974) 166.

17. John R. Loeschen, *The Divine Community: Trinity, Church, and Ethics in Reformation Theologies* (Kirksville, MS: Sixteenth Century Journal, 1981) 139.

Introduction: *Calvin's Theology of the Spirit*

For Calvin, the Spirit involves the sovereignty and freedom of God on whom the Christian life is based, so that the grace and power of the Holy Spirit renews and stimulates Christian life toward the glory of God, that is, the doxological aspect of the spiritual life (*Inst.* III.1.3–4). In the doctrine of creation, Calvin underscores Spirit as the *Spiritus Creator* at work in creation, through which the world is to be preserved, restored, and guided. Without the power of the Holy Spirit in preserving creation, the world will not sustain itself, and consequently degenerate into the chaos of bestiality (*Inst.* II.ii.12–20).

As for the nature and authority of Scripture, Calvin makes a most significant contribution for the doctrine of the internal witness or testimony of the Holy Spirit. This doctrine also becomes manifest in view of the inner working and witness of the Spirit concerning the knowledge of God, the authority of Scripture, and the right focus of preaching (*Inst.* I.ix.1–3). Here, preaching is not the speaking about Christ, but the event in which Christ himself comes to us. This is the Holy Spirit that affects the real presence of Christ through preaching. As Calvin writes, "We hold, therefore, that when God speaks, he adds the efficacy of his Spirit, since his word without it would be fruitless; and yet the word is effectual because the instrument ought to be united with the author of the action."[18]

Calvin displays the entire doctrine of Christian ethics (or the Christian life of spirituality) in light of the Holy Spirit. It is the Holy Spirit who connects the objective work of Christ (highlighted in Christology and soteriology) with our subjective benefit. Therefore, the function of the Holy Spirit effectuates the salvific benefits of Christ to us. The business of the Holy Spirit is the "power and efficacy" of God's activity in Christ (*Inst.* I.xiii.18), which brings us to the union with Christ. His doctrine of the mystical faith-union of the believer with his Lord (*Inst.* III.ii.24) is highlighted in pneumatological communication with one's spirituality. From this Christ-union aspect, double grace (justification and sanctification) comes about, and is associated with the ethical component of spiritual life.

For Calvin, it is important to integrate the Spirit's impact on Christian spiritual and ethical life. The regenerating and sanctifying Spirit of God, who directs human beings towards the love of God and neighbor, plays a key part in the formation of spirituality, as well as ethical responsibility.

18. John Calvin, *Commentaries on Ezekiel*, II.2; OC 40, 61–62. Cf. Richard, *Spirituality of John Calvin*, 155.

Calvin's *locus classicus* for the work and function of the Spirit is located in the opening sections of Book III. By the Holy Spirit, "we come to enjoy Christ and all his benefits . . . the Spirit is the bond by which Christ effectually unites us to himself" (*Inst.* III. I.1). For Calvin, regeneration, calling, conversion, repentance, justification by faith, and sanctification are associated with the reality and actuality of the Holy Spirit (*Inst.* III. ii.7–8.33–36). God's election is the most profound expression of God's love in Christ. Election is rooted in Christ, and only by the Spirit of Christ does one attain assurance of God's act in electing one in Christ (*Inst.* III.i.3f; II.11f; xxi.3). Therefore, the doctrine of election is not a metaphysical, deterministic speculation on God's arbitrariness. Rather, it is a confession of Christian faith looking back at God's trustworthiness in one's life, so that this teaching of election creates spiritual qualities in Christian life, namely, gratitude, humility and hope.

Calvin's emphasis on the Spirit is also evident in his doctrine of the church and sacraments. His ecclesiology highlights Calvin's spirituality in the following statement: "We cannot have God as our Father if we do not have the Church as our mother." In fact, Calvin begins Book IV of the *Institutes* with the following heading: "The True Church with which, as Mother of all the godly, we must keep unity." In a similar fashion, Joseph Bohatec has brought to light Calvin's organic concept of the church. That is to say, for Calvin the church is a living organism, a dynamic interaction between Christ the head and the members of his body. Therefore, Bohatec attempts to base the Christocratic view of the church on the "pneumatocracy."[19]

Likewise, Calvin's understanding of the sacraments as the visible form of the real presence of Christ by the power of the Spirit is, like preaching, the audible form of the Word. The Eucharist is a gift in which Jesus Christ himself is given by the power of the Holy Spirit. The notion of the Spirit being distinctly present in the Eucharist is a dominate and compelling theme in Calvin's thought. Spirituality based on the Eucharist is understood not only personally, but also socially, that is, spirituality serving God in the world.

As Howard Hageman has stated, "once we have been received into God's new people by baptism, we are given everything that Jesus Christ is and has and are enabled to appropriate it . . . by sharing Christ in the

---

19. Joseph Bohatec, *Calvins Lehre von Staat und Kirche: Mit besonderer Berücksichtigung des Organismusgedankens* (Aalen: Scientia, 1968) 183.

INTRODUCTION: *Calvin's Theology of the Spirit*

preaching of his Word, in the receiving of his Supper, and in the liturgical life of his body, the Church. From the power and the strength . . . we are enabled and expected for obedient service to God in the world which is under his promise."[20]

In briefly examining some aspects of Calvin's teaching of the Spirit, one must consider the words of Hendrikus Berkhof. "The famous third book of the *Institutes* contains great riches in the field of pneumatology, many of which have not yet been uncovered by Reformed Churches."[21]

Given the relationship of the Spirit to Christian life, we come to spirituality. In describing Calvin's spirituality, Lucien J. Richard writes. "Spirituality means the forms that holiness takes in the concrete life of the believer. The concept of spirituality implies that there is the possibility of progress in holiness, that there is a need for working toward perfection, and that there are certain means and ways of attaining such a perfection."[22] The fundamental concern for spirituality is clearly expressed by Calvin in his *Institutes*. "My intention is only to offer some basic rudiments (*rudimenta*) through which those who feel some interest in religion (*studio religionis*) might be trained to true piety (*ad veram pietatem*)"(*Inst*. I.9.).[23]

Piety, according to Calvin, is an important theological term, which describes knowledge of God and of ourselves, and further designates the aspect of the human seeking holiness with ardent fervor. The entire Christian life is a continual exercise of progress through piety. John T. McNeill has observed the significance of piety, highlighting Calvin's *Institutes*. Noting that Calvin preferred naming his book "a *summa pietatis*" to "a *summa theologiae*," McNeil states. "The whole work is suffused with an awed sense of God's ineffable majesty, sovereign power, and immediate presence with us men."[24] For Calvin, piety means "that reverence joined with love of God which the knowledge of his benefits induces" (*Inst*.I.ii.1). In this regard, Calvin accentuates the spiritual life in prayer,

---

20. Howard G. Hageman, "Reformed Spirituality," in *Protestant Spiritual Traditions*, ed. Frank C. Senn (Mahwah: Paulist, 1986) 71–72.

21. Hendrikus Berkhof, *The Doctrine of the Holy Spirit* (Richmond: John Knox, 1964) 22.

22. Richard, *Spirituality of John Calvin*, 1.

23. See also Richard, *Spirituality of John Calvin*, 97.

24. John T. McNeill, *Introduction to Calvin's Institutes* 1:1; cf. James M. Gustafson, *Ethics From a Theocentric Perspective*, vol.1 (Chicago: University of Chicago Press, 1981) 164.

because "our hearts may be fired with a zealous and burning desire ever to seek, love, and serve God."[25]

Prayer is the "perpetual exercise of faith" (*Inst.* III.xx). The prayer of faith means the prayer of humility and repentance. In prayer we have recourse to the death of Christ as Mediator, in which prayer is linked to the intercession of Christ. As the principle spiritual exercise of faith, prayer has to be grounded upon the Word of God. "A dauntless spirit of praying rightly accords with fear, reverence and solicitude" (*Inst*.III. xx.14). Regarding prayer as "the expression of the heart to God,"[26] one can petition for human needs. If prayer is the true exercise of faith, it should be filled with gratitude, which is "the chief exercise of godliness."[27]

Such prayer is based on the feeling of love. Therefore, prayer is not self-centered, but is done with love toward the other. It is the most powerful and spiritual way for believers to intercede for the other with love. Our strength to endure in true prayer is the gift of the Spirit. "Unless the Spirit instructs us in the right pattern for prayer (Rom 8:26)" (*Inst*.III. xx.34), we cannot pray to God. It is the Spirit which inspires prayer with love and piety for personal need and communal intercession. Thus, it is worthwhile to consider William Bouwsma. "That Calvin's religion has not been generally treated as 'spirituality' is largely a result of the widespread notion of Calvin as a systematic and dogmatic theologian." It says "more about the later Calvinism than about Calvin." Calvin found himself "as an exclusively biblical theologian." "He valued system . . . only for limited, practical, and pedagogical purposes." Otherwise he was suspicious of all human impulse "to systematize, above all in religious matters."[28]

When considering the relationship between spirituality and social ethics, it is vital to clarify the definition of Christian spirituality as a discipline by distinguishing it from other disciplines. According to Bernard McGinn, Christian spirituality is the lived experiences of Christian belief

---

25. Howard L. Rice, *Reformed Spirituality: An Introduction for Believers* (Louisville: Westminster John Knox, 1991) 75. See also, *Inst*.III.xx.3.

26. Ronald S. Wallace, *Calvin's Doctrine of the Christian Life* (Edinburgh: Oliver & Boyd, 1959) 281.

27. Ibid., 284.

28. Cited in Dennis E. Tamburello, *Union with Christ: John Calvin and the Mysticism of St. Bernard* (Louisville: Westminster John Knox, 1994) 102. Cf. William J. Bouwsma, "The Spirituality of John Calvin," in *World Spirituality: An Encyclopedic History of the Religious Quest*, ed. Jill Raitt (New York: Crossroad, 1987) vol. 17, *Christian Spirituality II: High Middle Ages and Reformation*, 318–33.

INTRODUCTION: *Calvin's Theology of the Spirit*

in both its general and more specialized forms. McGinn distinguishes spirituality "from doctrine in that it concentrates not on faith itself, but on the reaction that faith arouses in religious consciousness and practice." It is also distinguished "from Christian ethics in that it treats not all human actions in their relation to God, but those acts in which the relation to God is immediate and explicit."[29]

The difference between spirituality as a theological discipline and dogmatics and ethics does not always mean that it should be treated in an independent manner. Rather, spirituality needs to be investigated in relation to dogmatic and ethical reflection in an interdisciplinary manner. As Sandra Schneiders has stated, "Spirituality better denotes the subject-matter of this interdisciplinary field than narrower terms such as spiritual theology."[30]

From the beginning of the *Institutes*, Calvin makes a concerted attempt to integrate spirituality with theological reflection. Theological reflection is not merely supposed to articulate and explicate dogma, but also deal with the genuine human experience of God in appropriate ways, because Calvin refers to theological knowledge as vital and experiential.

In speaking of Christian spirituality, according to Calvin, we are required to begin with an experience of Christ (i.e., our mystical union with Christ.) Calvin begins with Jesus Christ and our union with Christ and makes it the starting point for discussing spirituality and socio-ethical praxis. Communion with Christ *(insitio in Christum)* indicates the significance of experiential reality from which justification and sanctification spring. This union plays an indispensable part in the formation of spiritual life. Therefore, we assign the highest rank to that union of the head and members which is the residence of Christ in our hearts, in the sense of a mystical union (in Latin, *mystica*; in French, *union sacrée*. See *Inst.* III.xi.10).[31]

In terms of a mystical union, Tamburello brings to light the positive relationship between Calvin and Bernard of Clairvaux. Unlike Kolfhaus,

---

29. Bernard McGinn, "Introduction," in *Christian Spirituality I*, eds. Bernard McGinn and John Meyendorf, in collaboration with Jean Leclercq (New York: Crossroad, 1987) xv–xvi.

30. Sandra M. Schneiders, "Spirituality in the Academy," in *Modern Christian Spirituality: Methodological and Historical Essays*, ed. Bradley C. Hanson (Atlanta: Scholars, 1990) 31.

31. Cf. Richard, *Spirituality of John Calvin*, 109.

who states the relationship in a negative manner, Tamburello contends that "for to him [Calvin] it was not the pious soul with its experiences that was central, but rather Christ and the life that his members received from him."[32] Tamburello uses a two-fold sense of mysticism to evaluate the mystical element in Calvin's thought in a more persuasive way. The broader one—based on Ernst Troeltsch's remark that "in the widest sense of the word, mysticism is simply the insistence upon a direct inward and present religious experience"—involves a fundamental dimension of Christian life as a phenomenon intrinsic to all religiosity.

The narrower one includes not every Christian, but more specifically mystics in the medieval sense. However, Tamburello is inclined to neglect Calvin's spirituality in connection with social and ethical sphere, because Calvin's understanding of the mystical union present in the sacraments retains such a social and ethical dimension. Considering the relationship between the spiritual element and ethical direction in Calvin's eucharistic theology, André Biéler states that Calvin's view of the Christian life renewed by the sacraments in mystical union with Jesus Christ, which is initiated by the Holy Spirit, cannot take the form of solitude and individualism, but always and necessarily the form of social life.[33]

Calvin never lost sight of emphasizing the Holy Spirit as the bond of our union with Christ. From this perspective, spirituality can be interpreted to imply the entire process of a believer toward sanctification in the power of the Spirit. Here is the primacy of love in Christian spirituality—love of God and the fellow person, as well as God's love for the world. This spirituality is not individualistic [34] but socially and publicly oriented. Christian life, which is characterized by spirituality in the context of one's union with Christ, is basically related to the believer in the concrete social life. This is a Christian spirituality in the service of God and neighbor in the world.

What distinguishes Calvin's theology is his integration of the vertical dimension with the horizontal. As Niesel writes, "The distinctive thing in the teaching is that he [Calvin] first of all lays the foundation, by speaking of our union with Christ, next he deals with the gift of sanc-

32. Tamburello, *Union with Christ*, 6.

33. André Biéler, *La Pensée Économique et Sociale de Calvin* (Paris: Michel, 1961) 271.

34. For the influence of the *Devotio Moderna* on Calvin, see Richard, *Spirituality of John Calvin*, 48–73.

INTRODUCTION: *Calvin's Theology of the Spirit*

tification and only then develops his doctrine of justification."[35] As far as we give priority to the personal and social aspects of Christian ethics, Calvin can be considered an important figure, in contrast with his contemporaries and most conservative Christian theologians who followed him; they remained silent concerning the social and political contexts of human life. Being keenly aware of socio-economic relationships and tensions, Calvin makes it a point to understand and analyze them from a biblical point of view.

It is Karl Marx who taught that the social economic dimension of human life is decisive and indispensable in understanding the ethical consequences. Although his diagnosis has proven fatally invalid in our times, his insight on human life remains provocative and still challenging in our global context. However, prior to Karl Marx, Calvin brought to the fore the idea of social humanism in the political and economic realm. In his exposition of 2 Cor 8:13–14, Calvin writes: "God wills that there be proportions and equality among us, that is, each man is to provide for the needy according to the extent of his means so that no man has too much and no man has too little."[36]

This ethical reflection, which elaborates the law in the threefold use and discipleship in the world, is expressed not only Christologically, but also pneumatologically. Furthermore, Christian freedom, as it is intertwined with spiritual gifts such as justification and sanctification, is regarded as an appendage of justification (*Inst.* III. xix. 1).

As a matter of fact, Calvin's critical social analysis is based primarily on biblical insights and resources, that is, God's loving concern in Jesus Christ toward the poor in the world. According to Calvin, Christian spirituality is not to be discussed without regard to Christian commitment for social emancipation and economic justice. Christian life in justification and sanctification co-exists in a dialectical relation implying growth and progress by the power of the Spirit in the direction of prophetic *diakonia* and social *koinonia* for our world, (i.e., world transformation.) Here, spirituality, when grasped in depth, informs socio-ethical reflections on emancipation and solidarity.[37]

---

35. Wilhelm Niesel, *Reformed Symbolics* (Edinburgh: Oliver & Boyd, 1962) 192.

36. Cf. "Foreword by W. A. Visser't Hooft," in André Biéler, *The Social Humanism of Calvin*, trans. Paul T. Fuhrmann (Richmond: John Knox, 1964) 8.

37. On the relationship between spirituality and liberation, see Robert McAfee Brown, *Spirituality and Liberation: Overcoming the Great Fallacy* (Louisville: Westminster, 1988) 116–21.

In deliberation of spirituality and social ethics, Calvin interprets spirituality as the human way of relating to God and the world. It embraces holistic aspects of life concerning politics and economics, liturgical practice and communal worship, and prayer and meditation. In this regard, it is preferable to use the term spirituality over piety, because the latter might sound too religious and individualistic. The preference of spirituality in a holistic manner serves to better describe Calvin's ethical concern for social responsibility and emancipation in light of the Holy Spirit.

Given this theological background, this monograph will attempt to make an ecumenical contribution by reclaiming Calvin's teaching on the Spirit as it pertains to the mutual relationship between spirituality and human social and ethical life. The purpose is to interpret and explicate the way Calvin integrates spirituality with Christian ethics in the light of the Holy Spirit. The argument of this study is to demonstrate the relevance of spiritual theology to Christian ethics in the context of Calvin's dogmatic reflection on the Spirit.

Chapters 1 through 3 will explore the cosmic dimension of the Spirit and the basic structure of Calvin's doctrine of the Trinity from a pneumatological perspective, explicating in particular the function and role of the Spirit in relation to the Father and the Son. In discussing Calvin's idea of natural knowledge of God, attention will be given to the debate between Karl Barth and Emil Brunner. Regarding the relation of the Spirit to salvation, an attempt will be made to analyze and articulate the social and ethical implications of Christ-union as it pertains to double grace (justification and sanctification) and election.

Chapter 4 will focus on Calvin's ethical and practical reflection on Christian life in regard to the work of the Holy Spirit. Here we will deal with theological issues like the law, Christian discipleship, and freedom. Following this, there will be an analysis of the relationship between the Holy Spirit and the church. Furthermore, Calvin's political thought concerning the connection between the church and the state will be discussed. The excursus will deal with Calvin's political thought involved in the persecution of French Calvinists. In the afterward, a discussion will be made for the ecumenical legacy of Calvin in view of Reformed-Pentecostal dialogue.

1

The Spirit in Cosmic Dimension

IN A THEOLOGICAL REFLECTION on creation, Calvin combines the fundamental purpose of creation with twofold knowledge: the knowledge of God and the knowledge of our own being. God reveals himself as the creator to us: "It is one thing to feel that God as our Maker supports us by his power, governs us by his providence, nourishes us by his goodness, and attends us with all sorts of blessings, and another thing to embrace the grace of the reconciliation offered to us in Christ" (*Inst.* I.ii.1). In this statement we find the *locus classicus* of Calvin's understanding of the twofold knowledge of God (*Duplex cognito Domini*).[1] That is, for Calvin, God is known through the creation of the world and in general revelation and as the Redeemer in the person of Jesus Christ.

The God of the Scriptures is identical with the Creator of all things. Furthermore, we may also recognize God's creative work in terms of God's saving action in Christ, because all things are created through Christ, the eternal Word of God. According to Calvin, the divine creation and providence belong to general revelation. This knowledge is distinguished from the knowledge of God, the source of which is Jesus Christ.

Calvin views the role of the Holy Spirit as being the mediator of creation's participation in the divine life. Here the Holy Spirit is understood as the One who is equivalent in dignity with that of the Father and the Son. God created the world with the potential for incarnation in history and the Spirit's indwelling in human beings. This implies that God's creation is conceptualized in relation to Christ's incarnation and the regenerating work of the Holy Spirit in human beings. The significance of the Sabbath thereby becomes clear in that the ultimate purpose of life is to live in

---

1. Cf. Edward A. Dowey Jr., *The Knowledge of God in Calvin's Theology* (Grand Rapids: Eerdmanns, 1994) 41–49.

holiness, which means the presence of God in the world. If Christ and the Spirit are fully and truly divine, their work should be no less than God's work in creation. Thus, Christ's incarnation and the Spirit's indwelling will primarily accomplish and fulfill God's aims in creation.

With regard to the doctrine of creation in Scriptures, Calvin interprets the Spirit in creation to be both that of the Father and of the eternal Son. God created the world through the eternal Word. However, this creation is in need of the power and efficacy of the Spirit, so that the world can be sustained and maintained against the falling back into chaos. In Calvin's view, it is necessary to grasp that God created heaven and earth out of nothing. This creation out of nothing is essential and central to *Creator Spiritus*, because Calvin understands *bara* as *creatio ex nihilo* in the exclusive sense. If we affirm that God the Father is the origin of all things and also the creator of the world, we also should remember that God created all things through the eternal Word and the Spirit. Scripture, according to Calvin, tells us "that God by the power of his Word and Spirit created heaven and earth out of nothing" (*Inst.* I.xiv.20).

Creatio ex nihilo shows God to be the One who alone is eternal and self-existent. Thus, *creatio ex nihilo* implies the fact that the world has only one ground, that is, the goodness of God. The expression "out of nothing" does not mean "out of the Nothing," that is, out of some dark and chaotic power threatening our life.[2] Calvin refers to creation of the invisible and the visible, including angels and demons (*Inst.* I.xiv.3–9). From this point of view we are aware that creation is not, for Calvin, under the sway of a certain fate, but under God's almighty providence.

How does God sustain the creation? For Calvin, *spiritus creator* is conceptualized in the threefold way of life in the scope and outreach of creation. Calvin refers to *universal life*, which consists only in motion and sense, *human life*, which one possesses as the children of Adam, and, finally, *supernatural life*, which the believer alone obtains.[3] In view of

2. Cf. Hendrikus Berkhof, "God as Creator and the World as Createdness," in *Major Themes in the Reformed Tradition*, ed. Donald K. McKim (Grand Rapids: Eerdmans, 1991) 81.

3. Cf. Peter de Klerk, ed., *Calvin and the Holy Spirit*, Sixth Colloquium on Calvin & Calvin Studies, ed. Peter De Klerk (Grand Rapids: Calvin Studies Society, 1989). Krusche's understanding, exposited in *Das Wirken des Heiligen Geistes nach Calvin*, can also be seen in this regard: the three major chapters of the book are under such rubrics as "Der Heiligen Geist und der Kosmos," "Der Heilige Geist und der Mensch," and "Der Heilige Geist und die Kirche."

The Spirit in Cosmic Dimension

Calvin's pneumatological framework, Werner Krusche makes an appropriate distinction between the cosmic but hidden power of God (*arcana Dei virtus*), the general, indiscriminate bestowal of various gifts (*dona*) upon all human beings, and the particular regenerating work of the Spirit (*spiritus adoptionis*).[4] In other words, Calvin discusses the work of the Spirit concerning the cosmos, all human beings, and the regenerate.

THE COSMIC AND UNIVERSAL DIMENSION OF THE SPIRIT

As for the cosmic and universal dimension of the Spirit, Calvin states that "the power of the Spirit was necessary in order to sustain it [the world]," cherishing the earth "by his secret virtue, that it might remain stable for the time."[5] Here we see the Spirit preserving order and giving life, which implies God's ecological concern within the mission of the Spirit. Put otherwise, this refers to a continuous action of God in the process of God's creation. "He [God] brought forth living beings and inanimate things of every kind, that in a wonderful series he distinguished an innumerable variety of things, that he endowed each kind with its own nature, assigned functions, appointed places and stations; and that, although all were subject to corruption, he nevertheless provided for the preservation of each species until the Last Day" (*Inst.* I.xiv.20). God's ecological care of the world, that is, the preservation of each species until the Last Day, is clear in that God "nourishes some in secret ways, and, as it were, from time to time instills new vigor into them" (*Inst.* I.xiv.20). Thus, God's blessing comes. "God blessed them, saying, 'Be fruitful, and multiply and fill the waters in the seas, and let birds multiply on the earth" (Gen 1:22).

In this regard, it can be stated that God's ecological concern in creation stands in connection with God's providential blessing for human beings. The dominion, which God gives to human beings over other creatures, is the human right to care for the creatures, which is a part of human ethical stewardship and mandate. Our confession that God is the Creator of all being is then associated with our appreciation of God's providence effectively at work in the present life (*Inst.* I.xvi.1). The spiri-

---

4. Krusche, *Das Wirken des Heiligen Geistes nach Calvin*, 14. See also de Klerk, *Calvin and the Holy Spirit*, 19.

5. John Calvin, *Commentaries on the First Book of Moses called Genesis*, vol.1, trans. John King (Grand Rapids: Baker, 1993) 73–74. Hereafter referred to as *Comm. on Genesis*.

tuality of a human being in creation is characterized by gratitude, praise, and cooperation with God's goodness and care for other living creatures.

God stands in a particular relationship to human beings as well as with every kind of creature, and nature itself. Nature, in Calvin's view, has a two-fold meaning; nature as created perfection (the state before the Fall) and nature as corrupt or fallen nature, that is, accidental under the conditions of sin. Calvin's praise of nature's beauty in itself becomes tremendously striking. The created world as "most beautiful theatre" endows "each with its own nature, assigned functions, appointed places, and stations" (*Inst.* I.xiv.20). The stamp of the divine glory in the created nature is found in heaven and on earth, because God "has written and as it were engraven the glory of his power, goodness, wisdom and eternity." All living creatures could be witnesses and messengers of divine glory to all human beings to do God service and honor. "For the little singing birds sang of God, the animals acclaimed him, the elements feared and the mountains resounded with him, the river and springs threw glances toward him, the grasses and the flowers smiled."[6]

Although Calvin interprets nature to be "the whole array of the physical world including human nature,"[7] nature is not supposed to become the divine source of validating the point of contact between God and human beings. Rather it is God's creature under the promise of covenant that is to be preserved and taken care of in the power of the Holy Spirit for the glory of God. In fact, the Spirit is a point of contact between God, human beings, and nature.

At this juncture, theological talk about nature should not be misunderstood or glorified as a natural theology in its independent way, i.e., "the autonomous rational structure which it develops on the ground of 'nature alone' in abstraction from the active self-disclosure of the living God."[8] Rather, in God's creation nature has its unique place in relation to human life. From nature comes cultural life. By human interaction with nature, political, social, and cultural realms are shaped and developed. If these domains threaten nature, God's care for life should question and challenge their proper place. The Spirit awakens human beings to their relationship with nature. Here lies the human socio-ethical mandate of

6. OS 9.793,795. Cited from Santmire, *Travail of Nature*, 128.

7. Edward A. Dowey Jr., *Knowledge of God in Calvin's Theology*, 66.

8. Thomas F. Torrance, *Karl Barth: Biblical and Evangelical Theologian* (Edinburgh: T. & T. Clark, 1990) 147.

stewardship as God's co-worker in nature with other creatures. We discern the orderliness or constancy of God's will within nature that is, the *ordo naturae*. In point of fact, the universe is a book, theatre or mirror, and God appears "in the garment of creation" (*Inst*. I.v.1).

Along this line, Calvin's language of the cosmic work of the Spirit can be conceptualized as a theological program for deepening the connection between human beings with nature. Justice, peace and integrity of creation stand in mutual relationship and interaction which are inspired and strengthened by the work of the Spirit. Christocentric theology thus needs to be extended and deepened by a theology of the Spirit which gives a cosmic breadth in eschatological openness. Calvin's theology of the Spirit, which emphasizes the cosmic breadth of the Spirit, leads the church to heed the Spirit in care of the ecosystems of the earth, while encouraging the church to solidarity with the life of creatures.

For Calvin, God has a particular care for each creature in which all species have some inner guidance according to the natural law. However, the inner counsel of God is not subject to the interplay of natural laws, because divine intervention moves and guides every creature toward God's will and providence. God's goodness in creation and providence drives all of us (including the whole of nature) to gratitude to and trustfulness in God. "It is to recognize that God has destined all things for our good and salvation but at the same time to feel his power and grace in ourselves and in the great benefits he has conferred upon us, and so bestir ourselves to trust, invoke, praise, and love him" (*Inst*. I.xiv.22). This statement implies that, for Calvin, Christian spirituality stands in relation to *Spiritus Creator*, and that the human being stands in parallel with the life of all creatures because of God's goodness.

On the basis of Gen 22:8, God's provision, for Calvin, points to the foreknowledge of God, as well as God's particular care for God's creatures, which is opposed to the concept of *providentia universalis*. The latter tends to "concede to God some kind of blind and ambiguous motion" (*Inst*. I.xvi.4). From this we may understand providence as the effectual action and involvement of God in our human life (*Inst*. I.xvi.4). As long as God created the world out of nothing through the eternal Word in the presence of the Holy Spirit, God protects it from degenerating into chaos through God's providence.

According to Calvin, "God not only drives the machinery of the world and all its parts in a universal motion, but sustains, nourishes and cares for every creature, even for the little birds" (*Inst.* I.xvi.1). Providence which refers to God's universal activity is likened to "the captain of a ship, holding the helm in order to cope with every event" (*Inst.* I.xvi.4). In his treatise *Against the Libertines* (1545) Calvin sees providence first of all through the order of nature, secondly through special providence, and thirdly through the interior witness of the Spirit. God conforms Godself to the laws of the nature, because God gives Godself to all creatures when they are formed. However, through special providence, God works in God's creatures, and through them God's constant intervention happens to the life of human beings. Finally, God governs, transforms, and regenerates believers by the internal work of the Holy Spirit.[9]

The Spirit of God in the process of creation sustains, preserves, and cares for the life of all creatures, because "with tender care [the Holy Spirit] supported the confused matter of heaven and earth, until beauty and order were added." (*Inst.* I.xiii.22) The creator is also the conservator,[10] or to use the formulation of E. Doumergue, God creates not of nothing, nor does God conserve it by perennial recreation out of nothing.[11] God takes care of *ordo mundi* through the Spirit.

It is also *arcana Dei virtus* (or *arcana inspiratio* of the Spirit) in the process of creation that is in control of the waters. It is the same Spirit, who functions as God's *providentia generalis* by inspiring, sustaining and, preserving the world, and who also divides the waters of the Red Sea as effectors of *providentia specialis*.[12] These are examples of God's providence which takes place in the Spirit of the promise.

Calvin considers the Holy Spirit as *arcana virtus Dei* in the preservation of the created world, which makes sure that the universe has its reality, meaning and purpose within the *Spiritus Creator*. Calvin's eschatological openness takes place through the power and efficacy of the *Creator Spiritus*, Spirit of God and of the eternal Word. It is also guaranteed by God's sustaining action as freedom (grace) regardless of the perverted status of the world. Therefore, *Spiritus Creator* reveals God as free and sovereign, working and reigning in the cosmic, ecological realm, just as in the historical, soteriological realm.

9. Cf. Wendel, *Calvin*, 177–79.
10. Krusche, *Das Wirken des Heiligen Geistes nach Calvin*, 16.
11. Ibid.
12. Ibid., 17.

The Spirit in Cosmic Dimension

As we have already mentioned, the power of the Spirit lies in the ability to maintain the order and stability of creation, and to keep it from dissolving into nothingness. This spirit is also the source and wellspring of all life. "For it is the spirit who, everywhere diffused, sustains all things, causes them to grow, and quickens them in heaven and in earth. Because he is circumscribed by no limits, he is excepted from the category of all creatures; but in transfusing into all things his energy, and breathing into them essence, life, and movement, he is indeed plainly divine" (*Inst.* I.xiii.14). Calvin comments further on this point. "The power of the Spirit was necessary in order to sustain it [creation] . . . He therefore asserts that this mass, however confused it might be, was rendered stable, for the time, by the secret efficacy of the Spirit."[13] This activity of preserving order can be expressed as *continua creatio* because Calvin took seriously the term *creatio ex nihilo*. A theocentric-ecological reading of nature is of pneumatological character in Calvin's thought.[14]

As far as the *Spiritus Creator* stands in relation to the preservation of the creature's life, the Holy Spirit is, in Calvin's view, the *fons vitae*, the well of life. In this regard Moltmann relates Calvin to Francis of Assisi. All creatures are aflame with the glory of the Lord, full of a wonderful hymn of creation.[15] Moltmann's trinitarian pneumatology, stressing the cosmic breath of the divine Spirit in terms of eschatological panentheism, leads to respect for all living things, because God is present through the Spirit in them. However, it is difficult to ascribe panentheism to Calvin's position, because Calvin's concern lies more in the Spirit of the creation in the hidden and revealed sense than Moltmann, because the accidental function of the revelation in creation is under the conditions of sin.

God is the God of the spirits of all flesh (Num 16:22). All of creation returns to the inexhaustible vivificator. The earth's capacity for producing is not of itself, but is of heavenly inspiration, of the Spirit. As Calvin comments, "Therefore, that Scripture must be fulfilled, 'Send forth thy Spirit, and they shall be created, and thou shalt renew the face of the earth,' (Ps. 104:30) so, on the other hand, as soon as the Lord takes away his Spirit, all things return to their dust and vanish away (v. 29)."[16]

---

13. *Comm. on Genesis*, 73–74.

14. Cf. Santmire, *Travail of Nature*, 128.

15. Cf. Moltmann, *The Source of Life: The Holy Spirit and the Theology of Life*, trans. Margaret Kohl (Minneapolis: Fortress, 1997) 134.

16. *Comm. on Genesis*, 74.

Animal life is distinguished from the life of plants in such a way that the former represents itself not only as a vigor, but also as *motus* and *sensus*. This animal life needs *continua inspiratio* (Ps 104:29) to have its life. Calvin asserts that through death and birth, the world falls and again renews itself, not in the sense of a circulation process, or reincarnation, but through the contingency of divine action in bestowing and taking away the divine powerful, life-creating spirit. That is to say, the Spirit of God decides on physical life and death (Ps 104:30). Here, Calvin clearly speaks of the impact of *pneuma* on the physical world in an extraordinary, Hebrew manner. In Calvin's thought, it is often said, that there is a theme of disparaging the world, or separating the Spirit from nature.

Although Calvin sometimes expressed the relationship between Spirit and nature dualistically, it should not be understood as metaphysical dualism (in a Neo-Platonist way), but rather conceived of in terms of biblical and theological categories. Metaphysical dualism between Spirit and nature means that God is conceptualized as Spirit in an other-worldly manner, so that nature stands against Spirit, and, what is worse from an ontological point of view, it is degraded and underestimated. Calvin's concern however, is not to assert a metaphysical dualism; rather, he expresses the biblical image of *pneuma*'s dynamic relation and impact on the physical world. In this regard Calvin's idea is motivated and framed in a Hebrew manner rather than a Greek metaphysical manner.[17]

Unless there is the sustaining power of the Spirit, the world falls into nothingness. Therefore, Calvin's understanding of the Holy Spirit as *spiritus creator*, who is at work in creation, stands in opposition to pantheistic and metaphysical concepts of God. With this theological direction in mind, Calvin attacks the Manichean assertion that recognizes two principles in the world, i.e., God and the devil. This notion undermines and threatens the creative glory and sovereignty of God (*Inst*. I.xiv.3).

In confrontation with the Libertines (a fanatic sect), Calvin admitted that God's eternal Spirit is the source and origin of all things,[18] but this sentence should not be understood in a pantheistic manner, in which human, animal, etc., could become gods through participation in God's Spirit and Being. The spiritualistic monism, which only recognizes the *pneuma* as eternal, uncreated Spirit of God, sees the unifying bond between God

---

17. Krusche, *Das Wirken des Heiligen Geistes nach Calvin*, 21.
18. "L'espirit eternel de Dieu est la source et origine de toutes choses," ibid., 22.

and cosmos through its entrance into the world. But it loses sight of the Spirit of God as the mode of being (*Seinsweise*) of *una simplex Dei essentia*, which is distinguishable but not separable in a trinitarian life (*Inst.* I.xiii.22). The Spirit, which Calvin articulates in a trinitarian context, is the fountain and source of all creatures' lives. God pours life into creatures and sustains their lives through divine power. All living things are in the power of the Spirit. Through the *continua inspiratio* the creature remains stable. This power and efficacy of the Holy Spirit is seen not as a spiritual monism, but in terms of a Christological, trinitarian formulation.

THE HUMAN LIFE IN THE DIMENSION OF THE SPIRIT

Human life stands on a higher level as compared to animal life. In his exposition of Acts 17:28, Calvin recapitulates the Spirit's cosmic dimension and next brings to the fore the dimension of human life. "We have our being in him, inasmuch as by his Spirit he keepeth us in life, and upholdeth us. For the power of the Spirit is spread abroad throughout all parts of the world, that it may preserve them in their state; that he may minister unto the heaven and earth that force and vigor which we see, and motion to all living creatures. Not as brain-sick men do trifle, that all things are full of gods, yea, that stones are gods; but because God doth, by the wonderful power and inspiration of his Spirit, preserve those things which he hath created of nothing." Human life is inspired and moved by the power of the Spirit. Therefore, human beings take root in the Spirit, and are under his/her care and support.

Furthermore, insofar as human life is more excellent than motion and sense, said Calvin, "life hath the pre-eminence in men, because they have not only sense and motion as brute beasts have, but they are endued with reason and understanding. Wherefore, the Scripture doth for good cause give that singular gift which God hath given us, a title and commendation by itself. So in John, when mention is made of the creation of all things, it is added apart, not without cause, that life was the light of men (John 1:4)."[19] Along these lines Calvin expresses: "Now, we see that all those who know not God know not themselves; because they have God present with them not only in the excellent gifts of the mind, but in their

---

19. *Comm. on Acts*, 2:168.

very essence; because it belongeth to God alone to be, all other things have their being in him."[20]

It is the *imago Dei* that exalts human beings over the common mass of other creatures (*Inst.* I.xv.3). "Since the image of God has been destroyed by the fall, we may judge from its restoration what it originally had been."[21] In accordance with Col 3:10 and Eph 5:23, Calvin interprets the restoration of *imago Dei* as becoming the foundation and goal for the spirituality of Christian life in terms of true holiness and righteousness. It is important to note here Calvin's insistence that the natural endowments of human beings are not totally destroyed regardless of corruption. It is important to make a sharp distinction between corrupted "natural gifts" and "supernatural gifts" taken away from human beings. "Since reason, therefore, by which man distinguishes between good and evil, and by which he understands and judges, is a natural gift, it could not be completely wiped out; but was only partly weakened and partly corrupted, so that its misshapen ruins appear" (*Inst.* II.ii.12).

In this connection, Calvin says that the human being has a "natural instinct to foster and preserve society;" in other words, "sparks" or a "few meager sparks" that "still gleam." These sparks, which include "government, household management, all mechanical skills, the liberal arts," clearly testify "to a universal apprehension of reason and understanding by nature implanted in men" (*Inst.* II.ii.13–14). In this sense, the Spirit of God is explicitly the source of human spirituality, the Spirit of God the source of such gifts:

> If we regard the Spirit of God as the sole fountain of truth, we shall neither reject the truth itself, nor despise it wherever it shall appear ... Let us be ashamed of such ingratitude, into which not even the pagan poets fell, for they confessed that the gods had invented philosophy, laws, and all useful arts ... Let us, accordingly, learn by their example how many gifts the Lord left to human nature even after it was despoiled of its true good (*Inst.* II.ii.15).[22]

---

20. Ibid., 168–69.

21. *Comm. on Genesis*, 94.

22. For Calvin, the soul of human beings consists of two faculties: understanding and will. Will is in control of choice, containing the freedom to choose. Understanding (or mind or intellect) is even called at one point God's "true image." Calvin said that "It is a sign of God's image and likeness when he has made us reasonable creatures. God imprinted his image on humans by giving them intelligence and discretion; they have prudence; a great many are acute, have wisdom and skill." See William J. Bouwsma,

The Spirit in Cosmic Dimension

Calvin understands the *sensus divinitatis* and the *conscientia* as natural endowments of human beings undestroyable even by sin. However, in his commentary on the Gospel of John (1:5) he notes that endowments of human nature apart from grace finally come to a monstrous birth in a thousand superstitions, and conscience corrupts all judgment, confounding vice with virtue. In short, nature or reason will never direct men to Christ.

Karl Barth, based on such passages in Calvin, declares natural theology a doomed enterprise. Consequently, Barth rejects any "point of contact" for revelation.[23] Against Barth, Tamburello, however, regards the *sensus divinitatist* (sometimes referred to as *semen religionis*) and the *conscientia* as a point of contact with redeeming grace, in which Bernard of Clairvaux is used to compare with Calvin.

To revive this point of contact, Tamburello cites Edward Dowey's statement. "The impious themselves exemplify the fact that some conception of God is ever alive in all men's minds."[24] Dowey's further remark—"if the *sensus* is a knowledge of God's existence, it is *mysterium tremendum*"— helps Tamburello see Calvin as recognizing a point of contact with redeeming grace. Therefore, the argument goes like this: Barth had no grounds to cite Calvin in his denial of the point of contact. Following in the footsteps of Dowey, Tamburello sees no reason for a Christocentric theologian like Karl Barth to cite Calvin to deny a point of contact for the gospel.[25]

Be that as it may, Barth's "Nein!" to Brunner was not merely theological, but politically motivated in the face of German Christian support for Nazism. The danger of natural theology lay in domesticating and naturalizing the knowledge of God through the self-revelation in Jesus Christ. In the face of Hitler's rise to power, an attempt was made to domesticate and absorb Christianity into the German nature and culture. The so-called

---

John Calvin: A Sixteenth Century Portrait (New York: Oxford University Press, 1988) 79. Understanding is "the leader and governor of the soul; and . . . the will . . . always mindful of the bidding of the understanding, even in its . . . desires [awaiting] the judgement of the understanding" (*Inst.*I.xv.7).

23. Karl Barth, "No! Answer to Emil Brunner," in *Emil Brunner and Karl Barth, Natural Theology*, trans. Peter Fraenkel (London: Centenary, 1946).

24. Downey, *Knowledge of God in Calvin's Theology*, 55; see *Inst.*I.iii.2.

25. Dennis E. Tamburello, *Union with Christ: John Calvin and the Mysticism of St. Bernard* (Louisville: Westminster John Knox, 1994) 37.

"Deutsche Christen" was in collaboration for advocating conciliation with the Nazi regime. In addition, Roman Catholic theologians who were misguided, misapplied St Thomas's dictum (*gratia non tollit naturam sed perficit et complet*) to provide a theological ground for the concordat between the Vatican and Hitler. In other words, grace does not destroy German nature (blood and soil), but perfects and fulfills it. The essence of Christian gospel is at stake in Barth's confrontation with the natural and ideological theology of the "Deutsche Christen." This is why Brunner's mediating pamphlet *Nature and Grace* led Barth to angrily reply with a radical "No" to Brunner.

According to Dowey, Barth's insistence on the basis of Calvin's commentary on John 1:5 (natural reason will not lead to Christ) has no ground, because natural reason or human natural gifts in this context are opposed to what comes by regeneration. For Calvin "the man is corrupted by a natural wickedness, which however does not proceed from nature" (*Inst.* II.i.ii). In fact, the sinfulness or natural disposition of a human being is opposed to the created goodness. Dowey's concern is about referring to Calvin's natural theology in the non-Christian's relation to God outside the walls of Christianity. Calvin does not want to condemn natural knowledge of God as pagan or heresy, but for him a connection between *cognitio Dei creatoris* (*Inst.* I) and *cognitio Dei redemptoris* (*Inst.* II) is of pneumatological scope and content in a universal and cosmic sense rather than a dialectic one in the sense of Kierkegaard.[26] It seems to me that Calvin integrates the hidden power and efficacy of the Holy Spirit and the *theologia naturalis* into a cosmic dimension of Christ in terms of *extra Calvinisticum*. This is a unique point of Calvin's in that the Spirit mediates the point of contact between general and special revelation.[27]

Be that as it may, Barth never lost his concern about the *theologia naturalis* in terms of his nominalist tone of "Gott kann" (*CD* I) and the universal cosmic work of Christ (*CD* IV/3). Even during the confrontation with the Hitler regime, Barth dared to reflect on God's strange voice outside the walls of Christianity. It refers to a cosmic dimension of the revealed Word as the third form of the Word of God. "God may speak to us through Russian Communism, a flute concerto, a blossoming shrub, or a dead dog" (*CD* I/1, 55). At this point, Torrance is right in saying that for

---

26. Dowey, *Knowledge of God in Calvin's Theology*, 241.

27. Christian Link, *Handbuch Systematischer Theologie: Schöpfung*, vol. 7.1 (Gütersloh: Gerd Mohn, 1991) 148.

The Spirit in Cosmic Dimension

Barth "natural theology (*theologia naturalis*) is included and brought into clear light within the theology of revelation (*theologia revelata*), for in the reality of divine grace, there is included the truth of the divine creation." In this sense, "grace does not destroy but completes it."[28]

Later, in the doctrine of reconciliation, Barth develops more explicitly his counter thesis to natural theology. Yet Barth is open to natural theology in terms of the theology of God's reconciliation and God's word in action outside an ecclesial sphere. Barth's exposition of "secular parables of the truth" is in parallel with Calvin's pneumatology in the creation. It is certain that Barth does not want to talk about words *extra muros ecclesiae* by recourse to the sorry hypothesis of natural theology, but by recourse to the universal reign of Jesus Christ. It can refer to Barth's way of "establishing natural theology by means of Christology" in terms of socially and materially renewing and transforming its inherited traditional structure and framework.[29] Therefore, Barth writes; "dangerous modern expressions like 'the revelation of creation' or 'primal revelations' might be given a clear and unequivocal sense in this respect" (*CD* IV/3.1, 140).

In view of debate over natural theology, it seems to me more important to consider Calvin's anthropology through the cosmic dimension of the Spirit. Endowments of human nature are supposed to be discussed as a gift of God in the cosmic dimension of the divine Spirit, and it is the hidden impulse of the Spirit that leads these endowments for God's good purpose. Like Dowey, Tamburello loses sight of the Spirit's relatedness to the *sensus divinatatis* and *conscientia*. There is no division of natural theology from revelation theology, but the theology of the Spirit in Calvin's thought integrates problems such as nature, religion, and culture, as an integral part.

In speaking of the two faculties of the soul as the understanding and the will, Calvin arranges them in a clear hierarchy. The will as "the leader and governor of the soul" is "always mindful of the bidding of the understanding, even in its ... desires [awaiting] the judgment of the un-

---

28. Karl Barth, *Theology and Church: Shorter Writings 1920–1928*, trans. Louise Pettibone Smith (New York: Harper & Row, 1962) 342.

29. F.-W. Marquardt, *Theologie und Sozialismus: Das Beispiel Karl Barths* (Munich: Kaiser, 1981) 264. Moltmann argues that natural theology in a Barthian sense lies in the universalism of his doctrine of reconciliation. Moltmann sees Barth in sympathy with Tertullian's concept of "the naturally Christian soul" (*anima naturaliter christiana*). Cf. Moltmann, *Experiences in Theology: Ways and Forms of Christian Theology*, trans. Margaret Kohl (Minneapolis: Fortress, 2000) 75–76.

derstanding" (*Inst.* I.xv.7). However, human will is indeed totally enslaved, even though human natural endowments are not wholly extinguished: "Similarly the will, because it is inseparable from man's nature, did not perish, but was so bound to wicked desires that it cannot strive after the right" (*Inst.* II.ii.12). To be sure, Calvin does not deny that there are virtues and the right conduct among unbelievers; there is a clear difference "between the justice, moderation, and equity of Titus and Trajan and the madness, intemperance, and savagery of Caligula or Nero or Domitian . . . between observance and contempt of right and of laws" (*Inst.* III.xiv.2). Moreover, "In every age there have been persons who, guided by nature, have striven toward virtue throughout life." Calvin attributes such virtue to God's grace "not such grace as to cleanse it, but to restrain it inwardly" (*Inst.* II.iii.3.). "These are not common gifts of nature, but special graces of God, which He bestows variously and in a certain measure upon men otherwise wicked" (*Inst.* II.iii.4).

In accordance with the threefold work of the Holy Spirit—in the cosmos, in all human beings, and in the regenerate person—Calvin also described God's action upon human beings in a threefold manner: "There are three ways in which God acts upon men. First, all of us move and exist by him . . . Secondly, he moves and turns the wicked in a peculiar manner according as he thinks fit . . . Thirdly, when he governs by his spirit of sanctification, which is peculiar to the elect."[30]

As long as the Spirit is the source in all human beings, God is also in a position to move and turn the wicked in an extraordinary manner. God still makes use of the wicked for God's sake. By a secret impulse of God "God chooses, forms, yokes and draws men's hearts by a secret impulse, so that even by the impious he executes what he has decreed."[31] The ungodly are restrained and governed by God's power, that is, a secret impulse of God, which directs them to be used in the service of God's will.

In this regard, the second dimension of the cosmic work of the Holy Spirit is social and political. Christians should honor the civil order because it is ordained and rooted in God's will. "It behooves us reverently

---

30. Cited by Benjamin Milner, *Calvin's Doctrine of the Church*, Studies in the History of Christian Thought, 5 vols. (Leiden: Brill, 1970) 41. Cf. John Calvin, *Commentary on the Book of the Prophet Isaiah*, 4 vols., trans. William Pringle (Grand Rapids: Baker, 1979) 1:340 (Isa 10:5).

31. Milner, *Calvin's Doctrine of the Church*, 200. See especially the appendix, "The Secret Impulse of the Spirit," 197–203.

to regard and respect the political order, because it has been appointed by God for the common benefit of mankind."[32] But Calvin discounts any efforts to identify political order with the direct work of the Spirit. What Calvin has in mind concerning the political order is that it is divinely approved and ordained, and there can be wise rulers gifted by the Spirit of God. As Calvin states, "Kings can keep themselves within the bounds of justice and equity only by the grace of God; for when they are not governed by the Spirit of righteousness proceeding from heaven, their government is converted into a system of tyranny and robbery."[33]

In this sense, a discussion of Calvin's understanding of civil government is necessary, because the cosmic work of the Spirit is for the profit of the church. Civil government is an external means having the responsibility of restoring the godly order and protecting and promoting true religion (*Inst.* IV.xx.3.9). The magistrates are ordained by God, equipped for service of God as well as public commonwealth by the Spirit of God (*Inst.* II.ii.17). We will discuss Calvin's political ethical reflection on the state in chapter 5 more fully.

THE SPIRIT AS THE SANCTIFIER OF HUMAN LIFE

Calvin also speaks of the third dimension of the Holy Spirit as the sanctifier of human beings. This is the work of the Spirit especially in the regenerate. As mentioned earlier, it is the *imago Dei* that exalts human beings over other creatures. Through the fall we have lost the image of God. From its restoration we are aware what it was in its original state. Calvin refers to the restored image partly as consisting of true righteousness and holiness. The restoration of the image of God characterizes a new beginning of Christian spirituality. It also retains socio-ethical implications, taking into consideration true righteousness and holiness in an interpersonal context. Calvin's theology of the Spirit embraces spirituality of Christian life in relation to personal-social justice and sanctification. Out of creation is an anthropological place derived for human life. The human being is at the center of God's whole creative purpose and process, which is why God created all things for the sake of the human being's good and

---

32. Ibid., 30. Cf. Calvin, *Commentaries on the Catholic Epistles*, trans. and ed. John Owen (Grand Rapids: Eerdmans, 1948) 82.

33. John Calvin, *Commentary on the Book of Psalms*, 5 vols., trans. James Anderson (Grand Rapids: Eerdmans, 1949) 3:104–5 (Ps 72:4); and in Milner, *Calvin's Doctrine of the Church*, 31.

well-being (*Inst.* I.xiv.22). Nonetheless, human being does not stand for the self-glory and self-righteousness, rather for the gracious deed of the eternal, self-existent God.

The divine similitude of the human being depends on one's relationship to the Lord, because human beings are divinely created to serve God in terms of freedom and responsibility. Insofar as this relationship is thrown away, the divine image in human beings is destroyed. We know that the divine image in Christ is the perfect image of God. It is Christ by whom we are restored (*Inst.* I.xv.4). Through him we are brought again into a true relationship with our Creator, restoring the image of God in "true godliness, righteousness, purity, and knowledge" (*Inst.* I.xv.4), which had been lost by the corruption of Adam. At this point, Calvin's understanding of human beings (anthropology) stands in unbreakable connection with his Christology, and can be called a Christological anthropology. However, Calvin is tireless in asking who makes Christ present to us, i.e., how are the benefits of Christ possible for our life?

Therefore, Calvin relates the work of the Spirit to the work of regeneration. "We have nothing of the Spirit, however, except through regeneration. Whatever we have from nature, therefore, is flesh" (*Inst.* II.iii.1). "But the Spirit comes, not from nature, but from regeneration" (*Inst.* II.ii.27). "Hence it appears that God's grace, as this world is understood in discussing regeneration, is the rule of the Spirit to direct and regulate man's will. The Spirit cannot regenerate without correcting, without reforming, without renewing" (*Inst.* II.v.15).

In terms of regeneration, human beings are filled with "faith, love of God and neighbor, desire and application to live in righteousness and holiness" (*Inst.* II.ii.12). "Illuminating their minds and forming their hearts to the love and cultivation of righteousness" (*Inst.* II.v.5), the Spirit makes people a new creation. A new life in the power of the Spirit means a spirituality of the regenerated. From regeneration, the human's spiritual relationship with God can be discussed in connection with the interpersonal relationship. Hence a true socio-ethical attitude is grounded in a new spiritual life as a new creation. The new life of the regenerated has significant consequences for human reconciliation and harmony with nature, which has suffered through the corruption of human beings. The Spirit as the sanctifier mediates a genuine relationship between human beings and nature by awakening ecological awareness and human responsibility for all living creatures in nature. The Spirit also moves us dynamically toward transforming and sanctifying our social and ethical situation; challenging, in the familiar terms of Martin Buber, the "I-It" relationship and moving human beings to the "I-Thou" encounter with neighbors and other creatures.

The purpose of Christian spirituality, according to Calvin, is to live in conformity with the will of God. The Christian life consists, on the one hand, of justification by faith, and, on the other hand, of sanctification. God's grace as forgiving mercy and God's grace as sanctifying power are essentially interrelated in understanding of *spiritus creator*. Therefore, a Christian is not only a forgiven, justified person, but also an ethically committed person, righteous and holy, both personally and socially. It refers to the proper ethical concern of Calvin. Concerning spirituality and ethical reflection in the context of sanctifying Spirit, Calvin put the emphasis on its relationship—respect for the image of God in fellow people and love for them: "It is that we remember not to consider men's evil intention but to look upon the image of God in them, which cancels and effaces their transgressions, and with its beauty and dignity allures us to love and embrace them" (*Inst.* III.vii.6).

Therefore, "we ought to embrace the whole human race without exception in a single feeling of love; here there is no distinction between barbarian and Greek, worthy and unworthy, friend and enemy, since all should be contemplated in God, not in themselves" (*Inst.* II.viii.55). This has implications for social ethics, for our love of, and solidarity with our neighbors. For Calvin, secular matters such as socio-economic activities and relations cannot be dealt with independently of Christian life in the power of the Spirit. For now, we shall turn to Calvin's discussion of the role of the Spirit within a trinitarian context.

2

The Spirit in the Trinity

IF WE WANT TO clearly understand the role and function of the Spirit in Calvin's theology regarding the incarnated God in Jesus Christ, it is necessary to pay attention to his theological concept of the Trinity. How is the Spirit articulated in trinitarian terms? Calvin's theological hermeneutic finds itself in this statement: "For he so proclaims himself the sole God as to offer himself to be contemplated clearly in three persons [*Inst.* I.xiii.2] . . . Indeed, how can the mind by its own leading come to search out God's essence when it cannot even get to its own? Let us then willingly leave to God the knowledge of himself . . . He is the one fit witness to himself, and is not known except through himself" (*Inst.* I.xiii.21).

When Calvin deals with theological doctrines such as the Trinity, or with the confessions of the church fathers, his concern does not lie in solidifying or formalizing some doctrinal methodologies, but in placing Jesus Christ at the center. To put it another way, all theological references and doctrines move toward one goal: to serve and bear witness to the truth of Jesus Christ revealed in Scripture. In this way, Calvin separates himself from identifying his position with the literal, verbal truths of the Bible, because "scripture must be confirmed by the witness of the Spirit" (*Inst.* I.vii.1). The secret testimony of the Spirit precedes all mechanical, verbal inerrancy.[1]

For Calvin, the inner testimony of the Holy Spirit became an essential part of understanding the power and authority of Scripture. It is only the Spirit that enables us to grasp and comprehend what we read. Calvin's delicate balance between Word and Spirit is expressed in the Westminster Confession, in which "the inward illumination of the Spirit

---

1. Cf. Calvin's doctrine of the inner witness of the Holy Spirit, see *Inst.*I.vii.4., III.i.3f., III.ii.15, 33–36. Cf. Niesel, *Theology of Calvin*, 30–39.

of God" is found to be necessary for the saving understanding of such things as are revealed in the Word.² Lucien Richard sees Calvin's contribution to a new spirituality in his correlation of the Word and the Holy Spirit. As Richard writes, "It differed radically from the *Devotio Moderna* on three essential points: it was a spirituality of service within the world; it was accompanied by a new religious epistemology which made possible a reinterpretation of ecclesiological models and laid sound foundations for individualism in spirituality; and it asserted the inner unity of Christian life and theology."³

As Calvin insists, if Scripture is not "inscribed by the finger and Spirit of God on the heart, it is but a dead letter, and as it were a lifeless thing."⁴ Although the Bible is validated as the criterion, in light of which dogmatic ideas must be examined and tested, it does not mean our "slavish confinement to Biblical expressions" or to "making an idol of the Bible" as a paper pope.⁵ This aspect is expressive of Calvin's Spirit-dynamism in relation to the living reality of Jesus Christ. It is also worth bearing in mind when it comes to dealing with the role and function of the Spirit in a trinitarian context.

THE SPIRIT IN TRINITARIAN LIFE

Calvin refers to the Trinity in reference to the witness of the church fathers. Here Calvin concurs with the statement of Gregory of Nazianzus: "I cannot think on the one without quickly being encircled by the splendor of the three; Nor can I discern the three without being straightway carried back to the one" (*Inst.* I.xiii.17). As far as the one God in threeness is concerned, Calvin has no hesitancy in making use of the traditional term "person" to demonstrate distinctions within the One God: "'Person,'

---

2. Westminster Confession of Faith, *Book of Confessions*, 6.006; cf. Howard L. Rice, *Reformed Spirituality: An Introduction for Believers* (Louisville: Westminster John Knox, 1991) 101.

3. Richard, *Spirituality of John Calvin*, 174.

4. John Calvin, *Commentaries on the Catholic Epistles*, trans. and ed. John Owen (Grand Rapids: Baker, 1984) 297, Jas 1:25. Calvin rejects rationalistic scholasticism demanding proofs prior to faith in Scripture, as well as the fanatic sectarians claiming of leading of the Spirit independently, even running counter to Scripture. Jack Rogers and Donald K. McKim, *The Authority and Interpretation of the Bible* (San Francisco: Harper & Row, 1979) 106.

5. Niesel, *Theology of Calvin*, 56.

therefore, I call a 'subsistence' in God's essence, which, while related to the others, is distinguished by an incommunicable quality" (*Inst.* I.xiii.6).

Struggling with some heretical ideas, Calvin made a concerted effort to vindicate the truth of the Trinity. First of all, it was necessary for Calvin to affirm "the three persons in God." He was opposed to his contemporary anti-trinitarian writers (Servetus, Gribaldi, Blandrata, and Gentile, for example), who viewed God's essence to be torn into three persons. Calvin bases his use of personal terminology on Heb 1:3, referring to the Son of God as "the stamp of the Father's hypostasis."[6] In this sense, Calvin used hypostasis in describing the Trinity. For Calvin it is absurd to refer to hypostasis as being equivalent to essence, because essence is simple and undivided, without portion or derivation, and in integral perfection.

Calvin sees God as Father, even though "distinct in his proper nature, expresses himself wholly in the Son;" thus, God has made God's hypostasis visible in the latter (*Inst.* I.xiii.2). The same is said about the Holy Spirit. "There are in God three hypostases," but it means "not a distinction of essence" (*Inst.* I.xiii.2). In the Greek usage, *prosopon* (*Inst.* I.xiii. 2., n.7a) is equivalent to "subsistence," or *persona*. The Greeks Fathers taught the same doctrine—three *prosopa* in God—although this concept was expressed differently yet still agreeing "in the essential manner" (*Inst.* I. xiii.2).

In confrontation with Servetus, Calvin was more concerned about validating the true Godhead of Jesus Christ. Servetus's thought is reflected in this statement: "Indeed, to be execrated far beyond all else is the fact that he indiscriminately mingles both the Son of God and the Spirit with created beings generally" (*Inst.* I.xiii.22). Calvin also stands in sharp contrast with the anti-trinitarians (Gentile and his collaborators) because their interest lay only in asserting that Christ is "a figurative God, a God in appearance and name only, not in reality itself" (*Inst.* I.xiii.23). According to them, "the Spirit is of the Father alone, because if he is a derivation from the primal essence, which is proper only to the Father, he will not rightly be considered the Spirit of the Son" (*Inst.* I.xiii.23).

Calvin's bone of contention in understanding the Trinity starts from the biblical core message of God revealed in Jesus Christ. The name Yahweh is an inseparable from Jesus Christ. However, in the unity be-

---

6. Cf. *Inst.* I. xiii.2., n.7., *carakthr ths upostasews autou*, in the Vulgate: *figura substantiae eius*, in the KJV: "the express image of his persons," and in the RSV: "the very stamp of his nature." In the NRSV: "The exact imprint of God's very being."

tween God and Jesus Christ there should still be a distinction of persons. This distinction is not of the divine essence, but of the divine person. The Son is to be distinguished from the Father who sent him to us. Likewise, we can say that the Son of God is to be distinguished from the Comforter, the Holy Spirit, who makes Jesus Christ present to us (*Inst.* I.xiii.17).

Attacking Arianism, which argued that Christ was merely a creature, Calvin emphasized the *homoousios* (consubstantial) which was central to the creed of Nicaea (325). From here Calvin refuted Sabellianism, which insisted that "the Father is the Son, and the Holy Spirit the Father, without rank, without distinction" (*Inst.* I.xiii.4). That being the case, what is Calvin's proper understanding of Trinity? It can be seen as follows: "Father and Son and Spirit are one God, yet the Son is not the Father, nor the Spirit the Son, but that they are differentiated by a peculiar quality" (*Inst.* I.xiii.5).

Speaking of three persons in the One God does not imply three human beings as three persons. In Calvin's view, the term *person* only serves to demonstrate the special qualities which exist in the triune God: "Now, of the three substances I say that each one, while related to the others, is distinguished by a special quality. This 'relation' is here distinctly expressed: because where simple and indefinite mention is made of God, this name pertains no less to the Son and the Spirit than to the Father" (*Inst.* I.xiii.6).

That God is revealed as the Father, the Son, and the Holy Spirit is, in Calvin's view, different from the notion that "God is strong, and just, and wise" (*Inst.* I.xiii.4). It is not meant to be a monarchial concept of Trinity, which means "the unity of God precedes the Trinity."[7] Rather Calvin wants to express at this juncture that "indeed, the words 'Father,' 'Son,' and 'Spirit' imply a real distinction—let no one think that these titles, whereby God is variously designated from his works, are empty—but a distinction, not a division" (*Inst.* I.xiii.17). The formulation "a distinction, not a division" plays a significant role in Calvin's doctrine of Trinity because this distinction is used to express a reciprocal fellowship in the triune God. It denotes the dynamism of the Spirit in distinguishing, but not dividing, the perichoretic triplicity.

---

7. Moltmann, *Spirit of Life*, 290.

If this formulation is neglected, "a slightly modalizing tendency" of Calvin's Trinity,[8] or a monarchial Sabellianism[9] might come to the surface. What did Calvin mean by modalism? For him it is "a way of thinking, which, in principle, does not distinguish among persons of the Trinity, but views other divine persons only in terms of the work of the one person."[10] Out of this understanding of modalism arises the monarchial concept of the Trinity or Sabellianism which means that "God's strong uniqueness is unable to see another preexisting divine person besides himself."[11]

Here, the Son and the Spirit are nothing but *modi* of God's *Seinsweise*. But Calvin exempts himself clearly from this tendency. There has been the greater emphasis on the oneness of the Trinity in the Western church tradition (especially in the case of Augustine, suspected of "disguised modalism") as compared to its triplicity, Calvin tries to comprehend the perichoretic formulation of "distinction," while at the same time securing "no division." Calvin considers the triunity of the persons as expressing the unity of God, while making clear that God's triunity does not by any means imply three gods (*Inst.* I.xiii.25).

As Calvin writes, "What, then, did Christ mean when he commanded that Baptism should be in the name of the Father, and of the Son, and of the Holy Spirit, except that we ought with one faith to believe in the Father, the Son, and the Spirit? What else is this than to testify clearly that Father, Son, and Spirit are one God?" (*Inst.* I.xiii.16)

If the Holy Spirit is conceptualized as being equivalent in dignity with the Father and the Son within the trinitarian context, what relation does the Spirit have concerning the Father and the Son? How does the Spirit function for Calvin as the Spirit of the Father and of the Son in an

---

8. Wolf, Neuser, and Krusche all cast critical eyes on Calvin's Trinity, which has *in nuce* a modality aspect. Cf. H. H. Esser, "Hat Calvin eine 'leise modalisierende Trinitätslehre'?" in *Calvinus Theologus: Die Referate des Europäischen Kongresses für Calvinforschung vom 16. bis 19. September 1974 in Amsterdam*, ed. Wilhelm H. Neuser (Neukirchen: Neukirchener Verlag, 1976) 113–29.

9. Moltmann favors this term, characterizing Western trinitarian theologians such as Augustine and Anselm through the Reformation and including Barth and Rahner. See Moltmann, *Spirit of Life*, 290–98; Jürgen Moltmann, *History and the Triune God*, 57–63.

10. H. H. Esser, "Hat Calvin eine 'leise modalisierende Trinitätwslehre'?," in *Calvin's Ecclesiae Genevensis Custos*, ed. Wilhelm H. Neuser, 116.

11. H. Karpp, *Textbuch zur altkirchlichen Christologie*, Neukirchener Studienbucher Bd. 9 (Neukirchen: Neukirchener Verlag, 1972) 62.

inner-trinitarian relationship? We turn now to this aspect of the Spirit as the bond mediating between the Father and the Son.

THE SPIRIT AS THE BOND OF THE FATHER AND THE SON

Describing the three modes of one God in their peculiarities, Calvin admits "the observance of an order" (*Inst.* I.xiii.18). But he also disallows any speculative thinking to "seek in eternity a before or an after." For this reason, Calvin affirms the truth of the *filioque* in the Western form of the Nicene Creed, because if the Son alone proceeds from the Father, then "the Spirit [proceeds] from the Father and the Son at the same time" (*Inst.* I.xiii.18). He favors the *filioque* to express properly the mutual relationship of the triune God rather than seek a monarchial subordination of the one God (*Inst.* I.xiii.19).[12]

The *filioque* addition is significant because it expresses the reciprocal relationship between the Son and the Spirit. The Son and the Spirit should not be understood like "two sons" of the one God. Therefore, the Spirit should not proceed from the Father only. Calvin's understanding of the Spirit might therefore be reformulated with regard to the *filioque* in the following way: the Spirit proceeds from the Son in the presence of Father. As mentioned above, Calvin adopts the starting point for understanding the Trinity in connection with Jesus Christ. Lacking an awareness of a reciprocal relationship within the triune God, Anabaptist enthusiasm or the danger of heresy would arise. Thus, Calvin conceptualizes the mutual relationship between Christ and the Spirit in a perichoretic manner: "We ought to know that He is called the 'Spirit of Christ' not only because Christ, as eternal Word of God, is joined in the same Spirit with the Father, but also from his character as the Mediator" (*Inst.* III.i.2). Thus, from the beginning, Christ may not be separated from the Spirit.

These distinctions in the triune God lead us to understand that "to the Father is attributed the beginning of activity, and the fountain and wellspring of all things; to the Son wisdom, counsel, and the ordered disposition of all things; but to the Spirit is assigned the power and efficacy of that activity"(*Inst.* I.xiii.18). This is the doctrine of *appropriation*, that is to say, the work most appropriate to each person. But at the same time, one must be cautious about the fact that seeking the economy of the Trinity

---

12. Cf. Lukas Vischer, ed., *Fallacy Controversy, Spirit of God, Spirit of Christ: Ecumenical Reflections on the Fallacy Controversy* (Geneva: WCC, 1981).

does not mean seeking "in eternity a before or an after" (*Inst.* I.xiii.18). In fact, there may not be any division in the perichorectic God.

The triune God as *perichoresis*, in which each distinct mode of being of God coinheres and interpenetrates the other, also acts *ad extra* towards us. These actions are one, the external works of the Trinity are indivisible (*opera trinitatis ad extra sunt indivisa*). The triune God as *perichoresis*, which means dynamic being of God, is not separable from the triune God as appropriations. In this way Calvin affirms Augustine's rule of the Trinity.

How is it possible that the perichorectic God is present dynamically to us? It is the "power and efficacy" of the Holy Spirit that unites and simultaneously distinguishes between the Father and the Son. The distinction signifies no separation of essence, but rather the mutual relationship of the one God in threeness (*Inst.* I.xiii.19). The Spirit functions as the dynamic bond of Father and the Son in an inner-trinitarian way. The Spirit as the dynamic bond unites us to Christ in the economy (*Inst.* III.1.1). Here regeneration and sanctification can be understood as double grace arising from the experience of the living Christ through the Spirit. The dynamic, reciprocal relationship among the persons of the Trinity challenges any individualistic interpretation of the persons, since the social dimension of the triune God has implications for the human community. It characterizes Christian spirituality "with experience in love, in friendship, in the community of Christ's people which is filled by the Spirit, and in the just society."[13]

It is also the Spirit who enables oneness and threeness of the triune God by distinguishing dynamically each mode of being, but not by dividing them. Thus, Calvin uses the perichoretic-appropriation framework to articulate his view of the Trinity with special emphasis on the dynamic efficacy of the Holy Spirit. Calvin's understanding of God is not oriented toward any metaphysical dualism, but it is biblically oriented. The aseity of the perichoretic God cannot be isolated from God's action in Jesus Christ through the Spirit for us. In this respect, Calvin writes: "The Son is one God with the Father because he shares with the Father one and the same Spirit; and that the Spirit is not something other than the Father and different from the Son, because he is the Spirit of the Father and the Son. For in each hypostasis the whole divine nature is understood, with

---

13. Ibid., 309. For the debate on the social doctrine of the Trinity, see Jürgen Moltmann, *The Trinity and the Kingdom of God*, trans. Margaret Kohl (Minneapolis: Fortress, 1993).

this qualification—that to each belongs his own peculiar quality" (*Inst.* I.xiii.19).

If the whole divine nature of God can be understood in each hypostasis, and communicated through the Spirit, to what extent has the Spirit to do with the hypostatic nature of Christ? How does Calvin formulate this problem? In what way is the Spirit, as the dynamic bond, involved in the two natures of Christ?

THE SPIRIT IN RELATION TO CHRIST'S HYPOSTATIC UNITY

Based on the dynamism of the Spirit in the trinitarian context, we refer to Calvin's understanding of hypostatic unity in the person of Jesus Christ. How does Calvin consider the two natures of the one person Jesus Christ? First of all, Calvin stresses the dynamic unity of true God and true man in Jesus Christ, so that he could clarify the biblical understanding of Christology. Jesus Christ is "true God and true man" (*Inst.* II.xii.2). What does this mean? It is in Christ, true God, that salvation and saving grace is revealed. In Christian understanding, it is impossible to mediate the gulf between God and human beings from the human side on account of the fall (*Inst.* II.xii.1).

From the start it is not human beings who come to God, but God who comes to us through the divine initiative and fellowship. Therefore, Calvin expresses a radical distinction between God and God's creatures: "Even if man had remained free from all stain, his condition would have been too lowly for him to reach God without a Mediator" (*Inst.* II.xii.1). Calvin affirms himself in line with Pauline Christology: "One mediator between God and men, the man Jesus Christ (1 Tim. 2:5) ... For the same reason ... it was his task to swallow up death ... It was his task to conquer sin ... Therefore our most merciful God, when he willed that we be redeemed, made himself our Redeemer in the person of his only-begotten Son (cf. Rom. 5:8)" (*Inst.* II.xii.2).

For Calvin, the humanity of Jesus Christ is also of significance as much as his divinity: "Because the Spirit speaking through his mouth knew our weakness, at the right moment he used a most appropriate remedy to meet it: he set the Son of God familiarly among us as one of ourselves" (*Inst.* II.xii.1). The man Jesus Christ, according to Calvin, is the way "God, to bring Himself within the reach of human understanding, humbles Himself and makes Himself small."[14] What "Christ became true man" means is that the true humanity of Jesus Christ is the presupposition for our communion with him and so also for our salvation: "We trust that we are sons of God, for God's natural Son fashioned for himself a body from our body, flesh from our flesh, bones from our bones, that he might be one with us" (*Inst.* II.xii.2).

Therefore, the encounter between God and us in the true humanity of Jesus Christ opens up a new life for us as children of God before God and neighbors: "We are assured of the inheritance of the Heavenly Kingdom" (*Inst.* II.xii.2). But it must be kept in mind that the true humanity of Jesus Christ is not to be considered in isolation from his divinity. "In short, since neither as God alone could he feel death, nor as man alone could he overcome it, he coupled human nature with divine that to atone for sin he might submit the weakness of the one to death; and that, wrestling with death by the power of the other nature, he might win victory for us" (*Inst.* II.xii.3).[15]

Calvin's focus on Christology consists not in any philosophical, metaphysical fusion of two natures, but in solidifying dynamically the Godhead and humanhood of the one person, Jesus Christ. For Calvin, "the Word was made flesh" (John 1:14) does not mean that the "Word was turned into flesh or confusedly mingled with flesh." The Word chose for himself the virgin's womb as a temple in which to dwell. The Son of God became the Son of man—not by confusion of substance, but by unity of person (*Inst.* II.xiv.1).

In exploring the unity between divinity and humanity in one person of Jesus Christ, Calvin stands in line with Chalcedonian orthodoxy. Even though Calvin accepted *communicatio idiomatum* (*idiomaton koinonia*, the communicating of properties), yet the communication of properties seems not to be fully adequate to explain Calvin's dialectical, dynamic structure of Christology. Based on some biblical passages (e.g., Acts 20:28, 1 Cor 2:8, 1 John 1:1) Calvin writes: "Surely God does not have blood, does not suffer, cannot be touched with hands. But since Christ, who was true God and also true man, was crucified and shed his blood for us.

---

14. *Corpus Reformatorum*, 55.227 (hereinafter *CR*). Cf. Niesel, *Theology of Calvin*, 113.

15. Here Calvin sharply opposed the scholastic theology of the Roman church (including Nestorius), which viewed God in disassociation from revelation (*Inst.* II.xii.6–7).

Accordingly, there also a property of humanity is shared with the other nature (*Inst.* II.xiv.2)."

Here we see a different approach to divine passibility than Martin Luther. The two reformers saw Jesus Christ as one person in two natures by way of a relationship of unity in distinction. Where Luther focuses on the unity, Calvin emphasizes the distinction. With this distinction, Calvin is not eager to construct a theology of divine suffering, because "God has no blood, nor does he suffer, nor can he be touched with hands" (*Inst.* II.xiv.2). In reflection on the crucified (1 Cor 2:8) Calvin interprets Christ to suffer in the flesh "as an abject and despised man" (*Inst.* IV.xvii.30), so that divine impassbility is safeguarded. If Calvin took seriously the role of the Spirit in the communion of divinity and humanity in one person of Jesus Christ, should he not have stated that Christ's divinity is fully communicated with the humanity of Jesus? In an ecumenical context, Reformed theologians such as Barth and Moltmann make recourse to Luther's theology of divine passibility for articulation of relationship between God and human life.

Nonetheless, in confrontation with some heretical errors of Nestorius, Eutyches, and Servetus, Calvin was concerned about keeping the unity of the two natures from their fusion or separation: "We, therefore hold that Christ, as he is God and man, consisting of two natures united but not mingled, is our Lord and the true Son of God even according to, but not by reason of, his humanity" (*Inst.* II.xiv.4).[16]

Calvin affirms the "hypostatic union" in order to explain the one person of Jesus Christ out of two natures. What did this union mean for Calvin? The *ensarkosis* of the *Logos* does not mean that the *logos asarkos* is dissolved into the reality of the *logos ensarkos*, so that the second person of the Trinity can exist only in the person of the Mediator. Rather it means that the second person of the Trinity is assumed in the new office, so that he has another mode of being in incarnation. The pre-existence of the eternal *logos* cannot be denied or abandoned in the existence of the *logos* who became flesh. In other words, the eternal Son pre-exists still in rela-

---

16. Cyril of Alexandria at the Synod of Ephesus (431) condemned Nestorius's sharp separation between the divine and human natures of Christ as heretical. The Council of Constantinople (448) condemned Eutyches's rejection of Christ's human nature. The doctrines of both were repudiated by the Ecumenical Council of Chalcedon (451). Cf. *Inst.* II. xiv. 5 n. 11.

tion to the *ensarkos* of Jesus Christ after the incarnation, and at the same time, he exists as the one who became flesh.

Who is then to make possible this dynamic hypostatic union of Jesus Christ (*ensarkos/asarkos* dynamism) as true man and true God? As already mentioned, the Spirit as the bond of the Father and the Son should be understood as the bond that dynamically unifies the divinity and humanity of Jesus Christ, without separating, or confusing. Calvin is not satisfied with accepting the status of Jesus Christ ontologically in terms of being. Rather he portrays Christology in light of the dynamism of the Spirit. As far as the two natures are concerned, these may not be conceived in a static and abstract way. Calvin's *Logos* Christology is endowed with the dialectical structure of Christology in connection with the actuality of the Spirit. In this regard, Krusche's statement is worth considering: "The *logos ensarkos* and *asarkos* is not two different *Logoi*. This is the one *Logos*, the second person of the Trinity, who is concerned with Father through the Spirit proceeding from the Father."[17]

For this reason Calvin insists that "the Son of God descended from heaven in such a way that, without leaving heaven, he willed to be born in the virgin's womb, to go about the earth, and to hang upon the cross; yet he continuously filled the world even as he had done from the beginning!" (*Inst.* II.xiii.4). Calvin opposes and rejects the ubiquity of Christ's body, which Luther frequently utilizes to explain the presence of Christ's body in the Eucharist.[18] What is important for Calvin is to underline emphatically that "the one person of Christ so consists of two natures that each nevertheless retains unimpaired its own distinctive character" (*Inst.* IV.xvii.30).

If Lutheran theology develops its Christology in terms of maintaining a perichoresis between the divinity and the humanity of Jesus Christ, the Lutheran statement about the enfleshment of the Word of God holds that the Word of God has reality only through and in the humanity of Jesus. Thus, there is nothing outside of the flesh (*extra cranem*). In Barth's view, Reformed Christology has its connection with Athanasius and Gregory of Nyssa. Even Luther considers the *extra* in due and proper form. The Reformed position is not directed against a Lutheran sense of

---

17. Krusche, *Das Wirken des Heiligen Geistes nach Calvin*, 129.

18. Martin Luther, "Confession Concerning Christ's Supper—from Part I (1528)," in *Martin Luther's Basic Theological Writings*, ed. Timothy F. Lull (Minneapolis: Fortress, 1989) 375–404.

totus intra carnem, but against its negative conclusion, the *numquam et nuspiam extra carnem*. Reformed concern regards the *extra* as distinctive, not as separate. Together with the Lutherans, the Reformed position asserts the permanent presence of the Logos in the flesh which is much closer to Luther's reflection of ubiquity of human nature in virtue of the glorious operation of the risen God-Man. Nonetheless, the Reformed position does not want to abolish or suppress the reality of the *logos asarkos* in view of the *logos ensarkos*. It indicates a Reformed dynamic-noetic interest in Christology.[19]

Any static fusion or separation of the two natures would endanger the hypostatic unity of Jesus Christ. Therefore, Calvin cites Paul's remark: "He suffered in weakness of the flesh but rose again by the power of the Spirit" (2 Cor 13:4; *Inst.* II.xiv.6). Therefore, a rigid christological formulation, *extra Calvinisticum* (*finitum non capax infiniti*; the finite is not capable of the infinite), has to be reinterpreted in light of the dynamism of the Spirit who mediates Christ's *munus triplex* (Christ's three offices) (*Inst.* II.xv.1–6).[20] Christological soteriology becomes the foundation in the transformation of human life and spiritual benefit for it.

In a nutshell, we can say that Christ's *munus triplex* is structured in a pneumatological framework because the threefold office is closely related to the anointing of the Holy Spirit. As for Christ's prophetic office, one must notice that "he (Jesus Christ) received anointing, not only for himself that he might carry out the office of teaching, but for his whole body that the power of the Spirit might be present in the continuing preaching of the gospel" (*Inst.* II.xv.2). From this office "the whole immensity of heavenly benefits" is given for the believers.

The kingly office refers to the eternity of Christ's dominion, which inspires us to have hope for blessed eternity and immortality. That is spiritual in nature: "The hope of a better life . . . the full fruit of this grace in the age to come" (*Inst.* II.xv.3). The benefit of Christ's kingly office for the believer lies in the fact that "Christ enriches his people with all things necessary for the eternal salvation of souls and fortifies them with courage to stand unconquerable against all the assaults of spiritual enemies" (*Inst.* II.xv.4). Christ is called Messiah by virtue of his kingship. Christ

---

19. *CD* I/2:168–70.

20. Cf. Bucer, "*Rex regnum Christus est, summus sacerdos, et prophetarum caput.*" *Enarrationes in Enagelia*" (1536) 607. Cf. *Inst.* II.xv.2, footnote.

was anointed by the Spirit to be herald and witness of the Father's grace for our sake.

Even in the midst of misery, reproaches and other troubles surrounding our life there will be divine consolation: "Our king will never leave us destitute, but will provide for our needs until, our warfare ended, we are called to triumph" (*Inst.* II.xv.4). Furthermore, the spiritual nature of Christ's kingly office refers to the sovereignty of Christ. "Christ's kingdom lies in the Spirit" (*Inst.* II. xv.5). God has given all power and authenticity to Christ so that God may take care of us through the Son. "Christ stands in our midst, to lead us little by little to a firm union with God" (*Inst.* II.xv.5). The prophetic dignity in Christ is just for our benefit, so the blessing of Christ's kingly office is also for us. Christ's kingly office is related to sanctification, as long as Christ as King rules us through his Spirit, by leading our struggle with the world toward victory.[21]

The priestly office is treated in the context of the reconciliation and intercession of the Mediator. This office implies that Christ as mediator brings for us reconciliation with God through his holiness. Obtaining God's favor for us and appeasing God's wrath, Christ performs this office through the sacrifice of his death. Beginning with his sacrificial death we are granted the efficacy and benefits of his priesthood. Through this office we obtain not only God's favorable and propitious action through reconciliation, but we are also accepted as God's companion in the great office (*Inst.* II.xvi.6). Our justification is possible only through the priestly office in which Christ makes an offering sacrifice and becomes the objective basis of our justification (*Inst.* II.xv.6). Where Luther represents *theologia crucis*, Calvin defends *theologia gloriae* in terms of *munus triplex*.

In light of what has been described, the Spirit lives and works in relation to the Father and the Son in a trinitarian context. Here the Spirit functions as the bond unifying and distinguishing the Father and the Son. "Distinction but no division" in the perichoretic triune God basically denotes the dynamism of trinitarian pneumatology. This Spirit is also at work in communicating the two natures of Jesus Christ in dynamic, dialectical, and actual manner. The Spirit as mediator unifies and com-

---

21. In this regard, Calvin states: "Christ enriches his people with all things necessary for the eternal salvation of souls and fortifies them with courage to stand unconquerable against all the assaults of spiritual enemies." . . . But "our King will never leave us destitute, but will provide for our needs until, our warfare ended, we are called to triumph" (*Inst.* II.xv.4).

municates the divinity and humanity of the one person of Jesus Christ. A hypostatic unity refers to Jesus Christ as truly God and truly man in a Spirit-dynamism. Furthermore, the Spirit in the Trinity reaches out to us, because the person and the work of Christ is not divided, but mediated and communicated for our benefit in the power and efficacy of the Spirit. Therefore, we can refer to the Spirit as communicator of Christ for us, which will be a topic of our next discussion.

3

The Spirit as Communicator of Christ for the Christian Life

THE SPIRIT AND SPIRITUALITY OF CHRIST-UNION

In order to explore and discuss what the Spirit in the trinitarian context brings for our benefit, Calvin begins book III of the *Institutes* under the title, "The things spoken concerning Christ profit us by the secret working of the Spirit." Here, as the sanctifier of human life, the Spirit stands in correlation with the person and the work of Christ: Christ works for the Spirit, while the Spirit works for Christ. Thus, there is a christological dimension in Calvin's theology of the Spirit, grounded as it is in the trinitarian communion, which is the ground of the spiritual event of Christ within us, centered in our union with Christ.

In Calvin's terminology, union with Christ is distinctly Christological, however this Christocentricism is not at all at odds with a doctrine of union with Triune God.[11] To the degree that Calvin thinks of the union in a trinitarian context in light of the different roles of the Trinity (appropriation in the economy of the Trinity), he prefers to use the term union with Christ. Calvin describes the Father as the One who sends the Son, Christ, in whom we are engrafted, and the Spirit, who sanctifies us.

To what extent does Calvin conceptualize union with Christ in a pneumatological sense? How can we become partakers in the salvation

---

1. "We are united to God by Christ and . . . we can only be joined to Christ if God abides in us;" and "Men are so engrafted into Christ by faith that Christ joins them to God." Calvin, *John 11–21 and First Epistle of John*, 293–94, quoted in Tamburello, *Union with Christ*, 93. See also *Inst*. II.viii.18., II.xv.5., II.xvi.3., III.vi.2, and III.xxv.2. Consider also Wilhelm Kolfhaus, *Christusgemeinschaft bei Johannes Calvin*: Beiträge zur Geschichte und Lehre der Reformierten Kirche 3 (Neukirchen: Buchhandlung d. Erziehungsvereins, 1938) 3:38.

of Christ? How can the historic Jesus become effective and actual for us here and now? With these questions in mind, Calvin calls our attention to Christ *extra nos* as the objective ground for our faith and salvation. We are allowed to share in what Christ has done for us, because the benefit, which Christ acquired from the Father, has been provided for us. "Therefore, to share with us what he has received from the Father, he had to become ours and to dwell within us" (*Inst.* III.i.I). Indeed, by nature we are hostile and rebellious against God, but if we "embrace that communion with Christ . . . we come to enjoy Christ and all his benefits" (*Inst.* III.i.I).[2]

However, it must be remembered that salvation takes place in Christ outside of us. This *extra nos* event is one of the dominant leitmotifs in Calvin's Christology. In speaking of the certainty of justification by faith alone, he takes account of Christ's *extra nos* as the fundamental ground: "Righteous—not in ourselves but in Christ" (*Inst.* III.xi.23). This starting point affirms Calvin's epistemology in understanding faith, justification, and salvation. We know our righteousness only because we become sharers in Christ: "By the intercession of Christ's righteousness" (*Inst.* III. xi.23), we are justified in the sight of God. Therefore, "this is equivalent to saying that man is not righteous in himself but because the righteousness of Christ is communicated to him by imputation— something worth carefully noting" (*Inst.* III.xi.23).

When it comes to justification, Calvin put the emphasis on Christ's righteousness *extra nos* in numerous places, for example, "'We are made righteous by Christ's obedience' (Rom 5:19) . . . We could not stand unless we are reckoned righteous before God in Christ and apart from ourselves" (*Inst.* III.xi.4.). From this objective basis, we understand our mystical communion with Christ. Calvin explains our union with Christ in emphatic terms, like the "joining together of Head and members," the "indwelling of Christ in our hearts," or the "mystical union."[3] Hereby "Christ, having been made ours, makes us sharers with him in the gifts with which he has been endowed" (*Inst.* III. xi.10). It means that we are engrafted into his body.

---

2. For Calvin's communion with Christ in comparison with Bucer's terminology. Willem Van't Spijker, "Die Lehre vom Heiligen Geist bei Bucer und Calvin," in *Calvinus Servus Christi: Die Referate des Internationalen Kongresses für Calvinforschung vom 25. bis 28. August 1986 in Debrecen*, ed. Wilhelm Neuser (Budapest: Presseabteilung des Raday-Kollegiums, 1988) 73–106.

3. The expression *mystica Communicatio cum Christ* is found in his numerous exegeses. See also Tamburello, *Union with Christ*, especially his appendix, 111–13.

Here, Kolfhaus's statement is worthy of consideration: "Justification and sanctification, faith and morality, are seen [by Calvin] in light of engrafting into Christ. Calvin thinks from this point out, and his thoughts always turn back to it."[4] Calvin himself characterizes the nature and essence of the union with Christ in more detail based on an experiential moment in his letter to Peter Martyr Vermigli: "I know only this: that through the power of the Holy Spirit the life of heaven flows down to earth, for the flesh of Christ is neither life-giving in itself nor can its effect reach us without the immeasurable work of the Spirit. Thus it is the Spirit who makes Christ live in us, who sustains and nourishes us, who accomplishes everything on behalf of the Head."[5]

Sometimes Calvin makes use of the concept of *koinonia* (translated as *sacra unitas*). This *unitas* comes about as soon as we accept Christ by faith, being implanted into his body. Occurring beyond the capacity of human comprehension, it is more a matter of astonishment than of understanding; it is mysterious. In his letter to Peter Martyr, Calvin again stresses: "How this happens far exceeds the limits of my understanding, I must confess; thus I have more of an impression of this mystery than I strive to comprehend it."[6]

However, Calvin opposes the vulgar idea of an ontological mingling of our substance with Christ. Calvin never implied "the absorption of the pious mystic into the sphere of the divine being."[7] A mystical component in Calvin exists in the Spirit's communication between Christ *extra nos* and Christ *in nobis* for us, placing the issue of mysticism in a pneumatological framework.

In the Protestant tradition, mysticism as a whole has been viewed in a negative way as it has been thought to be incompatible with the core message of the Gospel, i.e., salvation through faith in Christ alone. As Ritschl, for example, writes, "Wherever mysticism is found, the theology of justification no longer retains its true significance as the key to the

---

4. Kolfhaus, *Christusgemeinschaft bei Johannes Calvin*, 80. Also see Tamburello, *Union with Christ*, 87.

5. John Calvin, Letter 2266 to Peter Martyr Vermigli, August 8, 1555, C. O. 15:723. See also Tamburello, *Union with Christ*, 87.

6. Letter to Peter Martyr, August 8, 1555, C. O. 15:723: "Let us therefore labor more to feel Christ living in us, than to discover the nature of that communication." See Tamburello, *Union with Christ*, 89.

7. Niesel, *Theology of Calvin*, 126, cf. 144, 222.

The Spirit as Communicator of Christ for the Christian Life

whole domain of the Christian life."[8] According to Ritschl, Reformed faith rejects any possibility of equating human beings with God in an ontological sense. The mystical conception of salvation stands in contradiction not only with the ethical thrust of Reformation theology. Furthermore, mysticism is based on works righteousness associated with contemplative exercises. Kolfhaus also views mysticism as "the effort on the part of the person for an unmediated communion with God." This effort results in "sinking into the divinity with pleasures and pain and annihilation of the person through meditation, asceticism, prayer and enjoyment of the deepest 'entering into' God, no matter which form it takes—in ecstasies, visions or other forms of being outside oneself."[9]

For Tamburello, Friedrich von Hügel's understanding of the mystical element of religion (institutional, speculative, experiential and mystical) is helpful in taking issue with mysticism. Von Hügel defines the mystical element as "the ontological presence of, and the operative penetration by, the Infinite Spirit, within the human spirit," or of "some, however implicit, however slight, however intermittent, sense and experience of the Infinite," which is similar to Troeltsch's definition of mysticism as "direct inward and present religious experience."[10] Thus, Tamburello takes Gerson's definition of mystical theology as a guide to clarify his study: "Mystical theology is experiential knowledge of God attained through the union of spiritual affection with Him."[11] Tamburello's ecumenical contribution to mysticism, critical of the one-sided understanding of mysticism as "involving a union of essence or absorption into the divine" can be found in presenting a genuine mysticism in Calvin's thought, no matter how generic it is or in the more specific definition of Gerson. For Calvin, union with Christ is fundamental to Christian faith, justification, sanctification, and even election. At any rate, Tamburello remains silent about how Calvin develops the contemplative dimension in a social, ethical direction, and how union with Christ is related to charismatic experience from a pneumatological-ecclesiological perspective. In my view, Calvin takes the mystical urge, which is the last stage of contemplative life prior to purgation and illumination, as his starting point in discussing

---

8. Tamburello, *Union with Christ*, 3.
9. Ibid., 5.
10. Ibid., 9.
11. Ibid., 11.

his theology of the Spirit. Integrating mysticism, experiential awareness or knowledge of God's presence, which is fundamental to his pneumatology, Calvin no longer views mysticism as a domain alien to faith, but an integral part of it. Werner Krusche expresses the tension between Christ *in nobis* and Christ *extra nos* in a convincing way:

> We in Christ and thus *extra nos* and Christ *in nobis* is to Calvin entirely the same thing. The fact that our justification takes place from our union with Christ does not mean that our righteousness lies in us ourselves and not *extra nos*. For after all, also in *unio mystica* Christ continues to be *extra nos* in this sense that he does not become identical with us.[12]

In light of and with emphasis on Christ *extra nos* (alien righteousness of justification), Calvin distinguishes Christ *in nobis* from any mystical, ontological mingling between the human and the divine. Furthermore, Calvin articulates the aspect of the Christ-union in a sacramental perspective. For him, Christ-union is put into a more concrete context by using his favorite image of "engrafting." Calvin understood the Eucharist as "a help whereby we may be engrafted into Christ's body, or, engrafted, may grow more and more together with him, until he perfectly joins us with him in the heavenly life" (*Inst.* IV.xvii.33).

Calvin also combined baptism with this "engrafting," defining it as "the sign of the initiation by which we are received into the society of the church, in order that, engrafted in Christ, we may be reckoned among God's children" (*Inst.* IV.xv.1). This Christ-union expressed itself extraordinarily in his understanding of the Sacrament. Here Kolfhaus's statement is worthy of consideration: "The sacraments do not have any meaning of their own; they serve the goal of sealing an already existing *unio mystica cum Christo*, of making it more emphatic and clear, of strengthening communion with the Head, and of nourishing the soul as living food."[13]

The pneumatological communication between Christ *extra nos* and Christ *in nobis* can be understood as the heart of Calvin's union with Christ in the context of Christian life. How and in what sense then can Christ *extra nos* become Christ *in nobis*, indwelling within us? It comes

---

12. Krusche, *Das Wirken des Heiligen Geistes nach Calvin*, 274. See also Willem van't Spijker, "'Extra Nos' and 'In Nobis' by Calvin in a Pneumatological Light," in *Calvin and the Holy Spirit*, Sixth Colloquium on Calvin & Calvin Studies (Grand Rapids: Calvin Studies Society, 1989) 50.

13. Kolfhaus, *Christus-gemeinschaft*, 121. See also Tamburello, *Union with Christ*, 100.

about by *faith*. Calvin elucidates faith at length in his *Institutes* (*Inst*. III. ii.1–40). He demonstrates Christ as the object of faith (*Inst*. III.ii.1), because the promise of faith is fulfilled in Christ (*Inst*. III.ii.32).[14]

But the assumption that we gain access to communion with Christ through faith is in need of elucidation. How does the revelation of God in Christ become a living reality for and in us? How are we placed into relationship with the person and the work of the Mediator? Is it by our own spiritual capacity or insight? Through our subjective, anthropological faith we cannot yet recognize and accept God revealed in Christ. Neither through our intellectual or spiritual strength are we also not capable of setting up a relationship with Christ. How then does it occur?

It is the Holy Spirit, in Calvin's view, who effectuates our faith, because "faith is the principal work of the Holy Spirit" (*Inst*. III.i.4). The Holy Spirit is the bond that unites us to Christ, as much as the Spirit binds the Father and the Son: "Without the Spirit man is incapable of faith" (*Inst*. III.ii.35). When Jesus Christ baptizes us with the Holy Spirit, when the Spirit leads us to the faith, and regenerates us as new creatures, we become real partakers in Christ's salvation. Through the power of the Holy Spirit Christ inspires us to be in faith to say yes to Him. Through the Spirit Christ enables us to stand in communion with him. By "the secret energy of the Spirit, we come to enjoy Christ and all his benefits" (*Inst*. III.i.1). Because of this fact "the indestructible certainty of faith rests upon Christ's oneness with us" (*Inst*. III.ii.24).

Therefore, the event of Christ-union has nothing to do with our own spiritual endeavors, but only divine initiative for us. Through the Spirit, Christ *extra nos* becomes Christ *in nobis*. The Spirit plays a decisive part in communicating the death, resurrection, and parousia of Christ for our Christian life. In this regard, Calvin stresses: "This union alone ensures that he has not unprofitably come with the name of Savior . . . But he unites himself to us by the Spirit alone. By the grace and power of the same Spirit we are made his members, to keep us under himself and in turn to possess him" (*Inst*. III.1.3).

This statement affirms again the initiative of Christ's action, bringing us into oneness with himself. The connection between Christology and

---

14. "Faith produces confidence, which again, in its turn, produce boldness . . . To separate faith and confidence would be an attempt to take away heat and light from the sun." John Calvin, *Commentary on the Epistles of Paul to the Galatians and Ephesians by John Calvin*, trans. William Pringle (Grand Rapids: Baker, 1993) 257.

pneumatology characterizes and penetrates Calvin's spirituality in expectation of eternal life. There is an important link between faith and hope. Faith is the foundation for hope, while hope nourishes and sustains faith in expectation of Christ. "Hope refreshes faith, that it may not become weary. It sustains faith to the final goal, that it may not fail in mid course, or even at the starting gate" (*Inst.* III.2.42).

With this connection in mind, it is legitimate for us to speak of faith from the human side. Faith is our surrender to Christ. Faith binds us to Christ, incorporates us into the body of Christ, because the power of the Spirit inspires the seed of our faith. If faith were merely a human decision or an existential feeling, or if faith didn't rest entirely upon the grace of Jesus Christ, what Christ has done for us would remain useless. Faith in itself has no value, no meaning for our salvation, because "faith arises from God's promise of grace in Christ" which is "revealed to our minds and sealed upon our hearts through the Holy Spirit" (*Inst.* III.ii.7).

Here Calvin rejects Osiander's doctrine of essential faith, through which our union with Christ effects a merging and commingling of our being with Christ's own. After all, his critique of Osiander's "essential righteousness" can be seen as a critique of a mystical, ontological absorption into God (*Inst.* III.xi.5–12). As we have already seen, in Calvin's thought, a mystical union has a different direction from "the absorption of the pious mystic into the sphere of the divine being."[15] His understanding of mystical union correlates with his understanding of justification and sanctification. Calvin explains what the mystical union means: "Therefore, that joining together of Head and members, that indwelling of Christ in our hearts—in short, that mystical union—are accorded by us the highest degree of importance, so that Christ, having been made ours, makes us sharers with him in the gifts with which he has been endowed" (*Inst.* III. xi.10). Commenting on union of marriage in Matt 19:4–6, Calvin again employs the term "the mystical union with which he (Christ) graced the church" (Inst. III.xii.7).

For Calvin, a mystical union is grasped as a spiritual gift in the power and presence of the Holy Spirit[16] rather than a contemplative absorption or merging of our ontological being into the divine being. As far as the certainty of the faith rests upon Christ's oneness with us,

---

15. Niesel, *Theology of Calvin*, 126, 144, 222.
16. Tamburello, *Union with Christ*, 21–22.

it is not simply a matter of intelligence, but of experience. By faith "we ought to hold fast bravely with both hands to that fellowship by which he has bound himself to us ... Not only does he cleave to us by an indivisible bond of fellowship, but with a wonderful communion, day by day, he grows more and more into one body with us, until he becomes completely one with us" (*Inst.* III.ii.24).

For Calvin, "faith implies certainty" (*Inst.* III.ii.15–16), so Christian life is lived in the company of Christ. By faith we understand that Christ not only suffered for us and was risen from the dead for us, but also we receive him as personal savior and enjoy possessing Him. The communion which we have with Christ is a fruit of faith (*fidei effectus*). Faith is not a historical knowledge of the past. It is, rather, the personal relationship with Christ here and now guided by his Spirit. Through faith Christ dwells in our hearts—we live in Him. Here lies the foundation for assurance and hope, but this assurance or hope is to be lived practically in the spirituality of new life.

In this regard, we might discuss Calvin's understanding of charismatic manifestation in the context of the Christ-union. In opposition to the Roman Catholic theology of miracle as well as to Anabaptist fanatics, Calvin insists that "that gift of healing, like the rest of the miracles, which the Lord willed to be brought forth for a time, has vanished away in order to make the new preaching of the gospel marvelous forever" (*Inst.* IV.xix.18). Drawing upon this statement, the Reformed church has tended to favor a doctrine of the cessation of spiritual gifts. However, it seems to me that there would still be room for *charismata* in Calvin's mystical union with Christ, because these gifts are given for the remission of sins and newness of life. According to Calvin, the extraordinary gifts of the Spirit ended in disorder by ignoring the Word and creating "some sort of vague and erratic spirit."[17] It is not strange that God took away spiritual gifts like speaking in tongues and healing to protect their use from human ambition and corruption:

> But ambition did afterwards corrupt this second use, for as much as many did translate that unto pomp and vain glory which they had received to set forth the dignity of the heavenly wisdom. Therefore, no marvel if God took away that shortly after which

---

17. *Comm. on Acts* 10:44, 317.

he had given, and did not suffer the same to be corrupted with no longer abuse.[18]

Be that as it may, Calvin would be open to accept *charismata* in the genuine, broad purpose and use in the sense that we are spiritually enriched in the union with Christ, and gifted by the Spirit to build up the Christian community, "For although we do not receive the Spirit to the end that we may speak with tongues, or be prophets, or cure the sick, or work miracles, yet is He given to us for a better use, that our tongues may be trained to true confession (Rom 10:10) that we may pass from death to life (John 5:24)."[19]

The mystical union between Christ and human beings in Calvin's theology, corresponding to the union between God and the Incarnate Son, presents itself as a possible similarity to the Greek Orthodox doctrine of *theosis*, i.e., the participation of human being in divine nature. Like leaven permeating bread, divine life permeates human beings to restore the image of God. Calvin, reminiscent of Irenaeus and other Greek fathers, stresses: "We trust that we are the sons of God because the Son of God by nature assumed to himself a body of our body, flesh of our flesh, bone of our bone, that he might be one with us; . . . so might be in common with us both Son of God and Son of man" (*Inst.* II.xii.I.2).

Seen in this perspective, Calvin's *mystica unio* is viewed as analogous to the Greek Orthodox teaching of participation in the divine life. Calvin's sanctification can be seen in the perspective of *theosis*, and therefore, becomes a point of dialogue with the Eastern church. In the church—the body of Christ—human being participates in the divine life and becomes partaker of "the divine nature" (2 Pet 1:4). The way of Christian life, once justified, leads to a gradual progress toward deification. It means the process of growing in holiness or getting closer to God. With the grace of the Holy Spirit, deification takes place by faith, hope, and love. This aspect is

---

18. Ibid., 10:46, 318.

19. Ibid., 2:38, 82. See Paul Elbert, "Calvin and the Spiritual Gifts," in *Essays on Apostolic Themes: Studies in Honor of Howard Moward Ervin Presented to Him by Colleagues and Friends on his Sixty-Fifth Birthday*, ed. Paul Elbert (Peabody, MA: Hendrickson, 1985); Leonard Sweetman Jr., "The Gifts of the Spirit: A Study of Calvin's Comments on 1 Corinthians 12:8–10; Romans 12:6–8; Ephesians 4:11," in *Exploring the Heritage of John Calvin: Essays in Honor of John Harold Bratt*, ed. David E. Holwerda (Grand Rapids: Baker, 1976). Also see John Hesselink, "The Charismatic Movement and the Reformed Tradition," in *Major Themes in the Reformed Tradition*, ed. Donald K. McKim (Grand Rapids: Eerdmans, 1992) 377–85.

to be understood not merely as synergism. But the initiative of the grace of the Spirit does not exclude human good work rather, grace propels it. The initiative of the Holy Spirit working through Word and the sacraments in the church empowers the human will. In return, the cooperation of the human will is required as a necessary instrument to do God's will and command. This includes the ethical-practical dimension of *theosis*. Nonetheless, human deeds alone cannot justify or bring human beings to a mystical union with God.

In addition, *theosis* is not intended to mean *eritis sicut Deus* (the work of the serpent) or a vulgar ontological mingling with, or absorption into, God's nature (*theopoiesis*) in which the human being actually becomes a god. The core message of *theosis*, or divinization, consists in synergistic participation of the believer in the divine life toward restoration of the *imago Dei* and incorporation into the divine life of the risen Christ. The complete realization of this deification takes place only at the eschatological consummation along with the resurrection from the dead. There are two classical formulations: first that "Because of his great love [Jesus Christ] was made into that which we are, so that he might bring about that we be what he is" (Irenaeus), or second that "[Christ] became man so that we might become divine" (Athanasius).[20] However, the idea of *theosis* has been misunderstood as influenced by Greek ontology so that it has been distinguished from a personal-ethical understanding of justification in relationship with God in the theology of the Reformation. *Theosis*, in the tradition of the early church and in the Orthodox church, has remained a stumbling block in an ecumenical dialogue with Protestantism.

However, Karl Barth retrieved a dimension of deification in his discussion of Augustine and Luther. In speaking of faith and experience in the Reformation theology, Barth boldly contends that Luther and Calvin's notion of faith in light of Augustine would be analogous to the notion of deification. According to Barth, Luther speaks of a deification of human being in light of the indwelling Christ in Christian life. "God help us, what a boundless, rich and mighty thing is faith! For it maketh man

---

20. Vladimir Lossky, *Mystical Theology of the Eastern Church* (Crestwood, NY: St. Vladimir's Seminary Press, 1976) 133–34. For the recent ecumenical dialogue between Lutheran church and the Greek Orthodox church, see Carl E. Braaten and Robert W. Jenson, eds., *Union with Christ: The New Finnish Interpretation of Luther* (Grand Rapids: Eerdmans, 1998) 26; further, see Tuomo Mannermaa, *Christ Present in Faith: Luther's View of Justification*, ed. Kirsi Stjerna (Minneapolis: Fortress, 2005).

in all things a god, to whom naught is impossible ... (Sermon on Lk 2:21, WA 10 I. 518, 1.5)" (*CD* I/1: 240). Similarly, Augustine states that a deification takes place in the grace of justification in so far as it makes us God's children. Nonetheless, neither Augustine nor Luther argued that there is anything about a deification in faith in the sense of a changing of human nature into the divine nature. The dimension of deification is grounded in the apprehension of Christ or His indwelling in us or union of humanity with Christ, so that it takes place in faith according to Gal 2:20 which says "it is no longer I who live, but it is Christ who lives in me."

Calvin also stands in this line of thought. Barth argues that without the principle of deification or union with Christ we cannot adequately understand the Reformation doctrine of justification and faith. In Calvin's controversy with Osiander (*Inst.* III.ii.5f.), Calvin's idea of deification presents itself as Christ-union in which the self-presentation of Christ or the Word of God takes place in the believer rather than denoting the ontological mixture of Christ with us. Thus the concept of the indwelling of Christ which takes place in faith should not be reduced to an anthropological concept without reservation (*CD* I/1: 240).

In this light we see that Calvin's theology of union with Christ, the relation between sanctification and divinization is united dynamically and eschatologically opened by the Holy Spirit. Furthermore, faith as seen from the perspective of the mystical union implies that human beings participate in the person and work of Christ, or the divine life of God in eschatological expectation.

In the Orthodox view, deification is grasped in a two-fold sense: one is the final perfection of our communion with God in the proper sense, and the other denotes the entire process of sanctification in the wider sense (cf. Rom 8:30). Does Calvin allow himself to consider deification in the proper sense? If we affirm that participation in the divine nature (2 Pet 1:4) or mystical union does not abolish or mingle the fundamental difference between God and human beings, deification in the proper sense holds a place in Calvin's spirituality, without blurring out the eschatological reservation. Sanctification (deification) initiated by the Holy Spirit in whom the triune God indwells and is at work in the faithful Christian is related to our participation in the resurrection and glorification (Rom 8:30).[21]

---

21. Cf. Braaten and Jenson, eds., *Union with Christ*, 1–20.

The Spirit as Communicator of Christ for the Christian Life

The mystical union in Calvin's theology of the Spirit and spirituality, includes an openness to both *charismata* and fruits, so that it does not preclude divinization within an eschatological reservation. Although the Eastern church views deification as human sharing and cooperation in the divine life, it does not ignore a continual process reaching to eternity. *Theosis* occurs through receiving the Holy Spirit and thus allows Christians to experience spiritual gifts personally (encompassing both *charismata* and fruits). Likewise the sacraments participate in this experience by bringing human beings into participation in the divine life.[22]

Communicating the activity of Christ in us, the Spirit fills us with Christ's presence. It brings about a profound change in our lives. Hope for eternal life and love in this life, living soberly amidst the temptations of the world, a zeal for righteousness and piety, the struggle against temptation, etc.—these spiritual qualities arise out of union with Christ. The spirituality of Calvin expresses itself in this manner.

As usual, spirituality is seen as the process of sanctification towards perfection in the concrete life of a believer. Lucien Richard says: "It [*pietas*] is only acquired with great effort on the part of man, and must be pursued with zeal (the *pietatis studium*). Christian life is a continual exercise in *pietas* . . . the entire life of all Christians must be an exercise in piety."[23] In fact, Calvin has no intention of teaching a gradual state of Christian perfection, but rather the union with Christ should be rooted in eschatological openness. That is why "day by day, he grows more and more into one body, with us, until he becomes completely one with us" (*Inst*. III. ii.24). In dealing with Christ's oneness with us, however, we should not lose sight of eschatological reservation, which means not encapsulating our activity, but stimulating us dynamically toward the "not yet" of the kingdom of Christ. This creates an attitude of a new life full of gratitude, humility, and hope before God and neighbor.

We need to call attention to this eschatological reservation in Calvin, which is also an essential component in our relationship with Jesus Christ, emphasizing our life as faith journey on the way. Spirituality in Christian life is not static, but dynamic. It denies any allegiance to the status quo; rather, it is moved in an eschatological direction by the power of the Spirit, challenging the powers and principalities of our world. For

---

22. Stanley M. Burgess, *The Holy Spirit: Eastern Christian Traditions* (Peabody, MA: Hendrickson, 1989) 3.

23. Richard, *Spirituality of John Calvin*, 101.

this reason, Calvin is also critical of any mystical identification with the divine nature or essence. Calvin stimulates a mystical component in his pneumatological-eschatological perspective, revitalizing its spiritual significance for Christian life.

Seen in Calvin's eschatology, his entire perspective, focusing on an exalted and presently-reigning kingship of Christ, moves between the two points of advent and *parousia*. The perfected Kingdom, already existing in Christ, will appear perfectly and visibly at his final return, the final revelation of the perfected Kingdom. Therefore, Calvin rejects a chiliastic notion, a temporal, limited millennial messianic Kingdom on earth as a childish fantasy. Rather, in the eschatological reservation, we dare to live in struggle against the sinful reality of the world. In the context of eschatology (*Inst*. III.xxv), "the final resurrection," our longing for union with God becomes the leitmotif for the hope of Christ's kingdom: "Even on this earthly pilgrimage we know the sole and perfect happiness; but this happiness kindles our hearts more and more each day to desire it, until the full fruition of it shall satisfy us ... Whatever hardships distress us, let this "redemption" sustain us until its completion" (*Inst*. III.xxv.2).[24]

Given the eschatological expectation of Calvin, it is important to discuss Karl Barth's sharp critique of a theology of future and hope. A Christian theology of hope as expectation of the future tends to cover and explain the transcendent character of theology. In such a pan-eschatological framework, little importance and attention is be attached to the hope "as a particularly eschatological sphere of hope as Christian expectation of the future" (*CD* IV/3.2:912).

Commenting on Heb 11:1, Barth contends that faith is not actually defined as hope, rather it is depicted as the basis and presupposition of hope which denotes a particular dimension of Christian existence. At this point, Calvin was clearly aware of the unity and also distinction of faith and hope. "Faith believes that eternal life has been given to us (*data nobis vitam aeternam*) ... On the other hand, the weakness (*imbecillitas*) of our faith, which might grow weary and fall away, must be supported and cherished by patient hope and expectation" (*Inst*. III.ii.42; *CD* IV.3.2:913). With due respect to Calvin, however, Barth is suspicious of Calvin's notion of hope which "seems finally only to enhance or deepen faith by leading it to the *contemplatio aeternitatis*" (*CD* IV/3.2:914). Although Calvin

24. *Inst*. III.xxv.5. See David E. Holwerda, "Eschatology and History: A Look at Calvin's Eschatological Vision," in ed. Holwerda, *Exploring the Heritage of John Calvin*, 110–39.

understands hope, like faith and love, as a gift of the Holy Spirit, on what grounds and to what extent could Calvin distinguish it "from a work of supreme human endowment and skill"? (*CD* IV/3.2:914). For Barth, the positive expectation in a unilateral sense is only God in Jesus Christ who is the future of Christians, and thus, creates their expectation. In fact, a Christian theology of hope should not be based merely on the Christian's experience of awaiting his/her future. In this regard, Calvin is critiqued for not properly paying attention to the One hoped for, who is the basis of Christian hope.

Be that as it may, Calvin never ignores the presence of Christ in our faith and union with him. Christ who is really present in our faith and union is the driving force for us to have eschatological expectation. Christ justifies us through his righteousness, sanctifies us through his holiness, leads us to participation in divine life, and finally drives us in eschatological expectation of hope through his presence and action in the power of the Spirit.

We have seen what union with Christ implies for salvation. This is a living reality which comes about through faith. Christ-union is the object of our astonishment and experience rather than of our comprehension. Christ *extra nos* is the sole basis for this communion. However, Christ *extra nos* does not merely remain in a forensic sense, but becomes effective and transformative as Christ *pro nobis* and *in nobis*. Real presence of Christ in the faith of the believer which is the work of the Sprit finds itself in our experiential union with Christ.

Fundamentally, faith lies not in human capacity, but in the power of the Spirit. Through the power of the Holy Spirit the *extra nos* event of Christ really becomes an *in nobis* event. The Spirit joins us to Christ, so that we become flesh of his flesh and bone of his bone. Attaining the benefits of Christ, we are led to a new dimension of life. The spirituality of this new life is inspired and moved by the Spirit with the eschatological expectation of Christ's Kingdom. The spirituality of the Christian life lies in tension between the "already" and "not-yet" dimension of eschatology in a progressive sanctification and perfection. In this regard, Calvin discusses sanctification (regeneration), and then justification in an interesting and distinctive way: "Now, both repentance and forgiveness of sins—that is, newness of life and free reconciliation—are conferred on us by Christ, and both are attained by us through faith . . . nevertheless actual holiness of life, so to speak, is not separated from free imputation of righteousness" (*Inst.* III.iii.1).

CHRISTIAN LIFE IN *DUPLEX GRATIA*

Based on the Christ-union, we obtain the forgiveness of our sins and our sanctification, or justification and regeneration. In keeping this double grace in mind, Calvin writes: "Christ was given to us by God's generosity, to be grasped and possessed by us in faith. By partaking of him, we principally receive a double grace: namely, that being reconciled to God through Christ's blamelessness, we may have in heaven instead of a Judge, a gracious Father; and secondly, that sanctified by Christ's spirit we may cultivate blamelessness and purity of life. Of regeneration, indeed, the second of these gifts, I have said what seemed sufficient" (*Inst.* III.xi.1). This twofold grace provides us with the purity of imputed justification, and also an actual purity coming out of the process of sanctification and renewal of life.[25]

The reason Calvin conceptualizes such an order (from sanctification to justification) reveals his practical and ethical concern, which is a vital part of Christian life. The actual dimension of sanctification in the Christian life may not be separated from justification. That is to say, both repentance and the forgiveness of sins—in other words, newness of life and free reconciliation—which lie in the actual holiness of life, are by no means to be separated from the free imputation of Christ's righteousness.

At this juncture, we can see that Calvin's practical concern becomes clear in relation to faith. Calvin put regeneration prior to justification in order to emphasize our responsibility before God and others. Christ, from whom we receive communion in faith by the Spirit, does not leave our old nature unchanged, but rather effects in us a profound change. The Holy Spirit unites us to Christ's death and resurrection. Before dealing with justification, Calvin is concerned about distinguishing the practical, ethical dimension of one aspect of double grace.

When we are caught up by Jesus Christ, when such communion is actualized in the presence of the Spirit, we are partakers of benefits of Christ's grace. We are not supposed to remain uncommitted outsiders,

---

25. Ronald S. Wallace, *Calvin's Doctrine of the Christian Life* (Edinburgh: Oliver & Boyd, 1959) 23.

but are called and moved dynamically to be active life in the world. This theological interest and direction makes it possible for Calvin to put an emphasis on the actual holiness of life in view of the third use of the law. Justification is not reducible to a mere individualistic, spiritualistic concept expressing our relationship with God in a narrow sense. Such a concept of justification is a gross misunderstanding. In fact, justification is a spiritual, practical matter pertaining to the living Christ. We are incorporated into Christ's body. Therefore, we are summoned to live through the Spirit and to remain under Christ's control. Christ unites and binds himself to us.

To this initiative of Christ, we must respond in obedience and faithfulness. The previous life which we enjoyed in estrangement from God must be abandoned and transformed to the new life under the guidance of the Spirit. By nature we are aggressive and rebellious against God. But the sovereignty of Christ which takes initiative in our communion with himself fills us with the two gifts of sanctification and justification. Calvin makes use of this term in various ways: repentance, rebirth, penitence, renewal, sanctification, regeneration, conversion—all of which imply our right attitude towards God's grace.

Calvin tries to characterize repentance (or regeneration) within the context of sanctification in a threefold way. First he calls it "turning of life to God" in the sense that "we require a transformation, not only in outward works, but in the soul itself" (*Inst.* III.iii.6). Then he refers to the reason for repentance as our "earnest fear of God," our "thinking upon divine judgment" (*Inst.* III.iii.7). Finally, it consists of mortification of the flesh and vivification of the Spirit. Calvin explains "mortification and vivification as component parts of repentance" (*Inst.* III.iii.8). In view of this practical dimension of repentance, Calvin again clarifies the dependence of repentance upon our communion with Christ:

> Both things happen to us by participation in Christ. For if we truly partake in his death, "our old man is crucified by his power, and the body of sin perishes" (Rom. 6:6), that the corruption of original nature may no longer thrive. If we share in his resurrection, through it we are raised up into newness of life to correspond with the righteousness of God. Therefore, in a word, I interpret repentance as regeneration, whose sole end is to restore in us the image of God that had been disfigured and all but obliterated through Adam's transgression. (*Inst.* III.iii.9)

Jesus Christ is the crucified and risen Lord who brings us into communion with himself. We are accepted into his death and resurrection by our participation in such communion. The Spirit grants us the opportunity to experience this dying and rising in Christ. Because Christ is a living Lord, who triumphs over the dominion of sin and death, we are also awakened and quickened into a new creation. Therefore, our old nature is slain and we are restored into the image of God. At first this restoration of God's image in us is rooted in Christ himself, because Christ is the Second Adam.[26]

As long as Christ is the most genuine and complete image of God, we are called to be restored into his likeness in order to bear witness to Jesus Christ. It is worth noting that Christ alone has suffered and died once and for all, through which the image of God is restored in us. This comes about *extra nos*, but *pro nobis* and lives *in nobis*. Our role is to share in his death and resurrection. The death of the old nature and the renewal of the new are possible and available *extra Christi participatione*.[27] This event lies only in the reality of the living Christ, because it is not us, but he who died and has risen again from the dead.

In speaking of this christological basis for salvation, the Spirit is not only the bond of such union with Christ, but also the bond of communicating Christ's benefits to us. In this sense, Calvin's theology does not have a merely historical, revelational structure, but demonstrates dynamism and actualism of the Holy Spirit in connection with Christ. It should be grasped in an experiential dimension of the Christian spirituality in terms of the Holy Spirit.

It is the Spirit who awakens us, leading us in faith and obedience to say yes to Christ in gratitude, humility, and hope. Throughout our whole lives, we are required to practice penitence. As Calvin states,

> This restoration does not take place in one moment or one day or one year; but through continual and sometimes even slow advances God wipes out in his elect the corruptions of the flesh, cleanses them of guilt, consecrates them to himself as temples . . . that they

---

26. See footnote 17 in *Inst*.III.iii.9. "Calvin thinks here of regeneration as a restoration of the original but ruined image of God in man. The expansion of the passage in the 1539 edition stressing the conflict of flesh and spirit and the distinction between the natural and the regenerate man appears in *OS* IV.63." Niesel, *Theology of Calvin*, 128f.

27. Ibid.

may practice repentance throughout their lives and know that this warfare will end only at death. (*Inst.* III.iii.9)

It is not a gradual access to a state of Christian perfection attainable in this earthly life, but a dynamic movement of continually being changed and reformed. It is characteristic of his spirituality of *semper reformanda*.

To be sure, in the midst of this faith journey and spiritual struggle we can talk about the progress of sanctification in the sense of gradual growth. But what we realize finally in this struggle is our weakness and incapacity (*Inst.* III.iii.10). According to Calvin, we do not possess full freedom by which we can free ourselves from any annoyance of our flesh. "But there still remains in them a continuing occasion for struggle whereby they may be exercised; and not only be exercised, but also better learn their own weakness" (*Inst.* III.iii.10).

For this reason, God encourages us to live in humility and gratitude to keep us aloof from becoming proud and forgetting our dependence on the grace of Christ. In our world we remain still caught up by sin and death, although Christ broke out of its dominion: "In believers sin has lost its dominion; but it still dwells in them" (*Inst.* III.iii.11). We are summoned to engage in a constant struggle and confrontation with evil bondage. Penitence, conversion, rebirth, regeneration are set forth by the work of Christ. He restores us into God's image and calls us to a military struggle against the reality of powers and principalities. This denotes the character of Christian life, which stands in permanent struggle, referring to the struggling character of Calvin's spirituality.[28]

The significance of struggle in sanctification becomes dominant in Calvin's practical and ethical concern. That is why Calvin understands the nature of the fruits of sanctification as follows: "The duties of piety toward God, of charity toward men, and in the whole of life, holiness and purity" (*Inst.* III.iiiI.16). We come to the realization that the living source and basis of our new life does not consist in our own strength, but in God's grace revealed in Jesus Christ. The Holy Spirit reveals and awakens us to live up to this truth in terms of humility and obedience. It is not for nothing that Calvin accounts for progress in sanctification. In this context, progress means the proper recognition of our own lack and weakness toward progress. "The more a man is marked by the Spirit of holiness,

---

28. Krusche, *Das Wirken des Heiligen Geistes nach Calvin*, 282.

the more must he realize how far he is yet from the attainment of perfect righteousness, and is thus led to trust only in God's pure mercy."²⁹

It is not developmental progress inherent in our human nature, but solely the gift of God effected and communicated to us in the power of the Spirit. Nonetheless, human sanctified will becomes an important factor. In an eschatological sense, the return of the Lord will consummate and fulfill, finally, our communion with himself and bring the perfect life of heaven. Here we see again the structural relationship between Christ's kingly office and sanctification. Human sanctification should be shaped along the lines of Christ's work. The *Spiritus sanctificationis* who is present in regeneration thus becomes the agent of our good deeds. According to Krusche, the goal of regeneration is the restoration of the *Imago Dei* in us through the Holy Spirit. The likeness of God is the eschatological goal of Christian spiritual life. The movement driving this eschatological goal is carried out in the fulfillment of union with Christ. That is the double movement of *mortificatio* of the flesh and *vivificatio* of the Spirit.³⁰

The newness of life is the effect of sanctification in a pneumatological, eschatological framework. Therefore, Wallace points out the eschatological significance of the spirituality of the new life:

> In the new ordered existence and upright living manifested by the regenerate man, he sees true signs that the image of God is here being restored ... For the final restoration of true order both in man's heart and in the universe we have to wait for the second coming of Christ ... nevertheless the whole new attitude and behavior of the regenerate man in obedience to the word of God is indicative of the original pattern of man's life as he was created in Adam.³¹

How does then Calvin conceptualize justification in matters of sanctification? According to Calvin, the grace of justification also flows out of our communion with Christ in the presence of the Spirit. Calvin refers to it as follows: "Justified by faith is he who, excluded from the righteousness of works, grasps the righteousness of Christ through faith, and clothed in it, appears in God's sight not as a sinner but as a righteous man" (*Inst.* III.xi.2). Therefore, justification means the imputed righteousness which Christ brought through his sacrifice, and thus "simply as the acceptance

---

29. CR vol. 31, 317. See Niesel, *Theology of Calvin*, 129. Cf. *Inst.* III. iii.14.
30. Krusche, *Das Wirken des Heiligen Geistes nach Calvin*, 281.
31. Wallace, *Calvin's Doctrine of the Christian Life*, 110–11.

with which God receives us into his favor as righteous men ... It consists in the remission of sins and the imputation of Christ's righteousness" (*Inst.* III.xi.2).

This becomes realizable, because Christ bestows upon us his benefits in the presence of the Spirit and thus we are members of his body. Justification is an act of divine judgment upon Christ for our sake, in which God accepts us and imputes Christ's righteousness to us sinners. Thereby we sinners have communion with the one righteous human, Jesus Christ. This action of God can be seen in a twofold way: as the forgiveness of human sin and as the imputation of Christ's righteousness to human beings. Through Christ's work God justifies us by remission of our sins. God does not consider us any more as sinners, but considers us to be entitled to the righteousness and purity of Christ. The ground of our justification exists outside of ourselves because we are made just and righteous in Christ alone. Justification is the imputation of Christ's righteousness including the forgiveness of sins.

Jesus Christ is the truly righteous one. God considers us righteous by virtue of our communion with Christ in the presence of the Spirit. Calvin's pneumatological dynamism between *extra nos* and *in nobis* becomes clear in sanctification as well as in justification. The righteousness which is imputed to us is Christ's own for our sake in terms of his obedience and glory, especially in death and resurrection:

> As a pure and stainless Mediator he is by his holiness to reconcile us to God. But God's righteous curse bars our access to him, and God in his capacity as judge is angry toward us ... Thus Christ to perform this office had to come forward with a sacrifice ... We see that we must begin from the death of Christ in order that the efficacy and benefit of his priesthood may reach us ... Now, Christ plays the priestly role, not only to render the Father favorable and propitious toward us by an eternal law of reconciliation, but also to receive us as his companions in this great office. (*Inst.* II.xv.6)

Our righteousness, which Christ provides outside of us stands in connection with Christ's sacrifice as priest. According to Krusche, such connection is already suggested in the explanation of *munus triplex* in terms of Calvin's theology of the Spirit. Our justification would come about through the priestly service of Christ in a way that Jesus Christ, as *sacerdos*, becomes the *causa materialis* of our justification in giving himself as sacrificial offering for us.[32]

Where justification overlooks Christ's work, it imperils the foundation of Christian life.[33] Since God takes into account not our righteousness, but Christ's, we are completely justified; "Since God justifies us by the intercession of Christ, he absolves us not by the confirmation of our own innocence but by the imputation of righteousness, so that we who are not righteous in ourselves may be reckoned as such in Christ" (*Inst.* III.xi.3).

If the case were different—if God justifies us according to the achievement of our new life—Christ's righteousness *extra nos* would be then of no avail and of no benefit to us. That being the case, we need to bear in mind the grounds of justification *extra nos* is at the center of Calvin's theology of justification and sanctification in connection with the presence of the Spirit. If that were not the case, Christ's righteousness would be meaningless. As Calvin writes, ". . . I do not deny that Christ, as he is God and man, justifies us; and also that this work is the common task of the Father and the Holy Spirit; finally, that righteousness of which Christ makes us partakers with himself is the eternal righteousness of the eternal God" (*Inst.* III.xi.9).

We need to distinguish justification granted to humans in their estrangement from God and the justification which the believer needs during his or her lifetime. Hence there is a justification which pays no regard to the work of humans and a justification in regard to which works are considered as the fruits of faith (*Inst.* III.xvii.4–5). The grace of rebirth, which humans receive together with the grace of justification is a living reality, although we are again and again in need of forgiveness. It is evident that we still live in this world and are surrounded by the dominion of sin. The believer is being constantly renewed by the Spirit into the likeness of the Son. This living reality is more powerful than the fact that sin still lives in the human: "For the Lord cannot fail to love and embrace the good things that he works in them through his Spirit. But we must always remember that God 'accepts' believers by reason of works only because he is their source and graciously, by way of adding to his liberality, deigns

---

32. Krusche, *Das Wirken des Heiligen Geistes nach Calvin*, 277.

33. See Calvin's rejection of Osiander's "essential righteousness," *Inst.* III.xi.5–12. In this context, Calvin opposes the doctrine of essential righteousness with a view to safeguarding Christ as the sole basis of our justification.

also to show 'acceptance' toward the good works he has himself bestowed" (*Inst.* III.xvii.5).

The works of the regenerated are acceptable to God. Therefore, God "requires of his servants in return uprightness and sanctity of life, lest his goodness be mocked or someone be puffed up with empty exultation on that account" (*Inst.* III.xvii.5). In fact, "justification serves God's honor; and revelation, his justice" (*Inst.* III.xiii.1). The effect of our incorporation into Christ is so great that we are justified in our being as a whole, and thus our deeds become acceptable to God for Christ's sake. By this doctrine of a twofold justification, which stands for sanctification, Calvin deepens our spirituality in a practical and ethical direction.

Calvin discusses faith in connection with our communion with Christ before coming to regeneration. As long as faith goes only partially, it is always weak and imperfect. What is the significance of faith for justification? "For if faith justified of itself or through some intrinsic power, so to speak, as it is always weak and imperfect it would effect this only in part . . . we compare faith to a kind of vessel; for unless we come empty . . . we are not capable of receiving Christ. From this it is to be inferred that in teaching that before his righteousness is received Christ is received in faith, we do not take the power of justifying away from Christ" (*Inst.* III.xi.7).

It is dangerous to insist that "faith is Christ" (*Inst.* III.xi.7) in the sense that we are capable of being righteous by our own spirituality. Christ is the ground for the divine judgment that we are righteous; faith is nothing but an empty vessel, whose aim is to receive the decisive core—the mediator Jesus Christ—for our justification.

In discussion of sanctification and justification, we are aware that there is the juxtaposition between them. Calvin stresses this point. "Why, then are we justified? Because by faith we grasp Christ's righteousness, by which alone we are reconciled to God. Yet you could not grasp this without at the same time grasping sanctification also. For he 'is given unto us for righteousness, wisdom, sanctification, and redemption' (1 Cor 1:30). Therefore Christ justifies no one whom he does not at the same time sanctify. These benefits are joined together by an everlasting and indissoluble bond . . . ; those whom he redeems, he justifies; those whom he justifies, he sanctifies" (*Inst.* III.xvi.1). Therefore, justification and sanctification stand together, because God's honor and God's mercy becomes, according to Calvin, "motives for action" (*Inst.* III.xvi.3).

When one attempts to separate sanctification from justification, there is the danger of tearing the unity of the one Christ asunder. However, it does not mean establishing a direct nexus between justification and sanctification, like a fusion of the two which inevitably endangers the *ordo salutis*. However, to distinguish justification from sanctification without confusion does not necessarily mean the isolation of the practical implication of this twofold grace. We are justified for worshiping God in terms of the holiness in our lives:

> You cannot possess him without being made partaker in his sanctification, because he cannot be divided into pieces (1 Cor 1:13) . . . the one never without the other. Thus it is clear how true it is that we are justified not without works yet not through works, since in our sharing in Christ, which justifies us, sanctification is just as much included as righteousness. (*Inst*. III.xvi.1)

In a nutshell, our communion with Christ guarantees our justification and sanctification. The strong emphasis on *extra nos* (in the context of *Inst*. III.ii.23) is coupled with *unio mystica in nobis* as the basis of imputation of Christ's righteousness and our holiness within the pneumatological framework. In the *unio cum Christo*, justification and sanctification build an inseparable unity. In this regard it is important to recall Charles Lelièvres's remarks: "The imputation, therefore, the consequence of our union with Christ, or likewise of our intimate relationship with the Spirit of God."[34]

Justification and sanctification are *duplex gratia*, in which Christ guarantees our salvation as priest and king. As we cannot separate the priesthood and kingship of the one Christ regardless of its indissoluble distinction, we are also not to mingle or confuse *duplex gratia*. The *munus triplex* is coupled with *duplex gratia* in *unio cum Christo*. In this way Werner Krusche rightly articulates this point of fact:

> Calvin sees the order of justification and sanctification based in the unity of the salvation work of Christ in realizing the priestly and kingly office. It is the forgiveness of the sin, through which God imputes the justification and sanctification of the Spirit to us, and creates us to do good deed. Justification and sanctification are two parts of redemption. The whole benefit of redemption

---

34. Krusche, *Das Wirken des Heiligen Geistes nach Calvin*, 273.

comes, above all, from the two contents: *remissio peccatorum* and *regeneration spiritualial*.³⁵

In light of what we have described, Calvin's *duplex gratia* out of the Christ-union in the pneumatological point of view, we know that a Christian life in *duplex gratia* is a life in the movement inspired by the Spirit serving to glorify God's honor and responding to God's grace in terms of gratitude, humility and hope, expecting the Kingdom of Christ in eschatological openness.

Justification is related to what Christ has done for us (*Christus extra nos et pro nobis*), while sanctification relates to what he does within us through the Spirit (*Christus in nos*). Sanctification is the continuing regenerative work of the Holy Spirit in us, a work implying a gradual process toward holiness. If justification means the imputation of Christ's righteousness, sanctification means the process of continuing spiritual effort and struggle of human beings with the help of the Holy Spirit to fulfill the image of God. Therefore, justification is not only the initial moment, but also accompanies the gradual progress toward the restoration of the image of God. Given this fact, Calvin writes:

> Therefore, Christ justifies no one without also sanctifying him . . . But you cannot possess him without participating in his sanctification, for he cannot be torn apart . . . never one without the other. Thus we see how true it is that we are not justified without works, but yet not by works, since our participation in Christ by which we are justified includes sanctification as well as justice. (*Inst.* III. xvi.1)

The dialectical relationship between justification and sanctification includes a notion of spiritual growth in the life of the Christian. It is the *insitio in Christum* that links justification to sanctification inseparably. In this regard, Richard insists that "having based his concept of justification and sanctification on the doctrine of union and incorporation in Christ, Calvin preserved in his spirituality a genuine mystical element."³⁶

---

35. Ibid., 277.
36. Richard, *Spirituality of Calvin*, 116.

CHRISTIAN LIFE IN ELECTION

We have discussed the spirituality of Christian life in the context of pneumatological communion with Christ which embraces justification and sanctification as a twofold grace. In this discussion we came to the realization that it was not our righteousness or our good works, but God's righteousness in Jesus Christ that justifies (faith) and sanctifies us (love), leading us in hope to the kingdom of Christ. In other words, Christian life in communion with Christ is moved and inspired by the power of the Spirit, who points us toward Christ's *parousia* in the eschatological perspective. From this pneumatological, eschatological point of view, we are in a better position to comprehend what Calvin means in terms of God's eternal election.

For the purpose of this discussion we should be suspicious of any rigid emphasis on a dualistic concept of double predestination in which the election stands in strict contradiction to the reprobation. Thus, Wendel is right in stating: "He [Calvin] observes that the separation of the elect from the reprobate is effected by God, but . . . we cannot clearly distinguish the elect from the reprobate in spite of some 'sure signs' to that effect given us in the Scriptures."[37]

My strategy of interpretation in this regard is based on Calvin's comprehension of predestination as a gift of God's grace arising out of the union with Christ. As a matter of fact, Calvin treats and discusses Christian life in election along the lines of Christ-union. Predestination cannot be understood apart from Christ-union. Understood in this way, the doctrine of predestination points to the center of our faith, Jesus Christ, rather than becoming that center itself.

Given this fact, predestination itself does not have any central meaning; on the contrary, predestination, which is grounded in the union with Christ, can be understood as a confession of our assurance of salvation in Christ, full of gratitude, humility, and hope in pneumatological and eschatological perspective.

Let us consider the historical development of Calvin's doctrine of predestination from various stages and correction of the *Institutes* (1536, 1539, 1543, 1550, 1559). Calvin's earliest writings did not include any systematic treatment of predestination. This idea was developed in certain

---

37. François Wendel, *Calvin: Origins and Development of His Religious Thought*, trans. Philip Mairet (Durham, NC: Labyrinth, 1987) 266.

controversies with Jerome Bolsec (*Congregation sur l' election eternelle* of 1551) and Pighius (*Upon the Eternal Predestination of God* of 1552). In the *Institutes* of 1536, predestination was not fully dealt with as an independent doctrine. In consideration of the second article of the creed, and with regard to ecclesiology, however, it is mentioned. In the French Catechism of 1537, Calvin dealt with predestination between the Law and Redemption. In the *Institutes* of 1539 until 1554, predestination is more closely related to ecclesiology, in connection to preaching. In 1559, Calvin considered the treatment of predestination in relation to the doctrine of God to be inappropriate (*Inst.* I.xv.8). Here we also come to encounter the practical and ecclesiological point of view surrounding the doctrine of predestination because Calvin's ecclesiology "embraces above all the community of the elect" (*Inst.* IV.i.7).[38]

In parallel with the union with Christ, Calvin refers to the basis and ground of our election in Christ alone. We are elected in Christ. Therefore, any speculative, metaphysical approach to understanding God's election is basically blocked out. Calvin prohibits all human attempts to clarify predestination in terms of human curiosity because it is confusing and dangerous. Such an attempt is rejected as "seeking outside the way." "For it is right for the stupidity of human understanding to be thus punished with dreadful ruin when man tries by his own strength to rise to the height of divine wisdom. And this temptation is all the deadlier, since almost all of us are more inclined to it than any other" (*Inst.* III.xxiv.4).

Any metaphysical speculation about God's eternal election leads us after all to uncertainty and a labyrinth. If Christ is the only way to God, we look to Christ in speaking of the election. For Calvin, God's eternal election should be expressed and comprehended only on the basis of scripture, because "scripture is the school of the Holy Spirit" (*Inst.* III.xxi.3). On this basis, Calvin elaborates a hermeneutical approach to predestination: "For just as those engulf themselves in a deadly abyss who, to make their election more certain, investigate God's eternal plan apart from his Word, so those who rightly and duly examine it as it is contained in his Word reap the inestimable fruit of comfort. Let this, therefore, be the way of our inquiry: to begin with God's call, and to end with it" (*Inst.* III.xxiv.4).

God calls us in God's Word. Our election begins with God's calling through the Word. Calvin keeps strictly faithful to what the Bible teaches

---

38. Cf. Wendel, *Calvin*, 264–68. Paul Jacobs, *Praedestination und der Verantwortlichkeit bei Calvin* (Darmstadt: Wissenschaftliche Buchgesellschaft, 1968) 61–66.

on this matter because "to seek any other knowledge of predestination than what the Word of God discloses is not less insane than if one should purpose to walk in a pathless waste (cf. Job 12:24), or to see in darkness" (*Inst.* III.xxi.2).

In dealing with scriptural passages about predestination, Calvin focuses on Christ as the ground of the election. What does it mean, saying that we are elected in Christ before the foundation of the world? As God once made a covenant with the people of Israel, so now God makes a covenant of life with us in Christ. God has chosen us in Christ before the foundation of the world. It must be remembered that our election in Christ takes place regardless of human merit. Human merits are out of consideration when we speak of God's eternal election, because "according to his own purpose, the grace [was] given to us by Christ before time began" (*Inst.* III.xxii.3). When we are touched by Christ, we come to the realization that we are members of his chosen people. We are aware that our salvation is rooted unequivocally and solely grounded in Christ.

Along this line Calvin affirms our election in relation to Christ, in other words, Christ *extra nos* is the ground and basis of our election. The assurance of our salvation and of our election was predestined by God's grace in Christ before the foundation of the world. Here, faith is the work of election like it is the work of the Spirit in communion with Christ. Our holiness, our works have no value for our election in Christ, because election comes about totally and dependently through the grace of God. All this speaks to Calvin's radical understanding of election in light of God's grace. When Jesus Christ really calls us through his words, when we are united to him by faith through the Holy Spirit, our assurance of salvation in Christ is also our assurance of election in Christ. Our communion with Christ is also evidence of our election in Christ.

In this regard, Calvin's treatment of predestination is not fatalistic or deterministic, but rather points to the soteriological horizon grounded in Jesus Christ. "Election is to be understood and recognized in Christ alone" (*Inst.* III.xxiv.5). "But if we have been chosen in him, we shall not find assurance of our election in ourselves; and not even in God the Father, if we conceive him as severed from his Son. Christ, then, is the mirror wherein we must, and without self-deception may, contemplate our own election" (*Inst.* III.xxiv.5).

If we are in communion with Christ, we have assurance of election, which is also a benefit coming out of our communion with Christ. We cannot find out our election *extra Christum*. In Christ God has elected us before the foundation of the world, so that Christ is the mirror of our election. Accordingly, we should be holy and blameless before God. However, it is to be remembered that a holy and blameless life originates not from our own capacity, but from the grace of God's election. Calvin implies by no means a *syllogismus practicus* concerning election. What Calvin has in mind in speaking of *signa posteriora* (latter signs) (*Inst.* III.xxiv.4) does not lie in our election-producing praxis, but in solely Christ *extra nos*. Calvin's theology of predestination is different from the Calvinist Orthodox or the Puritan concept of predestination associated with a demonstration of signs of election through work ethics.

In this sense Wendel's statement is worthy of notice: "We know that some disciples of Calvin took a much more affirmative position with regard to the testimony of works, and that for a number of his spiritual successors the abundance and the success of our works provided the manifest proof of our election and our salvation. But this tendency ... is contrary to authentic Calvinist thought."[39]

In addition to the positive side of predestination (election), however, there is no denying its negative side (reprobation). When we turn our attention to the biblical witness to God in Christ, we also encounter the empirical fact that "God adopts some to hope of life, and sentences others to eternal death" (*Inst.* III.xxi.5). This statement leads us not to shrink from the negative side of election. To what extent do we understand this negative side in relation to the positive side of election?

At first, Calvin calls into question the universality of God's invitation, while accentuating the particularity of election. He writes about the negative reality of election as follows: "In actual fact, the covenant of life is not preached equally among all men, and among those to whom it is preached, it does not gain the same acceptance either constantly, or in equal degree. In this diversity the wonderful depth of God's judgment is made known. For there is no doubt that this variety also serves the decision of God's eternal election" (*Inst.* III. xxi. 1).

How do we understand and explain this distinction among human beings when the gospel addresses itself to all in general, but in fact the gift of faith is rare? This distinction maintains that God has not made salvation manifest to all. As Calvin explains, "With respect to the elect, this

---

39. Wendel, *Calvin*, 276–77. Niesel deals with the problem of *syllogismus practicus* in detail in *Theology of Calvin*, 169–81. Cf. *Inst.* III.xiv.18.19.

plan was founded upon his freely given mercy, without regard to human worth; but by his just and irreprehensible but incomprehensible judgment he has barred the door of life to those whom he has given over to damnation" (*Inst.* III.xxi.7).

Here, we are embarrassed by Calvin's statement on God's "irreprehensible but incomprehensible judgment." Is this God in judgment totally different from the God in Christ? Calvin attempts to defend God's righteousness from its misunderstanding. There are serious and difficult objections to be raised against the negative side of predestination: Is God not a tyrant? Does not predestination deny the human ethical responsibility or the endeavor for a holy, righteous life? Does not God have partiality toward persons? If so, are all admonitions meaningless?

Calvin makes an attempt to account for these questions on the basis of scriptural passages, including empirical facts, as well. The justice of God's judgment *in reprobatio* still remains a mystery to us. Drawing on Paul, Calvin is content to assert that "the reason of divine righteousness is higher than man's standard can measure, or than man's slender wit can comprehend. The apostle even admits that such depth underlies God's judgments (Rom 11:33) that all men's minds would be swallowed up if they tried to penetrate it" (*Inst.* III.xxiii.4). Calvin confines himself to the biblical witness on this subject in the strictest sense of the word. He defends the double nature of predestination (election and reprobation) grounded ultimately in divine determination not only in terms of biblical witness but also in terms of his observation of empirical facts. Unfortunately, Calvin calls the doctrine of predestination the eternal decree of God, in light of which eternal life is foreordained to some and eternal damnation for others (*Inst.* III.xxi.5).

At this juncture, Karl Barth is sharply critical of Calvin's theology of double predestination associated with *decretum absolutum* and the certainty of empirical facts. According to Barth, the doctrine of election is the "sum of the gospel," God as the One who loves in freedom elects humanity (*CD* II/2:3). For Barth, Calvin's limitation in the doctrine of predestination comes out of his attempt at gathering the doctrine of election with an absolute certainty from the fact of experience (*CD* II/2: 40). In this certainty put by experience, Calvin did not escape a pressing danger. Furthermore, Calvin's idea of *syllogismus practicus* has been misunderstood to justify Calvin's doctrine of predestination in a way that certain works of faith and existence should "give direct confirmation of faith and indirect confirmation of election" (*CD* II/2: 113).

Methodologically, Barth highly counts and values Calvin's approach in dealing with the doctrine of providence (*Inst.* I.16–18) in connection with that of creation and predestination (*Inst.* III.21–24). Taking seriously the Augustinian-Reformed concept of Christ as the mirror of election (*Inst.* III.22), Barth contends that "the basis of the election is to be found in Jesus Christ" (*CD* II/2: 70).

With due respect to Barth's creative proposal regarding the election of Christ, it should be asked whether Barth paid enough attention to Calvin's theology of union with Christ in connection with the idea of predestination. Did Calvin then block any space for the reprobate in support of God's eternal decree without reservation? What connection exists between the *Spiritus Creator* and the reprobate? Calvin expresses the dialectical tension inherent in the relationship between the universality of God's election and its particularity in an historical and empirical setting. "God is said to have ordained from eternity those whom he wills to embrace in love, and those upon whom he wills to vent his wrath. Yet he announces salvation to *all men indiscriminately*" (*Inst.* III.xxiv.17, italics added).

At stake here is for Calvin to affirm God's free and sovereign act for our salvation in distinction from human free will, which could decide finally on our election and reprobation.[40] "For this call is common also to the wicked, but the other bears with it the Spirit of regeneration (cf. Titus 3:5), the guarantee and seal of the inheritance to come (Eph 1:13–14), with which our hearts are sealed (2 Cor 1:22) unto the day of the Lord" (*Inst.* III.xxiv.8).

Furthermore, "If we are in communion with Christ, we have a sufficiently clear and firm testimony that we have been inscribed in the book of life (cf. Rev 21:27)" (*Inst.* III.xxiv.5). The first quotation above (*Inst.* III.xxiv.8) expressly speaks of the Holy Spirit, whereas the latter (*Inst.* III.xxiv.5) does not. But the first one sheds light on the second one. The second one can be understood as an implicit statement of the work of the Holy Spirit in justification and predestination.

What Calvin has in mind here indicates that election and reprobation become one reality of God's righteousness. How is it possible for us

---

40. Calvin already contrasts God's sovereignty for our salvation and Adam's free choice. See *Inst.*I.xv.8.

to be in communion with Christ in a special sense? It comes about by the power of the Spirit. Who were we who are led by the Spirit towards the union with Christ? Is there any "seed of election" for us to be elected? By no means! We as sinners are elected in Christ. In fact, we were Adam's children under reprobation. Now we are elected in the Second Adam, Jesus Christ, through the work of the Holy Spirit. Regardless of reprobation in Adam's universal sin, election in Christ is universally open towards human beings in general. But in reality there remain people who deny this grace of Christ. Are these people then predestined and eternally determined by God fatalistically to reject the gospel? Here, we need to pay attention to Calvin's reflection on the Spirit, which refers to a cosmic work of the Spirit even among reprobates in a hidden way. God's election remains still incomprehensible to us. But Calvin leaves a space for universal inclusiveness of election even toward the reprobates, although he has not managed to fully elaborate the doctrine of election in light of Christ.

Along this line, I propose a new understanding of Calvin's theology of election in favor of deepening and actualizing a term "the secret impulse of the spirit [*arcano Dei instinctu*]" in Calvin's thought. In many places in Calvin's commentaries,[41] he expresses the secret impulse or influence of the Spirit in connection with the pious as well as with the ungodly. In speaking of the universal work of the Spirit, Calvin recalls the vestiges of the *imago Dei* in all human beings, that is, "some remaining traces of the image of God, which distinguish the entire human race from the other creatures" (*Inst.* II.ii.17), even though neither common grace nor special grace has any bearing on the salvation of its possessor.

Therefore, Calvin expresses this hidden work of the Spirit in relation to reprobates:

> ... experience shows that the reprobate are sometimes affected by almost the same feeling as the elect, so that even in their own judgment they do not in any way differ from the elect ... But this does not at all hinder that lower working of the Spirit from taking its course even in the reprobate ... Yet the reprobate are justly said to believe that God is merciful toward them ... (*Inst.* III.ii.11).

---

41. Cf. *Comm.* Gen 20:2, 24:12, 40:12, 43:11, 48:17; *Comm.* Oba 1:2–4; *Comm.* Exod 2:10, 3:21, 8:10, 11:1, 14.17; *Comm.* Deut 28:28; *Comm.* Jer 28:14, 31:15–16; *Comm.* Ezek 3:12, 3:14; *Comm.* Dan 4:26; *Comm.* Matt 21:8, 27:57, 26:10; *Comm.* John 1:7; *Comm.* Acts 11:21, 20:22, 23:19.

The Spirit as Communicator of Christ for the Christian Life

Still, for Calvin, there is a sovereignty of the Spirit which can be at work even among the reprobate. The truth of predestination does not lie in denying the possibility of salvation among the reprobate. Were that the case, the doctrine of election would result in causing a spiritual egoism of the elect over the reprobate. On the contrary, Calvin's concern essentially becomes obvious in witnessing to the sovereign initiative of God in Christ through the work of the Spirit for our salvation.

What is characteristic of the spirituality of Christian life in election as compared to life in reprobation? Election as a gift is not given to people due to their own merits, but due to the total work of the Holy Spirit. Therefore, they are summoned to bear witness to this grace in the daily struggle with the reality of sin in this world. Drawing a strict, dualistic line between *electio* and *reprobatio* in one reality of God's righteousness is essentially of no significance to Calvin. Such a case would end up in either attributing to God an unrighteous one, or ascribing our merits as the cause of salvation.

There seems to be an analogy of the Spirit. The Spirit as the agent of the hidden presence of God's future works for all. As the elect in Christ are constantly in need of God's grace by the Spirit in justification and sanctification, so the reprobate outside Christ are still in need of the power of the Spirit, which is hidden in the secret of God. If the election is totally dependent on the work of grace, if the election has nothing to do with *syllogismus practicus* (*Inst*. III.iv.18–19), a deterministic, fatalistic distinction between *electio* and *reprobatio* is fundamentally of no value for Calvin. The elect as well as the reprobate are under the power of *Spiritus Creator* moving them towards communion with Christ in eschatological openness because the truth of predestination will be fully revealed only in the last day of Judgment. Thus, Calvin applies this idea very carefully to his idea of discipline of the church (*Inst*. IV.xii.9).

The spirituality of Christian life in election is moved in the eschatological perspective, embracing the reprobate. This is what Calvin really meant by the term *electio* and *reprobatio* as one reality of God's righteousness in Christ. In this regard communion with Christ is a dynamic union in movement under the guidance of the Spirit towards the Kingdom of Christ. If our ethical direction is anchored in the union with Christ, is God to be regarded as the cause of the sin regarding people outside of Christ-election? This problem remains very paradoxical and complicated for Calvin: "All of Adam's children have fallen by God's will . . . the cause of which is hidden in him. But it does not directly follow that God is subject to this reproach" (*Inst.* III.xxiii.4).

Adam cannot commit sin without the permission of God. But God's will is the rule of righteousness. God did not cause Adam to sin, but with God's permission Adam did. It is was not God, but Adam who broke his promise with God. This is what Calvin thinks in terms of God's sovereignty and human free will. According to Heinz Otten, with the will to choose right things or bad things, human beings choose the evil side spontaneously. The cause for corruption and sin is, therefore, to be sought and found in human beings themselves.[42]

In parallel with this argument, Calvin states. "For even though by God's eternal providence man has been created to undergo that calamity to which he is subject, it still takes its occasion from man himself, not from God, since the only reason for his ruin is that he has degenerated from God's pure creation into vicious and impure perversity" (*Inst.* III.xxiii.9). Therefore, "scripture proclaims that all mortals were bound over to external death in the person of one man" (*Inst.* III.xxiii.7).

Be that as it may, God's permission is indicated by Christ's election before the foundation of the world in a supralapsarian sense. From the beginning, God's salvation plan is open in the universal sense. In this context, the particularity of this salvation does not replace the universal tendency regardless of the historical, empirical facts. The Spirit is the Spirit of sovereignty beyond our reason. According to Krusche, *electio generalis* as such is not the election to salvation, yet. This is the room, inside which *electio specialis*, i.e., the actual election, is understood not as a qualitatively different thing, rather as being effective of general election.[43]

What is the ethical consequence of our election? The Christian life in election leads to "a holy and blameless life." The manifestation of the new life is the work of the Holy Spirit witnessing the sign of the election. "If election has as its goal holiness of life, it ought rather to arouse and goad us eagerly to set our mind upon it than to serve as a pretext for doing nothing. What a great difference there is between these two things: to cease well-doing because election is sufficient for salvation, and to devote ourselves to the pursuit of good as the appointed goal of election!" (*Inst.* III.xxiii.12).

---

42. Heinz Otten, *Praedestination in Calvin's theologischer Lehre* (Neukirchen: Neukirchener, 1968) 94.

43. Krusche, *Das Wirken des Heiligen Geistes nach Calvin*, 235.

The Spirit as Communicator of Christ for the Christian Life

This is the ethical horizon of election in Christ. The Holy Spirit, who makes predestination dynamic and actual in the eschatological sense, is not only *spiritus adoptionis,* but also *spiritus regenerationis* or *sanctificationis*. Therefore, we devote ourselves and are eager to pursue a holy and blameless life for ourselves as well as to be in solidarity with the reprobate in eschatological expectation.

In these initial chapters we have discussed the person and the work of the Spirit within a trinitarian framework in view of its spirituality and ethical implications. The Spirit in creation functions in a threefold manner: cosmic, ecological, and human. The Spirit as the agent of the hidden presence of God's future is preparing and preserving all reality for *regnum gloriae in advent,* into which *theologia naturalis* is included and brought up. The Spirit as *Spiritus Creator* is dynamically involved with the trinitarian fellowship. Here, the Spirit functions as the bond mediating the Father and the Son not only in an intra-trinitarian, but also an economic-trinitarian sense. In the dialectical and dynamic union of the two natures, Calvin put *Logos* Christology into a pneumatological framework. Out of this emerges his unique doctrine of *munus triplex,* which has to do with the ethical responsibility of a Christian life. The Christology of *munus triplex* is characteristic of Calvin's theological structure while *theologia crucis* penetrates and guides Luther's theology.

As far as the work of the Spirit is concerned, Calvin formulates the Spirit as the communicator of Christ to us. Here the pneumatological union with Christ plays a decisive role in creating his spirituality and ethical theology. This is also a starting point for helping us understand the spirituality of Christian life within the context of justification and sanctification that originates from Christ-union in an eschatological perspective. Therefore, the social and ethical component of Christian spiritual life in *duplex gratia* finds itself in struggle with the world as we bear our spiritual qualities of gratitude, humility and eschatological hope for the eternal life.

According to Calvin, election can also be localized within this pneumatological, eschatological context. In parallel with union with Christ, election is rooted in Christ *extra nos*. It is the Spirit who makes election in Christ *extra nos* appropriate and actual for us. Therefore, election is totally a work of grace. From the outset, this gift has nothing to do with our merits or racial nature. Like election, reprobation is also based on God's righteous judgment. Distinction between election and reprobation ought not result in the elect's spiritual egoism or judgmentalism against the reprobate. The *Spiritus creator* is beyond this deterministic, fatalistic division, working even among the reprobate. Certainly this work of the Spirit remains a mystery to Calvin.

However, if we take predestination seriously in a pneumatological, eschatological perspective, election and reprobation can be articulated as the one reality of God's righteousness in Christ. The spiritual quality of Christian life in election, therefore, is filled with gratitude, humility and hope pursuing a holy and righteous life not only for itself, but also for our neighbors. In the reflection of election for the Christian life, the spiritual life and the practical, ethical life comes together.

4

The Spirit and the Law

WHEN IT COMES TO the Spirit in relation to Christian life, Calvin understood spirituality to basically mean a new life in the power of the Spirit. When it comes to Christ-union, Calvin elaborates on the spiritual benefits, including the experiential dimension of human life with God. Drawing on this theological framework, I am interested in discussing Calvin's ethical reflection on the law in light of the Spirit. Furthermore, we must take into consideration the socio-ethical implications of the Decalogue, discipleship and freedom for Christian life.

Calvin's understanding of the law is not only related to Christ, but also to the work of the Spirit in the operation of the law. As Calvin asserts, "From the law, therefore, we may properly learn Christ, if we consider that the covenant which God made with the fathers was founded on the Mediator" (*Comm.* Lk 24:27). Revealing Christ in the law, the Spirit is involved in God's command. "If the Spirit of Christ does not quicken the law, the law is not only useless, but also deadly to its disciples. For without Christ there is nothing in the Law but inexorable rigor" (*Comm.* Ps 19:8). The exhibition of Christ in the law is intrinsically related to the role of the Spirit revealing the grace of Christ.

THE LAW IN CHRISTIAN ETHICS

What is Christian ethics? Although there are the various definitions and orientations in the field of Christian ethics, I understand ethics to be "the theory of the conduct of human life."[1] It involves practical purpose and the ethical meaning of life in reality, in which Christians are encouraged and stimulated to make proper moral judgments and to question "the

---

1. Trutz Rendtorff, *Ethics Vol.1: Basic Elements and Methodology in an Ethical Theology*, trans. Keith Crim (Philadelphia: Fortress, 1986) 3.

social arrangements of their societies and of the human community as a whole." Particularly within Protestantism, ethics is characterized by the prophetic claim "to establish a sound moral indictment of current practices or orders of life in light of the claims of biblical faith."[2] Hence, "Christian ethics will be more likely to guide persons to right action than more intuitive approaches will. Ethics is a process of giving reasons for action; the establishment of good reasons both prior to action and in the justifications of actions after the fact is likely to develop more appropriate actions and evaluations."[3]

By this definition, James Gustafson contends that ethics reflects more theoretically on the foundations and principles of action, and is concerned about moral choice for more appropriate conduct and evaluations. However, practical morality refers more to behavior or actual practice as such. Paul Lehman distinguishes the difference between Christian ethics and practical morality, stating that this difference "is derived from presuppositions upon which ethical thinking is based . . . Christian ethics, as a theological discipline, is the reflection upon the question, and its answer: What am I, as a believer in Jesus Christ and as a member of his church, to do? To undertake the reflection upon and analysis of this question and its answer—this is Christian ethics."[4]

When Christian ethics considers and analyzes human moral conduct and practice in the light of Jesus Christ, it can not preclude theological reflection, i.e., the dogmatic principle and idea regarding its ethical reflection of human behavior and attitude. In this sense Christian ethics becomes "an intensified form of theology, in terms of dealing with the ethical, practical questions which are central and basic to theology. Thus ethics does not abolish theology, but makes it necessary in a manner that is new and fresh."[5] When spirituality of Christian life and moral deed are discussed in terms of ethical reflection and analysis, Calvin does not ignore dogmatic perspectives. Christian dogmatic theology integrates and combines spiritual experience with ethical reflection. Based on this idea, Calvin as a Christian ethicist considers our relationship with God in terms of the law. He interprets the law to sharpen the meaning of the gospel, and

2. James M. Gustafson, *Ethics from a Theocentric Perspective*, vol. 1, *Theology and Ethics* (Chicago: University of Chicago Press, 1981) 69.
3. Ibid.
4. Paul L. Lehman, *Ethics in a Christian Context* (New York: Harper & Row, 1963) 25.
5. Rendtorff *Ethics*, 1:9.

furthermore to solidify ethical commitment and responsibility. Therefore, Calvin interprets the law to assume the office "to call us back from our wandering, and to lead us to the mark set before us."[6]

What does Calvin understand by the term "law"? He views the nature and content of the law by and large in a threefold manner: (1) the Mosaic religious law as a whole (*Inst.* II.vii.1); (2) the special revelation of the moral law given to Israel, i.e., mainly the Decalogue and Jesus's summary (*Inst.* II.viii); and (3) diverse forms of civil, judicial, and ceremonial law (*Inst.* IV.xx.14–16). It is evident that Calvin considers the moral law to be "the true and eternal rule of righteousness" (*Inst.* IV.xx.15). Even though the Mosaic ceremonial and judicial law is superseded by Jesus Christ, its basic spirit, the fear of God and peace between people, remains valid and effective in Calvin's spirituality and ethical life. The twofold law of love of God and neighbor is taken seriously when civil authority acts in the name of freedom and the common good of the people (*Inst.* IV.xx.15).

Moreover, a source of the law can be found in nature, but natural law does not stem from human reason or standards, rather from God. God basically created all things to be good and harmonious. For instance, conscience is the gift of God's universal grace in its natural state. Calvin writes: "The purpose of natural law, therefore, is to render man inexcusable ... natural law is that apprehension of the conscience which distinguishes sufficiently between just and unjust, and which deprives men of the excuse of ignorance, while it proves them guilty by their own testimony" (*Inst.* II.ii.22).

In this light, the law of nature makes man inexcusable before God, even though Calvin goes as far as saying that "there is nothing more common than for a man to be sufficiently instructed in a right standard of conduct by natural law" (*Inst.* II.ii.22). For this reason the law of nature renders us incapable of standing uprightly before God. As sinners we constantly need the power of the Holy Spirit and need to be illuminated by the light of the Spirit in order not to commit sin. "Our will cannot long for the good without the Holy Spirit" (*Inst.* II.ii.27). Thus, the law of nature bears witness to the divine law whose basis lies in Jesus Christ.

Within the context of divine law, Calvin assumes not only the Ten Commandments, but also "the form of religion handed down by God

---

6. John Calvin, *Commentaries on the Book of the Prophet Jeremiah and the Lamentations*, 5 vols., trans. from the Latin and ed. John Owen (Grand Rapids: Eerdmans, 1950) 1:264 (Jer 5:5).

through Moses" (*Inst.* II.vii.1). Here, moral and cultic laws are bound up together. Obviously God gives the law of religious ceremonies to support the Commandments and to foster the faith. The sacrifices and ceremonies of the religious cultus in Israel remind us of the fact that God is the lawgiver concerning God's gracious and faithful covenant, so that we may live uprightly in holiness before God and in accordance with the law.

The law, seen from the cultic point of view, has something do with the direction of God's commandments. Niesel is right in saying that "God guarantees by the gift of the Law the fulfillment of the commandments; there is a life in accordance with the will of God because He has bestowed Himself upon His people."[7] God gives the law in terms of the covenant with Israel, in which God takes the initiative. The law is, therefore, bound up together with the covenant. Due to this covenantal character, sacrifices and ceremonies are subordinated to spiritual worship. For Calvin, both the moral and ceremonial law become significant, because they point and lead us to Christ.

Calvin understands the divine law christologically by viewing Christ as a double mirror, which means the fulfillment and end of the law. Accordingly, the divine law is not completely realized until "Christ confers it by free imputation and by the Spirit of regeneration" (*Inst.* II.vii.2). The law, which needs the Spirit of regeneration, is to be seen as "the true and only preparation for seeking Christ" (*Inst.* II.vii.2) because the law finds its meaning only in "the covenant of free adoption" (*Inst.* II.vii.2). This act of adoption is grounded solely in God's mercy, so that divine law is embedded into God's covenantal grace.

God, taking the initiative of covenant with God's people, makes a divine claim and demand upon them. This divine claim is the meaning of the law. Here is the radical difference between the covenantal law and all others. Through Moses God summons God's people to be obedient and faithful to the divine claim. Moses is the prophet of the covenant God, bearing witness to God's mercy and trustfulness. God's covenant is not changeable, nor is it destroyed by the changeable conduct of the people: "Moses was not made a lawgiver to wipe out the blessing promised to the race of Abraham. Rather, we see him repeatedly reminding the Jews of that freely given covenant made with their fathers of which they were the heirs" (*Inst.* II.vii.1).

---

7. Niesel, *Theology of Calvin*, 95.

The Spirit and the Law

If the law is divine, and it teaches the perfection of righteousness, then "the complete observance of the law is perfect righteousness before God" (*Inst.* II.vii.3). But, the perfect observance of the law is beyond our spiritual capacity. We are not able to fulfill the claims and demands of the moral law. This fact makes us inexcusable and brings us into despair, so that we find out "only the most immediate death" in it (*Inst.* II.vii.3). If fulfillment of the law is impossible for us, how can we be free from the claim of the law? How is God as Judge of the law seen as a gracious God? It is only possible through Jesus Christ. Thus, we are entrusted and encouraged to seek redemption in Christ. The law is given to us for the sake of "foster[ing] hope of salvation in Christ until [His] coming" (*Inst.* II.vii).

The meaning of the law and ethical responsibility arise from Christ. What is the work of the Spirit in the law? What the Spirit provides is inward obedience, when "he has engraven his Law in our hearts, and by his Spirit renews men within to obedience to it" (*Comm.* Jn 1:17). It is in vain that God proclaims God's law by the voice of people, if we do not inscribe it by the Spirit on our human hearts (*Comm.* Heb 8:10). When the law is obeyed truly inwardly in the power of the Spirit, it discloses the presence of Christ in the law. Apart from the effect of the Spirit's work in our minds and hearts, the Scriptures are nothing but the dead letter: "The letter, therefore, is dead, and the Law of the Lord slays its readers where it both is cut off from Christ's grace and only sounds in the ears, without affecting the heart. But if it is efficaciously impressed on our hearts by the Spirit, if it exhibits Christ, it is the word of life" (*Inst.* I.ix.3).

It is true of the relationship between the Spirit and the gospel. In the gospel, human beings meet Christ, because Christ is the author of the gospel (*Comm.* Heb 2:11). Yet the gospel is useless without the effectual work of the Spirit: "The Kingdom of heaven is indeed set open to us by the external preaching of the gospel; but no man entereth in except he to whom God reacheth out his hand; no man draweth near unless he be drawn inwardly by the Spirit" (*Comm.* Acts 14:27). Preaching of the gospel and the efficacy of the Spirit is correlated, because "the doctrine of the gospel cannot be understood otherwise than by the testimony of the Holy Spirit" (*Comm.* 1 Cor 2:11).

Calvin extends the soteriological dimension not in terms of the law, but in terms of the radical *in Christo* phrase, so that he develops the discussion of the law in the context of the promise of the gospel. The terminology of *gospel* and law is more appropriate to describe Calvin's ethical and theological concerns than the terms of *law* and gospel. For Calvin, Jewish tradition and culture connected with the law is totally superseded by the gospel and consequently is no longer meaningful and useful. Rather, Jewish cult and tradition gain appropriate meaning in terms of Christ, because there is essentially no antagonism between law and gospel. The office of the law leads the people of covenant to expect the knowledge of God the Redeemer. The law is nothing but a foreshadowing outlining and promising what is to come. Leading the people to expect the fulfillment of the law in the Redeemer is the law's basic purpose. Apart from the expectation of the Redeemer, the law turns out to be meaningless.[8]

For this reason, Calvin stresses Christ as the fundamental basis of the law: "Without Christ, the law is valueless and offers no sure ground of hope."[9] "Since God cannot without the Mediator be propitious toward the human race, under the law Christ was always set before the holy fathers as the end to which they should direct their faith" (*Inst.* II.vi.2). Apart from Christ, the law in every part is meaningless and even in vain. The whole cultus foreshadowed the grace and the truth of Christ. Its power and efficacy is dependent on Christ himself (*Inst.* III.ii.32).

God's covenant culminates in the incarnation. The pre-existence of Christ proceeds before the historic Christ so that Calvin expresses the concept of the law on an inner-trinitarian basis, which is also connected with the eschatological expectation of the coming Christ. God's redemption in Jesus Christ liberates human beings from the curse and compulsion of the law, from its ceremonial and political ordinances. For Calvin, however, the genuine spirit of the law still remains valid—not its use, but its meaning—while some ceremonies have been substituted and abrogated. In this regard Calvin rejects the teaching of the total abolition of the law.

As a matter of fact, the law serves the spirituality of the regenerated to be faithful to Christ. The law has been integrated into and exalted to its fulfillment in Christ. Accordingly, Calvin put into effect his unique notion of *officium ususque legis* (threefold use of the law). Having in mind the

---

8. Cf. Jack H. Robinson makes a concerted effort to clarify Calvin's concern about the Jews in particular in terms of the covenant, law/gospel relationship. Jack Hughes Robinson, *John Calvin and the Jews*, American University Studies, series VII, Theology and Religion 123 (New York: Lang, 1992) 39–53, 55–67.

9. CR 47, 124. Cf. Niesel, *Theology of Calvin*, 96.

use of the law, Calvin insists that "the Law consists chiefly of three parts: first, the doctrine of life; secondly, threatenings and promises; thirdly, the covenant of grace, which, being founded on Christ, contains within itself all the special promises."[10]

In this light Calvin interprets the law as retaining the three functions relevant to Christian ethics. In Calvin's exposition of the law in a threefold sense, it is clear that the law has still a meaningful function for Jews as well as for Christians, in view of a normative, a pedagogical, and a sanctifying function.

In consideration of the first function, Calvin is engaged critically with the insistence of the Libertine sect,[11] or John Agricola, who abrogates all Christian obligations to fulfill the law. In contrast to abrogation of the law, Calvin likens law to a mirror disclosing "our sinfulness, leading us to implore divine help" (*Inst.* II.vii.6).

The law, which functions like a mirror, has the normative role of showing God's righteousness and goodness. Human beings are blind and drunk with self-love, so that they have to be healed from the disease of pride. In the mirror of the law we find ourselves incapable of fulfilling God's righteousness, and consequently we are mired in sin. Because we act violently against God's spiritual law, we are not qualified to enjoy the blessed life offered by the law. To the degree that we prove to be transgressors, we turn the law into an occasion for sin and death. The more brightly the law shines upon God's righteousness, the more it reveals our iniquity and abomination. The more certainly it renders salvation dependent upon the righteousness, the more surely it teaches the destruction of the wicked.

Nonetheless, we are not trapped in despair and anxiety due to the indictment of the law, because the grace of God goes beyond the claim and demand of the law. It makes the law sweeter and more lovely. Consequently, we come to know that God is tireless in benefitting us and in bestowing new gifts upon us (*Inst.* II.vii.7). Where can we find God's grace and love? It is Christ in which God reveals God's divine mercy. Therefore, we are

---

10. Calvin, *Comm.* Isa. 1:26. Cf. *Calvin and Christian Ethics: Papers and Responses Presented at the Fifth Colloquium on Calvin & Calvin Studies*, ed. Peter De Klerk (Grand Rapids: Calvin Studies Society, 1987) 25.

11. *Contra la secte phantastique des Libertins*, CR VII 206, 220, 229, 233. See also *Treatises Against the Anabaptists and Libertines*, trans. and ed. Benjamin Wirt Farley (Grand Rapids: Baker, 1982).

supposed to seek and long for it with true faith: "If the Spirit of grace is absent, the law is present only to accuse and kill us" (*Inst.* II.vii.7) … "The usefulness of the law lies in convicting man of his infirmity and moving him to call upon the remedy of grace which is in Christ" (*Inst.* II.vii.9). This Augustinian statement shapes Calvin's understanding of the law as the normative one in a Christological sense. At the same time, his ethical reflection of the law points to the universal inclusiveness of Christ's salvation. "In Christ his face shines, full of grace and gentleness, even upon us poor and unworthy sinners" (*Inst.* II.vii.8). Christ's salvation as the fulfillment of the law is still open to sinners, in view of the hidden work of the Spirit which engenders it.

The second function of the law is clear when the law serves as protection of the community from unjust, wicked people, restraining them from committing wrongdoing against the public community and fellow human beings. However, hindered by the fear of punishment, they still keep the rage of their lusts in their hearts. At this juncture, Calvin deepens his social and ethical concern in terms of illuminating the second function of the law. "This constrained and forced righteousness is necessary for the public community of men, for whose tranquility the Lord herein provided when he took care that everything be not tumultuously confounded. This would happen if everything were permitted to all men. Nay, even for the children of God, before they are called and while they are destitute of the Spirit of sanctification" (*Inst.* II.vii.10).

By restraining these people, the law serves to protect society. By reminding them of the consequences of their wrongdoing and its punishment, the law keeps the goodness and righteousness of God for the holy and peaceful life in society. In this regard Calvin put the emphasis on a civil function of the law, which has social and political meaning. "For Moses has admirably taught that the law, which among sinners can engender nothing but death, ought among the saints to have a better and more excellent use" (*Inst.* II.vii.13).

In addition, the law serves as tutelage leading us to Christ. It leads people full of self-righteousness to recognition of their misery, and makes them empty. Thereby, they are brought down to humility to the point of receiving Christ's grace. Those who are full of the lust of the flesh are also in need of tutelage to prevent themselves from indulgence and depravity. In this way "the bridle of the law restrained them in some fear and reverence toward God until, regenerated by the Spirit, they began wholeheartedly to love him" (*Inst.* II.vii.11).

Finally, as for the third and principal function of the law, Calvin refers to necessity of the law especially in the life of the believers, because they still need the law. In order to conform to and accommodate God, they receive the benefit of the law "by frequent meditation upon it to be aroused to obedience, be strengthened in it, and be drawn back from the slippery path of transgression. In this way the saints must press on: "For, however eagerly they may in accordance with the Spirit strive toward God's righteousness, the listless flesh always so burdens them that they do not proceed with due readiness" (*Inst.* II.vii.12). The third use of the law is geared toward a specific demand of the new life. In terms of obedience to the law God stamps God's image upon the believer, which is exemplarily shown in Jesus Christ, and it is also the essence of the law. "For God has so depicted himself in the law that if any person carries out in deeds what is enjoined there, he will express the image of God, as it were, in his own life."[12]

For believers the law shows the goal they seek. If they accept freely the law as the gracious invitation of God with gratitude for God's mercy in Christ, the law offers consolation and sweetness. From this standpoint, Calvin delves into the final, principal function of the law in light of sanctification. Consequently, the ethical discussion of the law would be, according to Calvin, inappropriate without regard to sanctified life of the believer. The proper use of the law exists for encouraging the believer to live up to the holiness of God and in conformity to God's will. This new life is the goal of spirituality of the regenerated in relation to the genuine third use of the law. It shapes and deepens our true spiritual relationship with God and fellow persons. It is the goal of the sanctified in relation to the genuine use of the law, as becoming possible through the sanctifying power of the Spirit. This sanctifying dynamism of the Spirit set Calvin's ethical concern for the law in motion. Without this foundation of the Spirit, there is no delight or sweetness in the law.

The law in Christ has no power to condemn us with its curse. Becoming himself a curse for us, Christ completes its function of judging and punishing (*Inst.* II.vii.15). Therefore, the law holds a proper place and function in Christ to prepare us for every good work by admonishing and

---

12. Robinson, *John Calvin and the Jews*, 60.

correcting us. In this sense, the law no longer condemns us due to our imperfection. "For the Lord then freely bestows all things upon us so as to add to the full measure of his kindness this gift also: that not rejecting our imperfect obedience, but rather supplying what is lacking to complete it, he causes us to receive the benefit of the promises of the law as if we had fulfilled their condition" (*Inst.* II.vii.4).

Calvin's ethical discussion of the law in a threefold manner has been treated in christological-pneumatological perspective. In the use of the law, we see its ethical implications. First it makes people aware of sin and reminds them of their punishment, then corrects them and protects human society from the wicked, and leads and invites them to the Christ's salvation. Finally, it equips and sanctifies human life through the power of the Spirit, so that the image of God in Christ could be restored for our life. The restoration of the image of God as the goal of Christian spirituality is central to Calvin's ethics, which is grounded in the power of sanctifying Spirit.

In this regard, Karl Barth states that ethics, as the doctrine of God's command, should interpret the law as the form of the gospel, in other words, as the norm of sanctification (*CD* II/2: 509). In dealing with the call to discipleship, Barth contends that God's grace has the form of the command, and the gospel has the form of the law while the gospel is its content. It is a grace that commands (*CD* IV/2: 535). Furthermore, Barth argues that Luther, in his later stage, referred to a relationship of justification to sanctification like Calvin's *duplex gratia*. Luther grounds new life on the grace of justification (*CD* IV/2:507). On being made holy, in *The Small Catechism* (1529), Luther stresses the dimension of the third article. The Holy Spirit sanctifies me, like the Spirit does to the Christian church (BC 355). Barth, in light of Chalcedonian Christology, holds that justification and sanctification must be distinguished, but not divided or separated. The forgiveness of sin should be accompanied by an actual liberation from the commission of sin. In a similar fashion, Calvin interprets faith to rest upon God's Word. "In understanding faith, it is not merely a question of knowing that God exists, but also—and this especially—of knowing what is his will toward us" (*Inst.* III. II. 6).

The Spirit and the Law
CHRISTIAN ETHICS IN THE DECALOGUE

The law, which points to Christ and shapes the ethical concern for one's neighbor, would be hopeless and meaningless if it produced any sort of legalism in fulfilling itself apart from the power of the Holy Spirit. Through the union with Christ we are not only involved in the spiritual death of the old nature with Christ, but this union also sharpens ethical consciousness in our hearts. Calvin holds that "It would be in vain for the feet and hands and eyes to be controlled to observe the Law unless obedience begins at the heart. It is the Holy Spirit's own particular office to engrave the Law of God on our hearts."[13] The Spirit, which engraves the demand and claim of God into our hearts, gives a sign of our adoption and sanctification. In this sense, Calvin underscores the ethical significance of the Decalogue, whose fulfillment is possible through the sanctifying power of the Spirit.

As already mentioned, the task of Christian ethics lies primarily in the restoration of the image of God in human beings, which means righteousness and true holiness (*Inst.* II.iii.9). This life of righteousness and holiness is summed up particularly in the Decalogue. Seeking the holy life as taught in the Decalogue is an ethical task of the regenerated. Here spirituality of Christian life is discussed and treated in terms of ethical reflection. Calvin interprets the purpose of the Decalogue to join "man by holiness of life to his God," and in making "him cleave to God." In other words, it is "the fulfillment of righteousness to form human life to the archetype of divine purity" (*Inst.* II.viii.51). Christ fulfilled and completed this aim, since Christ as the gospel-giver has restored the genuine meaning of the law (*Inst.* II.viii.5).

In order to pursue the goal of the law, first we are required to keep humility and self-abasement in mind owing to the severity of the law. Hence, Calvin admonishes obedience to the law: "Since the law is God's law, it makes a total claim upon us" (*Inst.* II.viii.6). Calvin's hermeneutical principle in interpreting the meaning of the Commandments becomes manifest where "the commandments and prohibitions always contain more than is expressed in words" (*Inst.* II.viii.8). At stake here is not our relationship to the literal rigidity of the law, but to its content and spirit, through which God intends to speak to us.

In order to explore this intention of God in the law, Calvin follows the biblical way to explain the Commandments (the two tables of Exod

---

13. *Comm.* Ps 40:8. Cf. Wallace, *Calvin's Doctrine of the Christian Life*, 121.

31:18 and 34:1ff., and Matt 22:34–40) in terms of two parts; the first part aims at serving God purely while the second part underlines the ethical and social relationship in all integrity and uprightness: "God has so divided his law into two parts, which contain the whole of righteousness, as to assign the first part of those duties of religion which particularly concern the worship of his majesty; the second, to the duties of love that have to do with men" (*Inst.* II.viii.11). Therefore, in the field of Christian ethics, the spiritual relationship with God cannot be considered apart from the socio-ethical responsibility for neighbor and society.

First of all, Calvin regards the worship of God as "the beginning and foundation of righteousness" (*Inst.* II.viii.11). This vertical dimension works together with the horizontal dimension of human life, because his ethics always focuses on the dialectical unity and relation between divine demand and human response. God's commandment is the spiritual basis for Christian ethics, while Christian ethics put into effect divine demand in human life.

From the fact that we "honor God as Judge of right and wrong," we "learn to live with one another in moderation and without doing injury . . . The Second Table prescribes how, in accordance with the fear of his name, we ought to conduct ourselves in human society" (*Inst.* II.viii.11). This aspect should be kept in mind when it comes to human response to the divine claim. Spirituality in relationship with God is directed basically toward social justice and responsibility.

In illustrating the name of God, Calvin reminds us of the Exodus, because God's name essentially means freedom and emancipation: "Our heavenly Vindicator, having freed us by the power of his arm, leads us into the Kingdom of freedom" (*Inst.* II.viii.15). When we apply the Egyptian bondage of Israel to our current spiritual captivity, worshiping God means confessing God as our Liberator from the devil's deadly power surrounding us in earthly life.

Hence, the reverence for God's name leads Calvin to take the charge of idolatry seriously. Because God is incomprehensible, the human being is inclined to worship any image available to our sense in the name of religion. The critique of idolatry also questions and challenges any kind of absolute human ideological claims of truth. We are forbidden to take the name of God in vain, because "we are not to profane his name by treating it contemptuously and irreverently." Our ethical commitment should be zealous and careful in glorifying and respecting God's name with godly reverence (*Inst.* II.viii.22).

The purpose of the Sabbath Day is to praise God's rest in us, stopping our endless inclination toward work. Calvin especially integrates this commandment with freedom and the rest of a servant's labor, because it implies an economic justice in labor relations: "God resolved to give a day of rest to servants and those who are under the authority of others, in order that they should have some respite from toil" (*Inst.* II.viii.28). Our rest is to be seen from the standpoint of self-denial. As far as sanctification includes mortifying our will, on the Sabbath we must rest ourselves from all activities, abandoning our fleshly desires, having God's rest indwelling in us (*Inst.* II.viii.29).[14] "Spiritual rest is the mortification of the flesh" (*Comm.* Gen 107).

For Calvin, the goal and completion of creation becomes manifest in the celebration of God's Sabbath rest on the seventh day. God blessed the Sabbath with love for the purpose of celebrating the excellence and dignity of God's works in the creation. God sanctified the Sabbath by rendering it illustrious. Thus, Calvin distinguishes it from human rest. "In the magnificent theater of heaven and earth" God appointed God's own rest, so that the celebration of the Sabbath as "the sacred rest "aims to give the human mind to the glory of God. A new precept as to the Sabbath is given in the Law, that is, "a legal ceremony shadowing forth a spiritual rest" (*Comm.* Gen. 106). The truth of the Sabbath is finally and completely manifested in Jesus Christ. In this light, Calvin's reflection on the Sabbath has to do with his social economic reflection on freeing human beings from the righteousness of works. However, Calvin has not managed to adequately develop his reflection on the Sabbath in favor of promoting interrelationship between human beings and other living creatures in light of the cosmic dimension of the Spirit. An understanding of Sabbath and its interconnection of all living creatures, which may clarify Calvin's thought on the Sabbath, needs to be rearticulated and redeveloped toward an ecological theology of nature in the face of a dying cosmos in a global context.

---

14. Calvin's uniqueness in this regard is seen in his socio-economic reflection of labor from a Christological basis, because "Christ is true fulfillment of the Sabbath" (*Inst.* II.viii.31). From this point of view, Calvin refuted any form of "Sabbatarian superstition" (*Inst.* II.viii.34).

In light of what has been described in the first part of the Decalogue, it is clear that the consecration of our whole life to God is the true meaning of the law. The sanctity involves the dedication and offering of our whole life as a living sacrifice to God. This sanctity girds our ethical responsibility and attitude towards our fellow people, demanding that we fulfill the second table of the law: "This means that all the virtues we show in our relation to our fellow men should spring from devotion and obedience to God Himself and should in their exercise be consecrated to God."[15]

Propelling the dialectical relationship between consecration of God and the relation of the neighbor, Calvin delves into the meaning of interpersonal and social ethics in his discussion of the second table. As for family ethics, Calvin's thought is in line with the divine claim to respect our parents with reverence, obedience, and gratefulness. Concerning the public safety of all, Calvin considers human beings in light of the image of God. We should see sacred images in our neighbors so that we protect the image of God in them. We should embrace our fellow persons as our own flesh. The aim of the sixth commandment is respecting God's image imprinted in a fellow person. The image of God plays a key part in Calvin's ethics regulating human interpersonal attitudes and relationships (*Inst.* II.viii.39).

Therefore, we shall not do injustice and violence to others. God forbids us to be murderers, and orders us faithfully to protect the life of our neighbor. To have respect for life is to have respect for human beings who stand in their own unique relationship to God. To do harm to human beings is to do harm to their Creator. We are required to see God in our fellow person. As Calvin contends, God "not only forbids us to be murderers, but also prescribes that everyone should study faithfully to defend the life of his neighbor and practically to declare that it is dear to him."[16]

With respect to the prohibition of adultery, Calvin develops his ethical reflection on marriage. For him, the purpose of marriage becomes clear where God sanctifies it with God's blessing. The companionship of marriage is to be understood as "a necessary remedy to keep us from plunging into unbridled lust" (*Inst.* II.viii.41).

---

15. Wallace, *Calvin's Doctrine of the Christian Life*, 116–17.

16. John Calvin, *Commentaries on the Fourth Last Books of Moses arranged in the Form of a Harmony*, 4 vols., trans. Charles Bingham (Grand Rapids: Eerdmans, 1950) 3:20.

As for the eighth commandment, Calvin mentions various kinds of thefts—in violence, in malicious deceit, in more concealed craftiness, in flatteries, etc.—and interprets this obligation with an emphasis on care for the other's good. He gives various illustrating examples: the governors should take care of their own common people, keeping public peace, protecting the good, and punishing the evil. Likewise, people have to respect their governors. The ministers of the church should be faithful to the Word of God, not falsifying the doctrine of salvation, but delivering it to the congregation in a pure manner. They should instruct the congregation not only through teaching, but also through the example of their lives. The congregation, in turn, honors them to the extent that Christ deserves, and supports their lives. The point is to love mutually and treat humanely, "in order that men strive to protect and promote the well-being and interests of others" (*Inst.* II.viii.46).

Bearing false witness against neighbors comes about through evil intent, lying or defamation. It involves perjury which makes God's name profane and violated: "Hence this commandment is lawfully observed when our tongue, in declaring the truth, serves both the good repute and the advantage of our neighbors" (*Inst.* II.viii.47). Furthermore, Calvin treated covetousness as the absence of love. Love must rule our will.

In the context of the Decalogue Calvin's principal concern is to interpret the commandments in light of Christ's gospel and love. Christian life is to be filled with the love of God and the love of our neighbor. In particular, the commandment to love our enemy is a genuine commandment (*Inst.* II.viii.57). Calvin's ethical concern is to articulate that the believer's union with Christ is rooted and grounded in love (Eph 3:17), because "the whole human race without exception . . . should be comprehended in the same affection of love" (*Inst.* II.viii.55). For Calvin, love stands as the principle and norm for ethical conduct, because "love alone is the rule governing our actions, and the only guide as to the right way to use the gifts of God. God approves of nothing that lacks it, no matter how magnificent man may think it."[17] Love involves doing justice to one's neighbor. This justice based on love becomes apparent and compelling in the Decalogue, because "justice is the name given to the rectitude and humanity which we cultivate with our brethren, when we endeavor to do

---

17. John Calvin, *The First Epistle of Paul the Apostle to the Corinthians*, trans. John W. Fraser, eds. David W. and Thomas Forsyth Torrance (Grand Rapids: Eerdmans, 1960) 276, 1 Cor 13:3.

good to all, and when we abstain from all wrong, fraud, and violence."[18] Love also judges because it is able "to stretch forth the hand to the miserable and the oppressed, to vindicate righteous causes, and to guard the weak from being unjustly injured. These are the lawful exercises in which the Lord commands his people to be employed."[19]

CHRISTIAN ETHICS IN DISCIPLESHIP

Concerning our spiritual relationship with Christ, Calvin believes that the Christian should undergo in union with Christ the process of mortification, following the example of Jesus's death. This is central to Calvin's concept of discipleship. There are two aspects of mortification, i.e., inward as well as outward. An inward process of mortification is a dying to self, corresponding to Christ's perfect obedience to God and God's complete control of ourselves. An outward process of mortification implies that our inward conformity to Christ should be brought to the neighbor and to society. Therefore, spirituality in Christian discipleship cannot be separated from the social life context.

For Calvin, there are two ethical motives for Christian life: the first is to love righteousness, while the second is to affirm our zeal for righteousness. Calvin regards holiness as the bond of our communion with Christ. Certainly he does not mean our holiness, but rather Christ's righteousness *extra nos* as the basis for our righteousness. For this reason, Calvin's ethical theology is first grounded in the person and redemptive act of Christ. We strive for holiness and righteousness because we have been adopted as children of God, so that our life expresses and represents Christ, who is the bond and basis of our adoption. If we do not give and devote ourselves to righteousness, we are rebellious against our Creator, with wicked intention, so that we abandon our Savior (*Inst.* III.vi.3).

In this sense, an ethical theology for Christian life is not a matter of speech only, but of actual discipleship, because the gospel is fully effective only as long as "it possesses the whole soul, and finds a seat and resting place in the inmost affection of the heart" (*Inst.* III.vii.4). What is most striking is Calvin's practical concern to transform interpersonal relations in light of the word of God, bearing fruits in daily life. What do we attain

---

18. John Calvin, *Commentaries on the First Book of Moses Called Genesis*, 2 vols., 1:482, Gen 18:19.

19. Ibid., 1:482, Gen 18:19.

The Spirit and the Law

as the goal of the Christian life? Is Christian life able to attain perfect holiness and righteousness on earth?

In response to this question, Calvin gives a pneumatological and eschatological impetus to his ethics. In view of the progress and goal of Christian life, Calvin writes that "We may surpass ourselves in goodness until we attain to goodness itself. It is this, indeed, which through the whole course of life we seek and follow. But we shall attain it only when we have cast off the weakness of the body, and are received into full fellowship with him" (*Inst.* III.vi.5). This is the bearing of eschatology on Calvin's ethics.[20]

In the discussion of leitmotifs for personal ethics, Calvin considers the spirituality of Christian life in light of self-denial, cross-bearing, and prayer. The scope of this chapter will discuss only the first two at length.[21]

To delve into the ethical meaning of self-denial, Calvin considers its process stage by stage. In the first stage, Calvin argues that because we belong to God, it is of special significance to follow the leading of the Lord alone. In this first step, we dedicate ourselves for the service of the Lord, distancing ourselves from the selfish desire. Service means not only obedience to God's word, but also "to the biding of God's Spirit" (*Inst.* III.vii.1). Therefore, self-denial involves the mortification of our natural concupiscence, denying all the selfish emotions and bad impulses arising out of the "flesh." In this process, the Spirit of God is under control and has authority over our hearts. This first step which we undergo through mortification in union with Christ enables us to enter into the spiritual life.

In the second stage we are to pursue God's will and serve to advance God's glory. Denying ourselves, putting aside our self-concern, we faithfully incline our zeal to God and God's commandments: "This, then, is that denial of self which Christ enjoins with such great earnestness upon

---

20. To be more faithful to the eschatological significance of Calvin's ethics we should pay attention to his reflection on "Meditation on the Future Life" (*Inst.* III.ix) and "The Final Resurrection" (*Inst.* III.xxv). The importance of eschatology to Calvin's theology and ethics is underscored by Gustafson who states: "Calvin's doctrine of eternal life is indispensable in his theology; its coherence crumbles without it." Gustafson, *Ethics from a Theocentric Perspective*, vol.1, 182.

21. In parallel with the personal social implication of the first two, prayer is also both communal and private for Calvin. Calvin wrote, "To sum up, all prayers ought to be such as to look to that community which our Lord has established in his Kingdom and his household" (*Inst.* III.xx.38).

his disciples at the outset of their service" (*Inst.* III.vii.2). Thus, Calvin connects the whole process of self-denial with the death of Jesus Christ. Jesus Christ is the example for our self-denial, because "He kept Himself in subjection to the will of the Father."[22]

Moreover, Calvin refers to self-renunciation as the third stage in order to enter into Christian life in reference to the teaching of Paul. Based on Romans 6 and Col 3:5, the inward process of self-denial and renouncing the works of the flesh is equivalent to mortification. According to Rom 8:29, 2 Cor 4:10, Phil 3:10, and 2 Tim 2:11, Paul teaches that Christians undergo not merely an inward conformity to Christ but also a conformity to outward conditions, like suffering and persecution. We are surrounded with ungodliness and worldly lusts in mundane life.

To the degree that we are separated from the iniquities of the world, godliness joins us in true holiness with God. However, self-renunciation from ungodliness and worldly desires is not complete until the Redeemer is to come. Therefore, "self denial involves the Christian in constant conflict with his own nature and reason" in the eschatological openness.[23] This is a vertical dimension of self-denial which holds an eschatological bearing, that is, our devotion and conformity to God's will. Frequently, Calvin advocates for poverty equipped with piety in contrast to worldly prosperity, which leads to the forgetting of God (*Inst.* II.x.12, n. 11; III.xx.46). What Calvin admonishes us to heed is concern for God's blessing alone. When we always "look to the Lord," "we may be led to whatever lot he has provided for us" through God's guidance (*Inst.* III.vii.9).

Led by God's guidance, we are entitled to "pursue only those enterprises which do not lead us away from innocence" (*Inst.* III.vii.9). It is necessary even in the midst of suffering and persecution to look to "God's kindness and truly fatherly indulgence." That is "the rule of piety," according to Calvin, "with most orderly justice [God] deals out good as well as ill to us" (*Inst.* III.vii.10).

After explaining personal and spiritual stages of the Christian life, Calvin connects the principle of self-denial with the horizontal dimension of social life. Self-denial provides us with the right attitude towards our fellow person. In this sense Calvin analyzes what stands behind the interpersonal conflict and competition based on self-love and pride: "If

---

22. Wallace, *Calvin's Doctrine of the Christian Life*, 63.
23. Ibid., 57.

others manifest the same endowments we admire in ourselves, or even superior ones, we spitefully belittle and revile these gifts in order to avoid yielding place to such persons. Here arises such insolence that each one of us ... wishes to tower above the rest, and loftily and savagely abuses every mortal man, or at least looks down upon him as an inferior" (*Inst.* III.vii.4).

This desire for gaining superiority leads to inequality of classes: "The poor yield to the rich; the common folk, to the nobles; the servants, to their masters; the unlearned, to the educated. But there is no one who does not cherish within himself some opinion of his own pre-eminence" (*Inst.* III.vii.4). Seeing that "the pride is the mother of the deadly sins," Calvin is very critical of a superiority-based consciousness and self-sufficient intellectualism in the light of divine judgment.[24]

How can we resolve and overcome the social and ethical conflict? The sole remedy which Calvin keeps in mind is "to tear out from our inward parts this most deadly pestilence of love of strife and love of self" (*Inst.* III.vii.4). To put it another way, we should go back to "a heart imbued with lowliness and with reverence for others" in order to attain the remedy of the social conflict (*Inst.* III.vii.4). Furthermore, Calvin tries to locate self-renunciation as the proper stance toward our neighbors. Calvin conceptualizes his ethical theology in pursuit of the common good and the sharing of all benefits with others. This ethic embodies personal character oriented for social *diakonia*.

The controlling principle in this ethics is to set up the common advantage of the whole body, which functions as the rule for generosity and beneficence. Hence, Calvin underscores its social implication: "We are the stewards of everything God has conferred on us by which we are able to help our neighbor, and are required to render account of our stewardship. Moreover, the only right stewardship is that which is tested by the rule of love. Thus it will come about that we shall not only join zeal for another's benefit with care for our own advantage, but shall subordinate the latter to the former" (*Inst.* III.vii.5).

In fact, communal benefits based on love are characteristic of Calvin's theological ethics. Calvin's concern for love of neighbor is not merely humanitarian, rather it is to look in depth at the image of God in our fellow person. Love of neighbor, which expresses itself as obligation to others,

---

24. Cf. *Inst.* I.i.2., II.i.1. See III.vii.4, footnote.

means participating in the image of God among all people. Image of God in all people refers to the fact that people surpass other animals and have not been utterly destroyed even through Adam's fall (*Inst.* II.viii.45). How is it then possible for us to love those who hate us, doing their unrighteous deeds on us, and to grant blessings instead of reproaches? Here, Calvin brings the relationship between love of neighbor and image of God into the foreground: "It is that we remember not to consider men's evil intention but to look upon the image of God in them, which cancels and effaces their transgressions, and with its beauty and dignity allures us to love and embrace them" (*Inst.* III.vii.6).

Therefore, mortification comes about only if we make complete the duties of love. Calvin's interpersonal ethics on the rich and the poor requires consideration: "Rather, each man will so consider with himself that in all his greatness he is a debtor to his neighbors, and that he ought in exercising kindness toward them to set no other limit than the end of his resources: these, as widely as they are extended, ought to have their limits set according to the rule of love" (*Inst.* III.vii.7).

Furthermore, Calvin treats cross-bearing as an indispensable component of mortification. The union with Christ leads us to the cross and the resurrection of Christ. Our cross-bearing is thus our conformity to Christ. When we are in union with Christ, we are sharing his death and resurrection. As followers of Christ, we are called to follow his example. When we know his suffering, we will also know the power of his resurrection: "By communion with him the very sufferings themselves not only become blessed to us but also help much in promoting our salvation" (*Inst.* III.viii.1). Why is it necessary that we bear the cross? By nature we are inclined to be in "stupid and empty confidence in the flesh," being proud against God (*Inst.* III.viii.2).

Through cross-bearing we are led to in-depth trust in God's power and grace. Thereby, we are allowed to experience God's faithfulness and have hope for the future. It is to hold fellowship with the sufferings of Christ. In turning away from self-love, we become aware of our incapacity to do this. To feel our incapacity is to learn to distrust ourselves. To distrust ourselves is to transfer our trust to God. To have rest with a trustful heart in God is to stand under God's preservation. To take our stand in God's grace is to comprehend the truth of God's promises. Finally, to have assurance of God's promise is to strengthen our hope (*Inst.* III.viii.3).

The Spirit and the Law

The close relationship with Christ which is brought through cross-bearing encourages the Christian to bear it with confidence: "How much can it do to soften all the bitterness of the cross, that the more we are afflicted with adversities, the more surely our fellowship with Christ is confirmed!" (*Inst.* III.viii.1).

In some cases, God trains us through the cross, because God instructs God's people to obey and to follow Godself, testing their patience. It is interesting to notice that Calvin in this context refers to the cross as the medicine of our disease. Calvin describes God as "the heavenly physician" (*Inst.* III.viii.5). "Cross-bearing is a powerful aid to self-denial and a test of obedience."[25]

In addition, Calvin links the meaning of cross-bearing with correcting our previous transgressions, so that we may be fully obedient to God. The cross is seen as fatherly chastisement. Finally, Calvin considers cross-bearing for righteousness' sake. The more we suffer under persecution, the more intimately we will be received into God, and the firmer root we have in Christ. The more we are cast down from this world, the fuller place we have in God's kingdom. For this reason, the cross for righteousness' sake finds consolation in God. What ethical implication does cross-bearing retain in Calvin's theology? Does not Calvin instruct here a passive accommodation to the life situation? How does his teaching of the cross differ from the Stoics? Although Calvin is indebted to the ancient stoic philosophy, nevertheless he had no hesitation in giving critical expression to its teachings, especially concerning the rejection of feeling.[26]

For Calvin, tears and anxiety have a proper place in the Christian life in view of suffering. But Calvin distinguishes himself from passive acceptance of this feeling, because he grounds himself finally not in our affliction itself, but in our salvation under God's righteousness. Therefore, cross-bearing should not be misunderstood as a form of medieval piety as expressed *in imitatio Christi*. But it is conformity of our old nature to God's righteousness so that we may live a joyful life under the grace of God in the presence of the Spirit. As a result, the cross enables our ethical life in gratitude and joy to remain sober and humble before God. Calvin maintains this point of view as follows: "Therefore, in patiently suffering these tribulations, we do not yield to necessity but we consent for our own

---

25. Wallace, *Calvin's Doctrine of the Christian Life*, 74.
26. Cf. *Inst.* I.xvi.8., III.iv.28, III.vii.15. See III.viii.9 footnote.

good. From this, thanksgiving also follows, which cannot exist without joy ... It thus is clear to how necessary it is that the bitterness of the cross be tempered with spiritual joy" (*Inst.* III.viii.II).

In the discussion of the personal-social bearing of Calvin's ethics in the context of discipleship, i.e., self-denial and cross-bearing, we meet again the significance of the Spirit in his ethics. The Holy Spirit mediates the death and resurrection of Christ to us in terms of self-denial and cross-bearing, "in order that the shedding of his sacred blood may not be nullified, our souls are cleansed by the secret watering of the Spirit" (*Inst.* III.i.1). The Holy Spirit renders the death of Christ with efficacy for the mortification of our flesh and self-pride. The work of the Spirit is very closely connected with the death of Christ for us, for "to participate in the death of Christ by virtue of the Holy Spirit means to participate in the power of the Holy Spirit to subdue and conquer the will of the flesh."[27]

In light of what has been described, we come to see what Calvin's ethical theology implies regarding the law and discipleship: self-denial and cross-bearing. Calvin's ethical theology is primarily Christ-centered. But his understanding of Christology always moved in a perspective of the Spirit. Besides, his eschatological reservation does not define his Christology in a narrow sense, but underscores the dynamism of his ethics in the presence of the Spirit in expectation of God's future. Calvin's adherence to the law is not related to a kind of obligatory legalism, but rather to the grateful response of the justified believer to the grace of God in Christ, as encouraged and inspired by the power and efficacy of the Spirit.

In Christ, the law finds itself completing its function and goal of punishing and condemning. The practical and ethical concern of the law arises from the new understanding of the law as a gift of God. Principally the law admonishes and leads us to pursue holiness and righteousness in accordance with the sanctifying Spirit of God. Here we no longer are encapsulated or harassed by the perfect demand of the law owing to our weakness, because the Spirit of Christ, fulfilling the perfection of the law, inspires us to live up to the righteousness and justice of God.

Basically, Jesus Christ becomes a norm and principle in considering the personal-social bearing of Calvin's ethics. Jesus Christ is at the center of his ethical reflection of the meaning of the law and mortification for

---

27. Wallace, *Calvin's Doctrine of the Christian Life*, 66.

The Spirit and the Law

the spirituality of our discipleship. Thus, love functions as prime mover before God and the fellow person. This love encourages us to look to the image of God in the fellow person. The love which is the basis for Calvin's ethics in this context has a universal tendency, because with a single feeling of love, believers embrace the whole human race without exception. Actually, for Calvin there is no distinction between barbarian and Greek, worthy and unworthy, friend and enemy, because we are all sinners before God. Love initiates us to see the image of God in all human beings. As Calvin writes: "if we rightly direct our love, we must first turn our eyes not to man ... but to God, who bids us extend to all men the love we bear to him, that this may be unchanging principle: whatever the character of the man, we must yet love him because we love God" (*Inst.* II.viii.55).

Love of God and image of God in the fellow person is an ethical basis for our human responsibility and solidarity with the poor and the weak in society. At this point, the Holy Spirit plays an indispensable role in constructing his ethical theology concerning the law and discipleship in the vertical as well as the horizontal dimension. Calvin's ethics is not exclusively *theonomous*, nor is it an "ethics of autonomy,"[28] but rather a communicative ethics, which, inspired by God's Spirit, seeks a prophetic *diakonia* in the field of our social discipleship.

CHRISTIAN ETHICS IN FREEDOM

We have seen that Calvin's concept of union with Christ is coupled with practical and ethical reflection, in his discussion of discipleship. Moreover, in the treatment of law in Christ, Calvin never lost sight of its relevance to social and ethical solidarity and responsibility for the poor and the weak. For Calvin, a dogmatic theology is ethically oriented and a Christian ethics is dogmatically structured.

In the context of regeneration and justification, Calvin also conceptualizes his ethical theology of the Christian life (*Inst.* III.vi–x). And he further proposes his special ethics of "Christian freedom" following the doctrine of justification. Therefore, in his ethical theology justification and sanctification stand basically in continuity with Christian freedom and liberation.

Before Calvin became the representative of predestination, he was basically a theologian of freedom. In the 1535/36 edition of the *Institutes*

---

28. Gustafson, *Ethics from a Theocentric Perspective*, 1:166.

Calvin highlighted and ended his theological point in describing Christian freedom. Without attention to freedom, it is impossible to understand Calvin's ethical theology. In the last edition of the *Institutes* in 1559, Calvin again discussed the significance of Christian freedom (*Inst.* III.xix). In parallel with the threefold use of the law, Calvin also underlines Christian freedom in a threefold way: a liberation of the believer's conscience from the law in seeking assurance before God, then a liberation from constraint of the law, and, finally, liberation from something trivial (*adiaphora*), against church or national customs, traditions and authorities, etc.

In parallel with the Christ-union aspect, in which "both justification and sanctification yield conclusions for ethics,"[29] Calvin's ethics of freedom does not preclude the importance of the law, but, rather, deepens the freedom that Christ brings us in terms of fulfilling the law. This aspect retains essentially a practical consequence, because Calvin considers freedom as an "appendage of justification" (*Inst.* III.xix.1). A right understanding of Christian freedom is fundamental to Calvin, because "unless this freedom be comprehended, neither Christ nor gospel truth, nor inner peace of soul, can be rightly known" (*Inst.* III.xix.1).[30]

As for the liberation of the believer's conscience from the law, Calvin writes: "Christian freedom, in my opinion, consists of three parts. The first, that the consciences of believers, in seeking assurance of their justification before God, should rise above and advance beyond the law, forgetting all law righteousness" (*Inst.* III.xix.2). The basis of this liberation lies solely in Christ, who surpasses all perfection of the law. If we seek assurance of the justification before God, we ought to "turn our attention from ourselves" in terms of looking only to God's mercy in Christ. However, it does not follow that the law is superfluous, because the whole life of Christians should be a practice of godliness; we are called to sanctification (1 Thess 4:7; cf. Eph 1:4; 1 Thess 4:3). Although the function of the law, which encourages people to a "zeal for holiness and innocence," remains a significant component for Christian life, there is no other basis than Christ alone (*Solus Christus*) concerning how we are rendered righteous. In this regard we are required to proceed beyond the law, "by forgetting all law righteousness" (*Inst.* III.xix.2).

---

29. Niesel, *Theology of Calvin*, 141.
30. See also *Inst.* II.vii.14–15, III.xi.17–18.

The Spirit and the Law

The first freedom from the law renders believers obedient without being coerced by the law. This leads to the second aspect of the liberation from the law: "The second part dependent upon the first, is that consciences observe the law, not as if constrained by the necessity of the law, but that freed from the law's yoke they willingly obey God's will" (*Inst.* III.xix.4). This "willingness" arises from our whole confidence in the goodness of God. For instance, the law requires perfection so that it condemns all imperfection. As long as we are imperfect according to the standard of the law, we become its transgressors. But if we are free from the entire yoke of the law, our services, which we render not as servant but as God's children, will be approved and accepted by the gracious God, "however small, rude, and imperfect these may be" (*Inst.* III.xix.5). Therefore, Christians do not have to be afraid of "the remnants of sin," because we are aware of being emancipated through God's grace. We are not under the law under the grace, so that God's grace in Christ emancipates us from the curse of the law.

The third aspect of Christian freedom refers to freedom concerning "outward things that are of themselves 'indifferent.'" For Calvin, the assurance of this freedom is central, because "we are not bound before God by any religious obligation preventing us from sometimes using them and other times not using them, indifferently" (*Inst.* III.xix.7). Indifference in anything frees Calvin from the orthodox, rigid picture of him as a stern legalist. The Christian is at liberty to use or not use things intermediate and indifferent like "unrestricted eating of meat, use of holidays and of vestments, and such things" (*Inst.* III.xix.7). If we lack this knowledge, our conscience tends to superstition with no end. In discussion of freedom in things indifferent, Calvin takes into consideration moderation in enjoying God's temporal gifts (*Inst.* III.x.1–4).

Seeing that the apostle Paul subjected all outward indifferent things to the freedom of believers,[31] Calvin goes as far as saying that we should use our freedom in the use of God's gifts for the purpose, according to which God gives them to us: "With such confidence our minds will be at peace with him, and will recognize his liberality toward us . . . Our consciences may not be constrained by any necessity to observe them but may remember that by God's beneficence their use is for edification made subject to him" (*Inst.* III.xix.8).

---

31. Cf. *Inst.* III.x.4.

In view of freedom in things indifferent, Calvin warns of the abuse of this freedom for gluttony and luxury, standing in defense of the weak and the poor. In this context, Calvin's personal and social ethics, which underlies Christian freedom, denounces "those who allege it as an excuse for their desires that they may abuse God's good gifts to their own lust." This denouncement is directed to "those who think that freedom does not exist unless it is used before men, and consequently, in using it have no regard for weaker brethren" (*Inst.* III.xix.9). People are required to clearly use God's gift with a clean conscience and heart, "with no scruple of conscience, no trouble of mind" (*Inst.* III.xix.8), distancing themselves from "uncontrolled desire, away with immoderate prodigality, away with vanity and arrogance" (*Inst.* III.xix.9).

What characterizes Calvin's ethics of freedom is his social concern for the poor and weak brothers and sisters. He constantly opposes the abuse of Christian freedom which injures such people. Calvin holds that "We must with greatest caution hold to this limitation, that we do not abandon the care of the weak, whom the Lord has so strongly commended to us" (*Inst.* III.xix.10). This social concern for the poor becomes manifest when he deals with Christian freedom in the context of two kinds of offense.[32] For Calvin, our freedom should not be exercised to ignore the weak brothers and sisters. It is not to tolerate "the rigor of the Pharisees at all" (*Inst.* III.xix.11). Calvin's concern about the weak brothers and sisters, which is expressed in the discussion of Christian freedom, is articulated in the following way: "Our freedom is not given against our feeble neighbors, for love makes us their servants in all things; rather it is given that, having peace with God in our hearts, we may also live at peace with men" (*Inst.* III.xix.11).

In this sense it is important to pay attention to Calvin's discussion of the political order in the light of Christian freedom, because consciences are bound by civil laws. For Calvin it is dangerous to "misapply to the political order the gospel teaching on spiritual freedom" (*Inst.* III.xix.15).

---

32. In the interest of caring for the weak, Calvin calls into question two kinds of offenses: an offense given, an offense received. The first one is understood as an offense which comes about by our fault, so that it might cause the ignorant and the simple to stumble. In some ways it takes place "from the doer of the thing itself" (*Inst.* III.xix.11). The other arises when "something, otherwise not wickedly or unseasonably committed, is by ill will or malicious intent of mind wrenched into occasion for offense." (*Inst.* III.xix.11). Because this brings "offense to persons of bitter and pharisaical pride," it is called the offense of the Pharisees, while the former is called that of the weak.

The Spirit and the Law

Conscience has the function of establishing the political order, but also a spiritual significance. Calvin's demand that subjects obey magistrates—even tyrants—comes out of the fact that they have been constituted by God's ordination: "Even though individual laws may not apply to the conscience, we are still held by God's general command which commends us to the authority of magistrates. And Paul's discussion turns on this point: the magistrates, since they have been ordained by God, ought to be held in honor" (*Inst.* IV.x.5).

Human conscience in the spiritual sense is thus politically bound and framed. Calvin's conception of political order may be most fully described in connection with his ethical teaching about neighbors: "For Christ included all, without exception, who labor and are burdened" (*Comm.* Lk 10:28). It is a sacred bond based on love and equity for the sake of mutually assisting of each other. Seeking after love and looking toward the edification of our neighbor can be seen as the principle of freedom. In Calvin's ethics of freedom love remains a priority.

As far as the political order is concerned, it is not surprising that Calvin deals with *ordo politicus* in view of the image of God: "When man alone is called by Paul the image and glory of God, and woman excluded from this place of honor (1 Cor 11:7), it is clear from the context that this ought to be restricted to the political order" (*Inst.* I.xv.4.; cf. IV. xx.24). Therefore, Calvin interprets the *ordo politicus* as deriving from and dependent upon the *ordnatio Dei*.[33] We shall later discuss this relationship in view of Calvin's political teaching about church and state in the next chapter.

In light of what we have discussed about Calvin's concept of Christian freedom, we see that Calvin treats freedom as the power and effectiveness of justification: No justification without freedom, while no freedom without justification. Therefore, justification and freedom are, in Calvin's *Institutes*, "breathing-in and out of Reformation people."[34] Christian freedom, which stands in connection with justification, means emancipation from the law. The justified and emancipated people find their identity in seeking sanctification in terms of Christ through the power of the Spirit. Freedom means emancipation from self-centeredness. From this perspective the law is understood no longer as compulsion or constraint, but as

---

33. Milner, *Calvin's Doctrine of the Church*, 29–37.

34. Hans Scholl, *Reformation und Politik: Politische Ethik bei Luther, Calvin und den Frühhugenotten.* Urban-Taschenbucher 616 (Stuttgart: Kohlhammer, 1976) 17.

a helpful signpost showing God's grace for the free, justified people, who as God's children are willing to obey divine commandments. Moreover, the third aspect of Christian freedom refers to the emancipation from so-called indifferent things, which means the protest of the subjugation of the conscience to indifferent things and external means of church authority. Regarding the dimension of freedom in Calvin's ethics, Scholl accentuates the following point in a convincing way: "Anyone who is justified as a child of God does not despise effort and commitment, but these are not subject to the law of achievement in the society. He oriented himself toward this deed in a rather meaningful way. That means freedom of reformation: liberation from the action of compulsion to blessed grace."[35]

---

35. Ibid., 20.

5

The Spirit and the Church

THE HOLY SPIRIT IN THE CREATION OF THE CHURCH

CALVIN UNDERSTANDS THE CHURCH as "the external means or aids by which God invites us into the society and holds us therein" (*Inst.* IV.i). Much can be said about the marks of the church, the sacraments, baptism, order of ministry and discipline, etc. But Calvin's doctrine of the church cannot fully be explored merely within the context of Book IV of the *Institutes of the Christian Religion*, because Calvin's treatment of worship (under the heading of prayer) and his discussion of the Christian life (deeply connected with the church) are found in Book III. The important teachings like Christ-union, faith, justification, sanctification, ethical life in the Law and freedom—all of these are indispensable to the life of the church. Additionally, Calvin develops and refines his theological idea of the church particularly in his commentaries on scripture. The order of the church cannot be separated from the work of the Holy Spirit. As Milner rightly states, "the church [order] can only be understood dialectically, as referring simultaneously to the Word and to the Spirit."[1]

In chapter one we have seen the work of the Spirit in the creation of the world and in restoring the integrity of the human being according to the image of God. For Calvin, the whole order of nature was perverted by the original sin of Adam (*Inst.* II.i.5), as characterized as pride and disobedience rooted in infidelity. Its restoration is commensurate with the salvation of the human being, i.e., the church. Consequently, the creation of the church is perceived as the peculiar providence of God to create out of nothing. "A most beautiful example of Divine providence . . . that the

---

1. Milner, *Calvin's Doctrine of the Church*, 4.

Lord ... brings forth the salvation of his Church, not from magnificent splendor, but from death and grave" (*Comm*. Gen 37:6).

The history of Israel is located in the covenant between God and Abraham. Calvin refers to this covenantal act of God as "adoption" (*Comm*. Matt 10:6) or "the election" (*Inst*. III.xxi.6). There is a twofold election of God: particular election and general election. Calvin characterizes particular election as hidden and secret, which is grounded in the secret counsel of God. It becomes manifest through God's calling of human beings.

According to Calvin, there are three callings, the outward call (preaching), the secret call (election), and individual calling, the three of which are intrinsically related to each other:

> The Lord is indeed said to call men when he invites them by the voice of the gospel; but there is what precedes that, a hidden call, when God destines for himself those whom he purposes to save. There is then an inward call, which dwells in the secret counsel of God, and then follows the call, by which he makes us really partakers of his adoption. . . . But that the election of God is not to be separated from the outward call. (*Comm*. Joel 2.32)

What is the work of the Holy Spirit in the creation of the church? As the world is shaped in Word and through the Spirit, the church is created in the Word and through the activity of the Spirit. To the degree that the church is perceived as the place where the regenerating activity of the Spirit becomes evident, the Spirit restores the image of God in the human being. As Calvin states, "He speaks of the restoration of the church, the chief part of which is the new creature by which God restores his image in the elect" (*Comm*. Isa 44:4. *Inst*. I.xv .5).

THE NATURE OF THE CHURCH

Calvin describes the church in a threefold way: the mother of believers, the body of Christ, and the elect community. As far as the church as mother of believers is concerned, Calvin points to the gospel and the means of grace as imparted to the church. The church has not received them for its own private edification or veneration, but it is the gospel that claims the church to be faithful to it. God speaks to us through the mouth of humans, and through the visible elements of water, bread and wine. None of these gifts has been promised us apart from the work of the Spirit. God ordained instruction in this world for imparting these gifts to the church. Because God is the author of the ordinance, God wants God's presence to be recognized in this promise (*Inst.* IV.i.5): "It is always characteristic of God that He works and creates by spiritual means, but as He uses the servant of the Word as His instrument He inspires in the latter His own spiritual message; for He unites with the efforts of man the power of the divine spirit."[2]

Furthermore, Calvin writes, "He has ordained pastors and teachers in order through their words to instruct His own, has invested them with authority, and in fact has left nothing undone which might serve the cause of the sacred unity of the faith and good order. Above all he has instituted the sacraments of which we in fact know that they are extremely useful means to preserve and strengthen our faith" (*Inst.* IV.i.1). Although God is not confined to God's own ordinances, God demands for us to be faithful to the preaching and sacraments. The spiritual food of the soul in the church offered by God should not be despised. Otherwise we deserve to perish from terrible hunger.

For this reason, Calvin characterizes the being of the church as the mother of believers (*Inst.* IV.i.1). Calvin makes a concerted effort to reach the one true church. Accordingly, Calvin is in line with the teaching of the early church and the church fathers. The church is placed in the service of Christ, so that God wants to meet us there. The church is a vehicle to serve the realization of Jesus Christ in terms of preaching and sacraments in the presence of the Holy Spirit.

As we have seen that the church is the sphere where Christ comes into our lives through word and the sacraments in the power of the Holy Spirit, Calvin relates the church to the body of Christ: "There arises an integrated structure of the congregation of the faithful, the body of Christ is built up, and we grow in every part in adhesion to Him who is the Head and become at unity among ourselves" (*Inst.* IV.iii.3). As there is the relationship between the priestly work of Christ and our justification, justification is related to unity in the body of Christ. This union is most fully realized in the celebration of the sacraments—as seen especially in Calvin's doctrine of real presence—not in a substantialist or physical manner, but in a distinctly spiritual manner (*Inst.* III.xi.5.10). In speaking

---

2. *CR.* 50.235. Cf. Niesel, *Theology of Calvin*, 184.

of the body of Christ, Calvin depicts Christ as the head, which determines the character of the body.

The ministry of the church is directed toward becoming one body with Christ. To the degree Jesus Christ alone is its ruler and head, this aspect is intrinsically integrated to the kingship of Christ. Furthermore, the unity of the body of Christ may be derived not only from the head, but also from the Spirit: "By the Spirit of sanctification, God spreads himself through all the members of the church, embraces all in his government, and dwells in all; but God is not inconsistent with himself, and therefore we cannot but be united with him into one body" (*Comm*. Eph 4:6).

For our service of God, Christ imparts the gifts of the Holy Spirit in full abundance upon the church. Each receives from him a special gift for the edification of the whole. The binding of the Christian with Christ as possible and efficacious through work of the Holy Spirit is not separated from the binding of the members with each other. We cannot be Christians without being brothers and sisters. The mutual fellowship of the believers stands under brotherly and sisterly love and sharing. "It cannot but be that those who are convinced that God is their common father and Christ their common head are united together in brotherly love and share their goods in common" (*Inst*. IV.i.3).

The mutual fellowship of life in the body of Christ is particularly expressed in prayer. The church is the sphere of prayer for one another: "Paul . . . exhorts all the members of the body of Christ mutually to pray for one another. Since the members have a mutual solicitude for each other, and if one member suffers, the rest sympathize with it. And so should the mutual prayers of all the members, who are still engaged in the labors of the present state, ascend on each other's behalf to the head" (*Inst*. III.xxx.20). Because we are members of the same body, prayer must be common, including all those who are "in Christ." In this regard, "the prayer of Christians ought to be public and to look to the public edification of the church and the advancement of the fellowship of believers" (*Inst*. III.xx.47).

Prayer springs from the operation of the Holy Spirit. It is the Spirit who takes effect within us through prayer. In Calvin's view, prayer is not regarded as a personal, subjective activity, but as God's initiative in the efficacy of the Spirit for us: "Before we can utter a prayer we must have received the first fruits of the Spirit. For he alone is the proper teacher of the art of prayer. He not only inspires in us the words but guides the movements of our hearts" (*Inst.* III.xx.5). Not only faith but also the fruit of faith, prayer springs from the work of the Spirit.

Calvin also describes the church as "the congregation of elect people" because "the secret choice of God is the foundation of the church" (*Inst.* IV.i.2). The Spirit plays a decisive role in calling the particular election of an individual. It is through the regenerating work of the Spirit that the general election becomes effectual calling: "Calling consists not only in the preaching of the word, but also in the illumination of the Spirit" (*Inst.* III.xxiv.2). Faith is grounded in the illumination of the Spirit, so that Faith is the decisive moment within the effectual calling.[3] The concept of election may not lead to idle speculation or a sense of fear: "It is not enough that with our understanding and heart should apprehend the church as the body of the elect, if at the same time we do not realize its utter unity, believing that we ourselves are incorporated into it" (*Inst.* IV.i.2). The concept of God's election does not give insecurity about salvation, but rather strengthens believers to live in assurance of faith and to be faithful to their task.

Calvin speaks of the visible church in connection with his concept of election (*Inst.* IV.i.7), but this should not be taken as a neglect of the invisible church. His argument of "no salvation outside church" refers to the visible church, which is the mother of all believers. The invisible church denotes that God is really the Lord of the church. To the degree the external state of the visible church becomes possible through the interplay between the general election and the non-sanctifying work of the Spirit, the internal state of the invisible church becomes through the interplay between the sanctifying work of the Spirit and special election. For Calvin, to believe that the church is invisible does not avoid a possibility that many hypocrites and despisers of God are mixed in the visible church. As Calvin states,

> The word church is used in the sacred Scriptures in two senses. Sometimes, when they mention the church, they understand that those who are children of God by the grace of adoption, and by the sanctification of the Spirit are the true members of Christ . . . Often, however, the name 'church' designates the whole multitude

---

3. Cf. Calvin's famous definition of faith, *Inst.* III.ii.7: "Now we shall have a right definition of faith if we say that it is a firm and certain knowledge of the divine benevolence toward us, which, founded on the truth of the gratuitous promise in Christ, is revealed in our minds and sealed in our hearts by the Holy Spirit."

of men dispersed all over the world who profess to worship one God and Christ . . . consent to the word of the Lord and preserve the ministry instituted by Christ for the preaching of it. Many hypocrites are mixed in this church, who have nothing of Christ but the name and appearance, many ambitious, avaricious, envious, slanderous and others impure in life, who are tolerated for a time . . . As it is necessary, therefore, to believe that church, which is invisible to us, and conspicuous to the eyes of God alone, so we are commanded to honor and maintain communion with that which is called church with respect to man. (*Inst.* IV.i.7)

The distinction of visible and invisible refers to the true and false church. The idea of invisible church held a critical function with regard to the empirical church: "Precisely if it is the true church of its Lord it will be ready to undergo the test of that critical idea and so will witness to the glory of its Head."[4] The preaching of the word and the due celebration of the sacraments (*Inst.* IV.i.9) is the mark of the true church.

THE MARKS OF THE CHURCH

After the resurrection of Christ and the outpouring of the Spirit upon all flesh, God deposited his covenant with all nations (*Inst.* IV.ii.11). In this light Calvin states that "the Lord has designated for us what we should know about it by certain marks and symbols" (*Inst.* IV.i.8). What are the marks of the church according to Calvin? "Wherever we see the Word of God purely preached and heard, and the Sacraments administered according to Christ's institution, there, it is not to be doubted, a church of God exists" (*Inst.* IV.i.9). When these marks appear, "the church comes forth and becomes visible to our eyes" (*Inst.* IV.i.9). The invisible becomes visible at the moment of preaching of the word and the right administration of the sacraments.

In order to be the instrument of the Holy Spirit, the preacher should be clothed with the Spirit who confirms his/her teaching to the biblical word. "Let us not be led to investigate God anywhere but in his sacred word, or to think anything of his except as his word precedes, or to speak anything concerning him but what is taken from the same word" (*Inst.* I.xiii.21). What marks the church is not only preaching of the word, but also hearing of the word. Faith and obedience are the fruits of Christian preaching, without which the gospel is of no avail for us. As far as preach-

---

4. Niesel, *Theology of Calvin*, 193.

ing works in the power of the Spirit, the word itself is the instrument of cleansing and purifying human heart. The Spirit plays a decisive role in the preacher and in the hearer as well. Preaching is bound to the Spirit, becoming effectual in the hearts of human beings, producing obedience and good work. Preaching should really be heard in faith and obedience through the efficacy of the Spirit.

As for the second mark of the church, two sacraments, baptism and the Lord's Supper have to be mentioned. In understanding sacraments, Calvin's concept of symbol is indispensable. He defines a sacrament as "an external symbol by which the Lord seals on our consciences the promises of his good will toward us, in order to sustain the feebleness of our faith, and we in turn attest our piety toward him in the presence of the Lord and of his angels and before men" (*Inst.* IV.xiv.1).

According to Calvin, the Lord is pleased to employ earthly elements as vehicles for raising human minds on high, so that the celestial arch which had before existed, is here consecrated into a sign and pledge (*Comm. Gen.* 9.13). A symbol is a natural element that has been consecrated by God to a higher usage for the confirmation of faith. However, symbols have no power as such; rather they are instruments in terms of which we are to ascend to God. There is no revelatory quality inherent in the earthly elements as such. To the degree that they are consecrated and ordained by God, they become vehicles for the self-disclosure of God. Symbols and signs as the command and promise of God are not to be separated from the clarifying Word. They are dependent upon the Word for its meaning: "God doth, indeed, apply himself to our rudeness thus far, that he showeth himself visible, after a sort, under figures" (*Comm.* Acts 7:40).

Owing to divine accommodation, symbols are a more efficacious power to penetrate the human mind, although not the self-revelation of God. They are a confirmation, pledge, or seal of that revelation in the word. Faith depends on the Word, not upon sign, but the sign strengthens faith. Based on this understanding of the symbol, Calvin deals with the sacraments, including baptism and the Lord's Supper as sacraments.

> To Abraham and his posterity circumcision was commanded (Gen 17:10). To it were afterward added purification, sacrifices, and other rites from the law of Moses (in Leviticus). These were the sacraments of the Jews until the coming of Christ, at which time these were abrogated, and two sacraments were instituted which

the Christian church now uses, baptism and the Lord's Supper (Mt 28:19, 26:26). (*Inst.* IV.xiv.20)

The change from the ancient sacraments in the Old Testament to baptism and the Lord's Supper is a change in form, but not in content: "The former foreshadowed Christ promised while he was yet awaited; the latter attest him as already come and manifested" (*Inst.* IV.xiv.20). The old sacraments are abrogated only in their use, not in their effect (*Inst.* II.vii.16). They were "temporary sacraments." Only baptism and the Lord's Supper constitute the ordinary and permanent sacraments of the church, because, first of all, they are the command and promise of God which mean seals of God's grace and as confirmation of faith (*Inst.* I.xix.1.2.5.17).

Calvin makes a fundamental distinction between the sign itself and the thing signified: "The sacred mystery of the Supper consists of two things: the corporeal signs, which thrust before our eyes, represent to us invisible things according to the feebleness of our capacity; and the spiritual truth, which is at the same time figured and exhibited by the symbols themselves" (*Inst.* IV.xviii.11). The symbols do not merely point to Christ, but our union with him: "Through baptism Christ makes us sharers in his death, so that we may be engrafted in it" (*Inst.* IV.xv.5). The sacraments are the seals and pledges of a salvation already achieved. It is the Word that ordains the sacraments and gives them character and power. Therefore, the divinely instituted order, the preaching of the Word and the administration of the sacraments are not to be separated from each other.

How does a sacrament become efficacious? The Holy Spirit plays a dominant role in the operation of the sacrament. The efficacy of the sacraments is dependent upon the Spirit:

> But the sacraments properly fulfill their office only when the Spirit, that inward teacher, comes to them ... hearts are penetrated and affections moved and our souls opened for the sacraments to enter in ... Therefore, I make such a division between the Spirit and sacraments that the power to act rests with the former, and the ministry alone is left to the latter—a ministry empty and frivolous apart from the action of the Spirit, but charged with great effect when the Spirit works within and manifests his power. (*Inst.* IV.xiv.9)

The elements in the sacrament as such do not confer the grace which they promise; that comes about only through the efficacious work of the Holy Spirit. As that occurs, they become marks of the church. Apart from the agency of the Spirit, they would be literal and even poisonous in their effect. *Distinctio sed non separatio* is true of the relationship between sign and reality (Christ and his benefits).

As far as the word "this is my body" is concerned, Calvin suggests that "this" cannot refer merely to the "form" of the bread (*Inst.* IV.xvii.20). Calvin does not accept any sort of literalism: "Not Aristotle, but the Holy Spirit teaches us that the body of Christ from the time of his resurrection was finite, and is contained in heaven even to the last day" (*Inst.* IV.xvii.25). If the body of Christ is regarded as invisible, or as being in many places at once, we have to search for a new definition of the word "body" (*Inst.* IV.xvii.29). Calvin's thought in this regard has a very strong sensibility for the finitude of Christ's body: "We must not dream of such a presence of Christ in the sacrament as the craftsmen of the Roman curia have fashioned-as if the body of Christ, by a local presence were put there to be touched by the hands, to be chewed by the teeth, and to be swallowed by the mouth" (*Inst.* IV.xvii.12). All erroneous notions about a real presence of Christ in the sacraments are based on an idea of local presence. The Roman Catholic doctrine of transubstantiation obscures the finality of Christ's ascension, endangering once and for all sacrifice of Jesus Christ for our salvation. Calvin resists this Catholic teaching in light of Christ's divinity. Likewise, the doctrine of the ubiquity of Christ's body is rejected in light of Christ's humanity.[5]

If Christ does not descend from heaven, and if his body does not lie invisibly in, with or under the elements, how is the body of Christ truly present? In commenting on Paul's First Letter to the Corinthians, Calvin states

> that participation in the body of Christ, which, I affirm, is presented to us in the supper, does not require a local presence, nor the descent of Christ, nor infinite extension, nor anything of that nature, for the supper being a heavenly action, there is no absurdity in saying, that Christ, while remaining in heaven, is received by us. For as to his communicating himself to us, that is effected through the secret virtue of his Holy Spirit, which can not merely bring together, but join in one, things that are separated by distance of place, and far remote. (*Comm.* 1 Cor 11:24; cf. *Inst.* IV.xvii.10)

---

5. Cf. The two rejected views are to be found in *Inst.* IV.xvii 11–17.

The Spirit joins us to Christ and enables a true participation in and communion with Christ's body and blood, bringing us into the presence of Christ. Calvin's opposition to the Roman and Lutheran view of the real presence can be seen not only from the standpoint of Christology, but that of pneumatology, as well. As Kolfhaus correctly insists, "the *unio cum Christo* never means identity," but he obscures the role of the Spirit when he attributes this to "an act of Christ on the believer." "It is a question about a spiritual communion—always coming down from the Head. It is, to be sure, not a spiritual communion, but rather one in which the Spirit elevates us to be with Christ, a 'coming up'—*sursum corda*—rather than a 'coming down.'"[6]

Because the Lord's Supper is a heavenly action, we are elevated by the Spirit to be united with Christ. It was established of old that before consecration, the people should be told in a loud voice to lift up their hearts (*Inst.* IV.xvii.36). The Holy Spirit is the bond of our union with Christ, and the effective agent of this action. Calvin's understanding of Christ's real presence is not essentially Zwinglian, which downplays the real presence of Christ due to their excessive emphasis on faith and the Spirit.

Furthermore, Calvin contends that the Lord's Supper is a symbol not only of our union with Christ, but also of our union with each other (*Inst.* IV.xvii. 38). Christ has only one body, in which he makes us all participate, so that by such participation, we also are all made one body. The union as represented in the Lord's Supper embraces fellowship of the brothers and sisters in the sacrament. Therefore, "private masses are diametrically opposed to the institution of Christ," because they "divide the people from one another, who ought to have united in one assembly to know again the mystery of their unity" (*Inst.* IV.xviii.8). The invisible becomes visible when, through the right administration of the sacraments, we are all gathered together and led by the guidance of the Spirit into the presence of Christ.

God has ordained both the preaching of the Word and the administration of the sacraments. When coupled with the efficacious working of the Holy Spirit, they constitute the order which marks the reality of the church. The Spirit is the dynamic factor in preaching and sacrament. The church is to be defined dialectically as existing in union with Christ

---

6. Milner, *Calvin's Doctrine of the Church*, 180 n. 3.

through the preaching and sacraments, in which the Spirit makes it effective to bring us to Christ.

Additionally, for Calvin, the power of the keys has reference to discipline and excommunication, which is the third mark of the church. The discipline of the church depends on spiritual jurisdiction, namely the power of the keys. Calvin is anxious to prevent the profanation of the Lord's Supper as caused by the participation of the unworthy and unfit person. The order of the Lord's Supper should not be profaned by indiscriminate administration. His anxiety is basic and decisive to his emphasis on the discipline of the church. Calvin promotes the right to bar from the communion of the Lord's Supper (Inst. IV. XI. 5). However, Calvin's anxiety remains a problem when he regards the expelled from the church as estranged from Christ, interpreting Matt 18:18 in a way that "they are assured of their everlasting condemnation unless they repent" (*Inst.* IV.XII.10).

CHURCH AND STATE

In light of Calvin's ecclesiology, we need to examine how Calvin understands his political ethics concerning the relationship between church and state. How does Calvin conceptualize religious matters in regard to political matters? There is mutual respect between them by existing side by side, serving the same people with reciprocal support under the one Lord. The church should not prescribe civil laws, nor the state usurps spiritual discipline and order. Basically, the church has to be distinguished from the state, yet without separation or confusion.

In consideration of this problem, Calvin stresses "that Christ's spiritual Kingdom and the civil jurisdiction are things completely distinct" (*Inst.* IV.xx.1). In Calvin's opinion, this distinction does not mean the total separation, because these two governments are not antithetical, but standing under the rule of one Lord Jesus Christ: "Yet this distinction does not lead us to consider the whole nature of government a thing polluted, which has nothing to do with Christian men" (*Inst.* IV.xx.2).

Furthermore, Calvin interprets the state as the instrument which accomplishes and fulfills its function as God's agent for the service of Christ's Kingdom. Thus, the secular power has meaning only on the condition that it exercises something good and useful for the public life.[7] In turn,

---

7. Calvin began with the fourth book of the *Institutes* based on our communion with

the task of the church is to appeal to the civil authority for promoting true religion and enforcing ecclesiastical discipline. The reason that civil government is necessary is that its origin and institution is sanctioned "by divine providence and holy ordinance . . . For God was pleased so to rule the affairs of men, inasmuch as he is present with them and also presides over the making of laws and the exercising of equity in courts of justice" (*Inst.* IV.xx.4). Therefore, the magistracy is ordained by God so that "they have a mandate from God, have been invested with divine authority, and are wholly God's representatives, in a manner, acting as his viceregents" (*Inst.* IV.xx.4).

In reference to Paul's letter (1 Cor 12:28), Calvin legitimizes civil power and authority in regard to serving and exercising every kind of just rule for the service of God. Therefore, civil power and authority must not go beyond their barrier, but must be faithful as God's vice-regents to Christ's Kingdom. Christ, in fact, is "the vice-regent of God" and every secular dominion symbolizes "the kingly authority of our Lord Jesus Christ." In speaking of civil government as the divine institution, Calvin's intention is to make clear the universal foundation of the one Lord Jesus Christ for the secular world, because the latter is grounded in and sustained by Christ. In this context, Calvin integrates civil government to the doctrine of the kingship of Christ. All magistrates and princes subject themselves to Jesus Christ with "humility and recognition of a common humanity in the exercise of all forms of earthly authority."[8]

As far as they are aware of being "vicars of God . . . they should watch with all care, earnestness, and diligence, to present in themselves to men some image of divine providence, protection, goodness, benevolence, and justice" (*Inst.* IV. xx.6). This statement demonstrates what their government should accomplish as God's deputies for Christ's Kingdom. Once these obligations are done according to the Word of God, they are in harmony with what the kingdom of Christ orders. There is a constructive cooperation between church and state.

As for the task and responsibility of civil government, Calvin interprets it in a twofold way, vertical as well as horizontal: first, "to cherish and protect the outward worship of God, to defend sound doctrine of piety and the position of the church, to adjust our life to the society of men, to

---

Christ concerning outward means or instruments, by which God calls us to and holds us (*Inst.* IV.i.1).

8. Wallace, *Calvin's Doctrine of the Christian Life*, 162.

form our social behavior to civil righteousness, to reconcile us with one another, and to promote general peace and tranquility" (*Inst.* IV.xx.2).

The task and responsibility of the civil government embraces not only all the activities (breathe, eat, drink, etc.) necessary for our living, but also prevents "idolatry, sacrilege against God's name, blasphemies." It keeps public peace and personal property safe and sound. "In short, it provides that a public manifestation of religion may exist among Christians, and that humanity be maintained among men" (*Inst.* IV. xx. 3).

As the appointed end of the state, the state is really under obligation to protect Christ's church from false teaching. To the extent that the secular government is faithful and obedient to its essential obligation, it belongs to Christ and Christ's eternal Kingdom. The civil government is indispensable and helpful for the wellbeing of the church.[9]

For Calvin, the obligation of secular government is defined not only in terms of its religious aspect, but also in terms of its social and political aspects. These two aspects are essentially inseparable from each other. This interrelationship should be kept in mind under all circumstances. The duty of civil power is to preserve and protect the wellbeing of citizens as well as the church. For Calvin, its meaning and significance can be found in the service of God. Thus Calvin refers to the pre-eminent responsibility of the civil authority in protecting and securing the right worship of God: "All have confessed that no government can be happily established unless piety is the first concern; and that those laws are preposterous which neglect God's right and provide only for men" (*Inst.* IV.xx.9). In Calvin's political ethics, spirituality and social justice remain united so that these two aspects belong to the one reality of Christian life.

If the first duty of secular power (which is also a concern of the First Table) is concerned about caring for the church, letting it preach the pure gospel, its second duty (that of Second Table) is to "do justice and righteousness . . . to deliver him who has been oppressed by force from the hand of the oppressor . . . not to grieve or wrong the alien, the widow, and the fatherless or shed innocent blood" (Jer 22:3).

---

9. By theocracy Calvin tries to show only the close connection between the two powers. For him "theocracy" does not mean "the domination of the church over the state, or in the sense of the domination of the clergy over the political government." Cf. Graham, *Constructive Revolutionary: John Calvin & His Socio-economic Impact* (Atlanta: John Knox, 1978) 63.

Based on the admonition of Jeremiah, Calvin states that the duty of magistrates is that "they are ordained protectors and vindicators of public innocence, modesty, decency, and tranquility, and that their sole endeavor should be to provide for the common safety and peace of all" (*Inst.* IV.xx.9). Exercising force, magistrates are required to be compatible with piety of God. Calvin sees the task of the magistrates in ensuring freedom, because "nothing is more desirable than liberty." In this regard he favored "aristocracy bordering on democracy," or "a system compounded of aristocracy and democracy" (*Inst.* IV.xx.8). Calvin's option for such combination is to guarantee secure and ordered liberty of church and human life in society better than both tyranny and anarchy.

Based on a discussion of the task and responsibility of civil authority, Calvin articulates the responsibility of citizens for the secular government, that is, obedience. The reason that they show obedience to the magistrates is that their office is bestowed as a jurisdiction by God. On that account they have "to esteem and reverence them as ministers and representatives of God" (*Inst.* IV.xx.22). At stake here is not magistrates as such, but the order itself which is "worthy of such honor and reverence that those who are rulers are esteemed among us, and receive reverence out of respect for their lordship" (*Inst.* IV.xx.22).

If the institution of secular government is grounded in God's providence, and its authority is granted for our good, without it, there would be chaos and confusion in the world. Therefore, we give thanks and obedience to the persons bestowed with authority as the representatives of God. No matter what form it takes, we are supposed to obey them. But civil obedience towards authority is limited, because in return, kings must be concerned about the commonweal. God creates kingdoms and the order of this world not to give privilege and preeminence to some people in the powerful institution, but to grant us to live peacefully according to such means of help.

Rulers are not appointed for their own sake, but to improve the common good. The rule which the authority exercises over the people is nothing but a service. Niesel's remarks in this regard deserve consideration: "The people are submitted to authority and authority is subject to the people it serves. This reciprocal relationship of mutual service is founded

The Spirit and the Church

on the fact that the sovereign Lord Himself stands over rulers and ruled and has established civil government for the good of men."[10]

Along this line, civil obedience to authority implies that God vindicates the right and sets up the authority of the rulers, while at the same time this divine vindication becomes a cornerstone to limit secular government. On what grounds? The legitimacy of a secular government arises from the mutual relationship in which the ruler also stands in obedience to God. If rulers are in a position to evade the command of God and see themselves as demigods, what would happen to civil obedience to the authority? If rulers tried to eliminate their obedience to God, and disposed of everything for their own purpose, they would have been illegitimate. Nonetheless, this does not mean that they are no longer entitled with authority.[11]

For Calvin, the worst tyranny would be better, more bearable, and more available than anarchy because it still serves to some extent to hold human society together. But it does not mean that there is an intrinsic quality and legitimacy in such tyranny. It is rather due to the grace of God who does not withdraw God's sanction from those rebellious rulers. If the corrupt secular authority performs a service for civil life to some extent, it is based on the grace of God. Therefore, citizens are required to give obedience even to a bad government. It is our own fault if God permits the wicked ruler of the government, because God judges us by sending evil rulers: "They who rule unjustly and incompetently have been raised up by him to punish the wickedness of the people" (*Inst.* IV.xx.25).

In such cases, Calvin recommends subjects under bad rulers to do penitence and prayer. By confessing our sins and misdeeds, we should pray to God so that God will bring again something good and benevolent changing the minds of bad rulers. The prayer of the church for the civil authority belongs to the task of the church: "Since God appointed magistrates and princes for the preservation of mankind, however much they fall short of the divine appointment," we must not stop loving what

---

10. Niesel, *Theology of Calvin*, 240.

11. For Calvin, there was a difference between secular and ecclesiastical authority. If the latter rebels against God, it not only loses its legitimacy but also every kind of claim to civil obedience. But if the former causes distress and confusion, even if they are declared as enemies of God, it still should be recognized, because God sets up kingdoms and principalities for our peaceful life. Cf. Niesel, *Theology of Calvin*, 241–42.

belongs to God.[12] Believers must not only obey the laws and the government of magistrates, but also supplicate God for their salvation through their prayers.

Be that as it may, Christ's Kingdom essentially means a stone of stumbling that brings ruin the powers of the world when they rebel against the majesty of Jesus Christ. How does God as liberator intervene in the midst of rebellion? "For sometimes he raises up open avengers from among his servants, and arms them with his command to punish the wicked government and deliver his people, oppressed in unjust ways, from miserable calamity. Sometimes he directs to this end the rage of men with other intentions and other endeavors" (*Inst.* IV.xx.30).

When the first type of human being carries out the taking up of arms against kings, which is a special and lawful call inspired by God, they should not violate by their action the majesty and dignity divinely implanted in civil authority. The second type of person executes their work leading a revolt against legitimate authority, but unwittingly they do the work of God. In either case, God accomplishes the divine liberating work "through them alike when he broke the bloody scepters of arrogant kings and when he overturned intolerable governments" (*Inst.* IV.xx.31).

The fear of God is the foundation of obedience from both sides of subjects and of magistrates. It is God that princes are to fear:

> . . . next to him we are subject to those men who are in authority over us, but only in him. If they command anything against him, let it go unesteemed. And here let us not be concerned about all that dignity which the magistrates possess; for no harm is done to it when it is humbled before that singular and truly supreme power of God. (*Inst.* IV.xx.32)

Thus the minister, the "mouth of God," has the duty of speaking out sharply against all injustice, all neglect of duty. From here occurs denial of obedience to civil power. In the context of tyranny, Calvin is concerned with political emancipation reflected in a political right of resistance. The church is to warn the authorities when they are at fault. A legitimate rebellion against the bad rulers should be led by lesser magistrates (*Inst.* IV.xx.31). Constitutional magistrates ought to check the tyranny of kings for the deference of the people's freedom when the rulers violate the freedom of the people.

---

12. *Opera*, 52, 267. *Comm.* 1 Tim 2:2. Cf. Graham, *Constructive Revolutionary*, 61.

The Spirit and the Church

For this political matter, Calvin takes into account historical examples in ancient time (the *ephors* of Sparta, the tribunes of Rome, and the demarchs of Athens, etc.) which restrained the willfulness of kings. Regardless of this fact, Calvin does not hesitate to warn resistance of private individuals against tyrants. Even though Calvin is very cautious to grant any endorsement to the popular revolution, his position in his Daniel commentary (Dan 6:22) is less firm: "For earthly princes lay aside their power when they rise up against God, and are unworthy to be reckoned among the number of mankind. We ought, rather, utterly to defy them (*conspuere in ipsorum capita*, literally, "to spit on their heads") than to obey them" (*Inst.* IV.xx.31, footnote).[13]

He is also not hesitant to urge constitutional magistrates to assume the duty of caring for the people's interest, and to provide for the people the "inestimable boon" of liberty: "I am so far from forbidding them to withstand, in accordance with their duty, the fierce licentiousness of kings, that, if they wink at kings who violently fall upon and assault the lowly common folk, I declare that their dissimulation involves nefarious perfidy, because they dishonestly betray the freedom of the people, of which they know that they have been appointed protectors by God's ordinance" (*Inst.* IV.xx.31).

Therefore, the church encourages the state and magistrates to protect the poor and weak against the rich and powerful. Preaching the gospel is linked with the demand for social justice, and political emancipation, denouncing all economic injustice and dethroning social privilege. The duty of magistrates is to observe justice for all people.[14]

Given this fact, Calvin's ethics of freedom, which is centered on Jesus Christ, understands also Christ as the Liberator who brings us freedom in the social and political realms. Based on Christ's love of God and of the neighbor, compassion for the weak and the oppressed is underlined in Calvin's ethics of freedom. This liberating ethics becomes also manifest

---

13. Calvin writes, "On this consideration, Daniel denies that he has committed any offence against the king when he has not obeyed his impious edict (Dan 6:23)" (*Inst.* IV.xx.32).

14. As Calvin writes, "A just and well-regulated government will be distinguished for maintaining the rights of the poor and afflicted ... it is obvious why the cause of the poor and needy is here chiefly commended to rulers; for those who are exposed and easy prey to the cruelty and wrongs of the rich have no less need of the assistance and protection of magistrates than the sick have of the aid of the physician." See *Comm.* Ps 82:3.

in his socio-ethical reflection and analysis of human economic activities and political problems.

Basically Calvin's socio-economic ethics pointed to a radical democratic idea, in which economic justice for equality and social concern for the poor comes into the picture on favor of the economic redistribution between the rich and the poor. Here Calvin's thought focuses on overcoming interpersonal conflict and social class antagonism in terms of mutual solidarity and love. This is an aspect of personal-social humanism in Calvin's social ethics. State intervention plays a significant part in setting up the public interest and commonwealth.

Calvin's political ethics, which is grounded in theocracy, shows how carefully and deliberately he takes up the issue of political resistance to tyranny. For Calvin, theocracy is a political, theological reality that takes seriously God as liberator, King of kings. Therefore, the sole ground for civil obedience as well as that of magistrates or rulers, lies in Christ's kingdom. In light of Christ's Kingdom, which is the Kingdom of all kingdoms, Calvin critically examines the authority of civil power and the legitimacy of civil obedience.

At the critical moment when this political power violates God's command and restrains the civil freedom, Calvin is still hesitant to grant any endorsement of rebellion until God intervenes in the political matter. Prayer and penitence is also an important component for his political ethics, which is characteristic of an aspect of confession and resistance in Calvin's political thought. In the end, God who is the King of kings challenges and corrects the fierce licentiousness of kings in terms of calling constitutional magistrates to defend the people's common good. God requires obedience from the side of the magistrates to resist for the sake of promotion of people's emancipation and freedom. Magistrates are called to defend and liberate the weak and the poor from political oppression. The church is entitled with warning the authorities, battling over interest rates, employment opportunities, and everything related to social justice.

Under all social political circumstances, Calvin keeps in mind that obedience to God is the priority. This aspect characterizes Calvin's political direction for emancipation and freedom in promotion of the common good in society. This political thought gains a more radical, democratic shape and contour through historical development among his followers in Scotland and France, as well.

Excursus

Christian Politics in Confession and Resistance

THE HISTORY OF FRENCH Calvinism can generally be taken as a history of martyrdom, which underwent various dramatic stages. Its historical development can be classified by and large as follows: first, from religious wars to the edict of Nantes under Henry IV; second, Richelieu-Mazarin and the decline of Huguenots; third, the end of Calvinism under Louis XIV with the Edict of Fontainebleau in 1685; and fourth, the new beginning after the French Revolution.[1] To deal with Calvin's stance on the right of political resistance, it is necessary to examine Calvin's personal relationship with the French Calvinists and his attitude toward the first French Huguenot war. In this light there should be a discussion of the more radical resistance theory of French monarchomachs (three significant Calvinists, Theodore Beza, Franz Hottman, and Philippe Du Pleissis Mornay).[2] However, in this chapter my attention will be given to Calvin's personal relationship with the persecution of French Calvinists. This history of persecution characterizes Calvin's political theology in the confession.

Calvin's later time in Geneva was preoccupied with socio-economic problems related to refugees and political-religious struggles, particularly in France. He kept in touch with the daily political events in his home country and, from this, constructed his own idea of the relationship be-

---

1. Cf. Joseph Chambon, *Der Französische Protestantismus: Sein Weg bis zur französischen Revolution* (Zurich: EVZ, 1943).

2. Additionally, Althusius, a German Calvinist, deserves to be considered in this context, because he was the second generation of Calvinist monarchomachs radicalizing the right of resistance in defense of populist revolution. In this regard he stands in parallel with the political philosophy of Rousseau. Cf. For the debate of the ambivalent relationship between Althusius and Rousseau. See Leopold Cordier, *Jean Jacques Rousseau und der Calvinismus: Eine Untersuchung über das Verhältnis Rousseaus zur Religion und religiösen Kultur seiner Vaterstadt* (Langensalza: Beyer, 1915).

tween church and state. During this time he wrote many treatises and letters regarding the political situation in France. Among them, his confrontation with the Nicodemites in France deserves to be understood in order to more fully grasp his political views.

From 1515, King Francis I maintained a policy of indifference toward French Calvinists, not because of his religious tolerance, but as a political power strategy. Around 1525, Pierre Leclerc began to organize a reformed community in Caen. In La Rochelle and Poitiers, Orleans, Tours, Blois, Dauphine and Languedoc many believers turned from Catholicism to Protestantism. However, in the 1540s, because of Francis I's political strategy, many French Calvinists (Du Chemin, G. Roussel, etc.) began to stand in collaboration with French Catholicism.

In order to understand Calvin's position of Reformation, it is important to take for example Calvin's correspondence with Jacob Sadolet (1477–1547), who was bishop of Carpentras in the district of Avignon and cardinal presbyter of St. Calixtus at Rome. Influenced by the humanism, Sadolet, a reform-interested Catholic Cardinal of North Italy, called for church reforms, being open toward Protestantism. In 1537 he wrote a friendly letter of invitation to Melanchthon, asking him to return to Rome. In his letter to Geneva (March 18, 1539), Sadolet openly admitted the partial corruption of the Catholic church, showing his interest in the people of Geneva in confusion and apostasy. During his exile from Geneva, Calvin was asked to reply to Sadolet's strategy of convicting Geneva to return to the Roman church.

Against Sadolet's letter, Calvin clearly gives an account of the Reformation teaching on justification. Although the church is important, its sole concern has to be for God's Word. Calvin refutes Sadolet's argument that the Reformation caused strife and division. Reformation is to set up the oldest and true church that is now almost destroyed rather than erecting a new church. As Karl Barth paraphrases Calvin's position, "the truth is that it seeks peace for the kingdom of Christ, but no other peace ... The only bond of church unity is for Christ the Lord, reconciles us to God the Father, to unite us in the fellowship of his body, so that by his Word and Spirit we grow to be one heart and one soul."[3]

In the midst of the naive confusion or collaboration, Calvin's confrontation with so-called Nicodemites characterizes his political view:

---

3. Karl Barth, *Theology of John Calvin*, 409.

Excursus: *Christian Politics in Confession and Resistance*

"Christianity without confession and also suffering is a 'phantom.' In order for us to become one they should stop to play a dirty game."[4] By the term "Nicodemites" Calvin means those French Calvinists with higher class and privileges.[5] They are categorized in four groups: one, the Reformed theologians blended with Catholicism, above all in case of Du Chemin, G. Roussel; two, "noble *prothonotaires,* who are quite content to have the gospel;" three, the early French humanists; and four, "the merchants and the common people."[6]

In this polemic against the Nicodemites, Calvin's sharp political stance is aimed at uncovering the hypocritical attitude of pseudo-Nicodemites. Hans Scholl's statement is in need of consideration: "The anti-Nicodemite writings of Calvin introduced and sharpened the famous politicizing of French Protestantism. At this point, the prophet's warning in the Old Testament is important for Calvin: 'How long will you hesitate between two parties?'"[7]

When it comes to political resistance, which arises out of our spiritual relationship with God, Calvin's anti-Nicodemite arguments brings his political stance to the fore, a stance which is characterized as a politics of freedom in confession under the presence and comfort of the Spirit.

Henry II, who succeeded his father as king in 1547, tried to destroy all Protestant groups. In the first three years of his reign, five hundred Protestants were arrested, and sixty among them were sentenced to death. A notorious *Chambre Ardente* was set up in France, which resulted in the extraordinary civil inquisition. With this inquisition, the civil authorities were in a better position to treat directly many Protestant followers and associations. In 1551, the Edict of Chateaubriand was introduced in defense of the Roman Catholic doctrine, giving a strong impulse to persecution. Five young students who trained themselves as preachers in Lausanne and worked in France were placed under arrest and sentenced to be burned alive in May, 1553. Nevertheless, in 1555, a congregation in Paris was set up by a pastor sent from Geneva and according to the Geneva church pattern, including a pastor, elders and deacons. On May 25, 1559, 72 representatives from twelve churches met each other and

---

4. C. O. 6, 606. Cf. Hans Scholl, *Reformation und Politik, Politische Ethik bei Luther, Calvin und den Frühhugenotten* (Stuttgart: Kohlhammer, 1976) 71.

5. Ibid., 71.

6. Ibid., 73.

7. Ibid., 78.

organized a General Synod of the Reformed Church in Saint-Germain-des-Prés, which is called *petite Genève*.[8]

The December 1559 martyrdom of Anne Du Bourg, who was executed in Paris as a young student, played a decisive role in deepening the political resistance of French Calvinists. It became significantly a "prologue of the night of Bartholomew" and "milestone in politicization of the French Protestantism."[9] Regarding this political event, Scholl has demonstrated that the political implication of the Du Bourg case is that she made a contribution through her martyrdom to solve "the task and calling, integrating the repentance to the politics." In a nutshell, Du Bourg's significance was pointing to the fact that "righteous and integral politics, good politics means—repentence."[10]

During this period of persecution Calvin stood in deep solidarity with these French Calvinists. His later correspondence was full of diplomatic advice and pastoral concern and was addressed to members of the French upper nobility, many of whom adopted the Reformed faith. His correspondence partners were people like Antoine de Bourbon, King of Navarre, Louis the Prince of Conde, Francis d'Andelot and Admiral Gaspar de Coligny, and their wives.

The sister of Francis I, Margarete of Angoulème, deserves consideration in the context of Huguenot persecution. After being remarried to Henry d'Albret in 1527, she became queen of Navarre. In her childhood she was educated and influenced by her Protestant mother. From 1544 on she led an independent government. Her religious writing *Miroir de l'âme de la pécheresse* showed her Protestant character, and was prohibited by Sorbonne Catholic scholars. Regardless of this fact, she had no hesitation in accepting the Protestants, who were under persecution, and granting them asylum in her territory.

Her daughter, Jeanne d'Albret also was associated with her mother's Reformed faith. She introduced Protestantism officially to her country, Navarre. Her son, Henry IV, who would become king of France, would play an important role in promulgating the Edict of Nantes on April

---

8. Hugenotten, *Geschichte eines Martyriums*, Ingrid und Klaus Brandenburg (Leipzig: Leipzig edition, 1990) 33.

9. Scholl, *Reformation und Politik*, 88. For a detailed analysis of the political impact of Du Bourg's case on Hugenotten political direction, ibid., 87–102.

10. Ibid., 102. Cf. Calvin's letter to his friend Ambrosius Blarer concerning Anne Du Bourg' confessing death. See Scholl, *Reformation und die Politik*, 61.

EXCURSUS: *Christian Politics in Confession and Resistance*

13, 1598, while his statement "Paris is worth a mass" was controversial. Besides, there were other people with high status who were oriented for the Reformed faith: Philippe Duplessis-Mornay, Louis I. de Conde, Gaspard de Coligny, and Theodore Agrippa d'Aubigne are prime examples.

The Reformed communities in France placed their trust in Calvin, asking for his advice on various religious and political problems with which they were confronted in the midst of persecution. Beza wrote to Calvin during his stay in France: "Dear brother, as you are unable to aid us by your presence, guide us like children by your counsel! . . . I would that our Lord would glorify the praise of his wondrous wisdom by your mouth."[11]

Calvin's advice to the members of the Reformed Church in France was related to life and death matters. He never gave up his uncompromising attitude toward people who were afraid of confessing boldly the Reformed faith. For example, in his letter to a lady who was placed under arrest while emigrating to Geneva, Calvin wrote: "If we find ourselves in such necessity that no other means can be found to deliver us from the tyranny of the enemies of the truth, but those subterfuges which might turn us from the right path, there can be no doubt that God has called upon us to seal our faith with our blood."[12]

During the period of the persecution, Calvin moved very carefully into active resistance, even indicating the possibility of breaking the law. "Assemble here and there in little parties," he wrote to the congregation at Poitou, "till all the members of the Church are united in the Kingdom of heaven . . . Fear of persecution must not deter us from seeking the living pasture, and following our good shepherd." Given this statement, Calvin's counsel is to take "a middle way between rashness and timidity." In this letter (to the Brethren of Poitou, September 1554) Calvin mentioned "a quiet and deliberate civil disobedience."[13]

But Calvin rejected the use of violence when he became aware of the violent rebellion at the church in Anjou. Calvin counseled them to "abandon such designs which will never obtain the blessing of God so

---

11. *Letters of John Calvin*, vols I–IV, edited by Dr. Jules Bonnet, English Translation of vols. I and II, Edinburgh 1835–37, of vols. III and IV, Philadelphia 1858, August 30, 1561. Cf to Peter Martyr, May 22, 1558, cited in Wallace, *Calvin, Geneva and the Reformation*, 160.

12. C. L. September 13, 1553. Cf. Wallace, *Calvin, Geneva and the Reformation*, 161.

13. Ibid., 162.

as to come to a happy issue, for He does not approve of them ... There is no excuse for Christians under these circumstances to refuse "to suffer for Him who died and rose again that we might dedicate our lives as a sacrifice to Him." To endure such sufferings is to be involved in our call in conformity to Christ.[14] This is also our genuine resistance, because "our only secure refuge against the heat, the stormy wind and every other danger, is under the shadow of his wings. As soon, however, as we begin to resist by force we put away his hand and his help from us." Though God "will always cause the ashes of his servants to fructify ... excesses and violence will bring with them nothing but barrenness. We must therefore, never abandon the conviction that the hairs of our head are all numbered, and that if God does permit us to go through extremities of suffering he will ensure that not a tear is in vain."[15]

Before the war occurred, there was a conspiracy in Amboise. In March 1560, La Renaudie marched with an army against Amboise, where the king's residence was located. This military action proceeded without Calvin's consent, and finally the Guises defeated La Renaudie with ease. The family of the Guise made good use of this victory to seize and exercise more political power. Upon the death of Francis II on December 5, 1560, ten-year old Karl IX assumed the monarchy under the regency of Catherine de Medici, who would hold power for about twenty-five years. Calvin's tone towards the conspiracy was very serious and he warned in his letter to Coligny, "If a single drop of blood were spilled, floods of blood would soon deluge Europe. Thus it were better that we should all perish a hundred times than expose the name of Christendom and the Gospel to such opprobrium."[16]

After the failure of the Amboise conspiracy, Calvin was asked about the possibility of open rebellion. In Calvin's view, especially under the gloomy situation of France, "if several of the princes of the blood royal sought to maintain their rights for the common good, and if the Parliament joined with them, it would then be lawful for all good subjects

---

14. C. L. to Church at Anjou, April 19, 1556. Cf. Wallace, *Calvin, Geneva and the Reformation*, 162–63.

15. C. L. to Church in Paris, September 16, 1557, to the Church at Aix, May 1, 1561, cited in Wallace, *Calvin, Geneva and the Reformation*, 163.

16. C. L. to Coligny, April 16, 1561. Cf. Wallace, *Calvin, Geneva and the Reformation*, 163–64.

Excursus: *Christian Politics in Confession and Resistance*

to lend them assistance."[17] In this case Calvin's reflection on the duty to resist is still alluding to his *Institutes* (IV.xx.30–31); however, he leaves a space for open resistance in emergency situations. The war of religion in France took place intermittently from 1562 to 1598.[18]

The first Huguenot war broke out in 1562. On March 1 the Duke of Guise led a brutal massacre on a Protestant congregation at Vassey, where the Protestants worshiped. The Reformed leaders had now reached the point at which they were justified in resisting with arms. Louis I, Prince of Condé and Admiral Gaspard de Coligny led the military resistance. A battle took place at Dreux on December 19, 1562 in which the Protestants were defeated, but the other side did not gain much. The Duke of Guise was eventually murdered by a Huguenot, De Merey. Negotiations took place between Catherine de Medici and Condé, the Protestant leader, which finally resulted in the Edict of Amboise in March 1563. This edict by example granted personal freedom of religion to Protestants, but not for common worship. But later the Edict of Vincennes (1563) and of Roussillon (1564) were promulgated to limit this freedom of religion.

With regard to this first war, where certain rules and doctrines could no longer hold, Calvin's attitude was situational, contextual and no longer doctrinaire. Once the first war occurred, French Calvinists were admonished to make a fresh judgment concerning what action to take in a legitimate self-defending manner. Calvin was supportive of the side of equity, even taking into account financial expenses for mercenaries, and talking over strategy most available to the situation.[19]

Furthermore, Calvin approved of Beza's involvement as a chaplain, and leader on the battlefield.[20] When the Treaty of Amboise was negoti-

17. Ibid., 164.

18. Cf. 1) 1562–1563 battle in Dreaux, December 19, 1562: Protestants lost, Edict of Amboise, March 12, 1563; 2) 1567–1568 battle in Saint Denis, November 10, 1567, Protestants lost, Edict of Longjumeau, March 23, 1568; 3) 1568–1570 battle in Jarnac, March 14, 1568, Protestants lost, the death of Conde, battle in Moncontour, October 3, 1569, Protestants lost, Edict of Saint-Germainen-laye; 4) 1572–1573 Edict of Boulogne; 5) 1574–1576 peace of Beaulieu; 6) 1577 peace of Bergerac; 7) 1579–1580 peace of Fleix, Edict of Nemours, 1585, which forbade Protestantism, treating them with death sentence; 8) 1586–1598 battle in Contras, Win of Protestants, murder of Heinrich III, August 1, 1589, battle in Arques, September 20/21, 1589, battle in Ivry, March 14, 1590, battle in Doullens, July 24, 1595.

19. C. L. to Bullinger, August 15, 1562; to the Churches of Languedoc, September 1562. Cf. Wallace, *Calvin, Geneva and the Reformation*, 164.

20. C. L. to Coligny, April 16,1561. Cf. Wallace, *Calvin, Geneva and the Reformation*.

ated, Calvin regarded it as "execrable," but he immediately advised that the arms should be laid down because of a "legitimate" council.[21] In fact, Calvin's political ideas gained more democratic shape alongside the Huguenot resistance movement. Stankiewicz formulates Calvin's influence in the following manner: "He [Calvin] had engendered in people's minds certain ideas which produced unpredictable effects. His ardent plea for religious autonomy carried the seeds of revolt into social and political matters, revolutionizing the whole of contemporary life."[22]

In light of what has been discussed, Calvin's theological stance towards political issues may well be characterized by the fact that political ethics comes out of confession, obedience, and resistance. This direction is not created in abstract table talks, but came to the fore through Calvin's passionate solidarity and involvement with his French associates. He was no longer a doctrinaire thinker, but a prophetic thinker, who related an eschatological dimension to the whole of political problems.

At this point Calvin's commentary on the book of Daniel is significant for his political thinking grounded in the eschatological dimension. In his truly prophetic foreword of this commentary, Calvin proclaimed no two kingdoms, but one kingdom and one reality which belong to God. Thus, there is no way to separate "hearing and doing," "praying and acting," but bring faith and deed together to realization. This dialectical dynamism is the mechanism of the Holy Spirit. Calvin's political theology in confession made the influence regarding the question about the resistance right. Such influence also gives clear indication about the political duty of resistance of faith among his followers in France as well as in Scotland in the subsequent historical development.[23]

---

21. C. L. to Soubise, April 5,1563. Cf. Wallace, *Calvin, Geneva and the Reformation*, 165.

22. W. J. Stankiewicz, *Politics & Religion in Seventeenth-Century France: A Study of Political Ideas from the Monarchomachs to Bayle, as Reflected in the Toleration Controversy* (Berkeley: University of California Press, 1960) 17.

23. Cf. Scholl, *Reformation und Politik*, 65.

Conclusion

In this study of Calvin's theology of the third article, I have made a concerted effort to shed light on his relevance to spirituality and social ethics. For this task, my focus was given to the Holy Spirit in creation. The Holy Spirit participates in the creation of the natural order, in establishing and restoring the integrity of human beings, *imago Dei*, and in the establishment of God's social and political ordinances. Understanding the Spirit as the Spirit of creation, Calvin's concern was clear in that creation is not a static, once-and-for-all event belonging to "a momentary and vanishing power of God" in the past. Rather it refers to a *creatio continua* particularly coupled with the providence of God in the dynamic activity of the Holy Spirit: "It would be absurd to circumscribe creation within such narrow limits, as though it were witness to a momentary and vanishing power of God, rather, it ought to be extended to a continuous administration" (*Comm*. Is. 37.16). It is not only from the Word of God, but also from his power, from the Holy Spirit that the creation and preservation of the world derives: "The world is no less the work of the Holy Spirit than of the Son" (*Inst*.I.xiii).

The Spirit as *Spiritus Creator* is a life-giving Spirit. Living in harmony with God as the Spirit, the source of life lives in harmony with all creatures. This concept of harmonious life leads to the ethical charge and stewardship of the regenerated, whose living stands in harmony with creation. God's ecological concern for creation goes hand-in-hand with reconciliation and the peace of human beings with creation. The Spirit as life-creating Spirit is not dualistically or pantheistically understood, but it expresses a biblical realism in terms of the Spirit, who is involved in our earthly life.

God as the *Spiritus Creator* enables life to be protected from secularization and the exploitation of nature, defending it from the destruction of the world through human violence. Therefore Barth is right in holding that the "pneumatological doctrine of creation" is a "special doctrine of

Calvin's." As Barth writes, "in this respect we may recall the striking doctrine of Calvin, on which research has thus far shed little light, concerning the Holy Spirit as the principle of life which rules not merely in the history of the saved community but also in the whole created cosmos as such" (CD IV/3.2:756).[1] Calvin's theology of the Spirit can be appropriated and discovered as a new theological paradigm for the program of reconciliation and harmonious life with nature in the ecological realm.

Calvin's theology of creation is similar to the ecological theology or cosmic Christology (Colossians 1). The sanctifying Spirit of Christ is not in contradiction to the life-giving and caring Spirit of God. Experience of the *Spiritus Creator* in faith is not limited to inner spiritual life, but leads Christian spirituality toward loving and caring for nature, plants and animals as God's creatures.

This life-giving dimension of the Spirit is not merely universal, but is an integral part of human life. The integrity of human beings lies in *imago Dei*. It is the soul, the human inner life, which is the "primary seat" of the *imago Dei*. "The image of God is engrafted in the soul in creation. It can be regarded as "inner good of the soul ... the perfect excellence of human nature" (*Inst*. I.xv.4). The *imago Dei* was, in Calvin's view, recognized "from the reparation of corrupt nature," and it is Christ "the most perfect image of God, who "restores us to a true and solid integrity" (*Inst*.I.xv.4). Like the order of creation, the image of God in human beings is dependent upon the work of the Holy Spirit. Not only through life-giving power, but also through conferring gifts, the Spirit regenerates and sanctifies the original order of human beings. "Natural," "super-natural," and "spiritual" gifts in this regard are mentioned (*Inst*. II.ii.12).

Calvin differs here from Augustine, who affirmed that some triadic structures in nature and in the human soul which a Christian can understand as analogies to the divine Trinity. That is, *vestigia trinitatis*, namely traces of the Trinity. This amounts to a similarity between Trinity and nature, God and creature. For Calvin, however, there is only one basis of salvation through God's action in historical revelation, but God as the creative spirit is operative in nature with the cosmic, hidden power.

Here, it is worthwhile to note the hidden, secret impulse of the Holy Spirit in Calvin's thoughts. Even though the whole order of nature is described as "perverted" by the fall of Adam (*Inst*. I.1.5), the Spirit operates

---

1. For Moltmann's criticism of Barth's statement, see Moltmann, *History and the Triune God*, 134.

Conclusion

not only as the sanctifier of human beings, but also as the impulse-giver for people outside the walls of Christian church: "Nor is there reason for anyone to ask, what have the impious to do with the Spirit, since they are utterly alienated from God? For when it is said that the Spirit of God dwells only in the faithful, that is to be understood of the Spirit of sanctification" (*Inst.* II.ii.16). The reprobates are to live within the operation of the Spirit. "The reprobates are sometimes endowed by God with the gifts of the Spirit, to execute the offices with which he invests them ... But this is widely different from the sanctification of the Holy Spirit, which the Lord bestows on none but his own children" (*Comm.* John 13:18).

Along this line, we are aware that two dimensions of the Holy Spirit, i.e., the sanctifying work and non-sanctifying work of the Holy Spirit, are correlated. This aspect uniquely characterizes Calvin's theology of the Spirit, integrating the knowledge of God and the knowledge of human beings in dynamic and actual sense.

It is the Spirit who, proceeding from the Father and the Son (*Inst.*I.xiii.18), who "sustains, quickens and vivifies ... in all things transfusing his vigor, and inspiring with being, life and motion" (*Inst.* I.xiii.14). The Spirit as the virtue and efficacy of all action involves the trinitarian fellowship through the dynamic bond between Father and the Son. For Calvin, God's revelation in Jesus Christ is the starting point for reflecting of the Trinity: "A mode of being (*subsistentia*) in the being (*essentia*) of God, which when contrasted with the other modes is distinguished from them by such characteristics (*proprietas*) as cannot be communicated to any other mode" (*Inst.* I.xiii.6). With this explanation, Calvin maintains that "in each several modes of being, the whole nature of the Godhead must be understood to be included together with what is proper to each" (*Inst.* I.xiii.19). Calvin's trinitarian thought in this regard is concerned about maintaining the trinitarian dogma in its integrity. Father, Son and Holy Spirit are not conceived of as different titles attributed to God merely to signify Godself in several manners.

In this light Calvin's theology of the Trinity is not to be understood as one alluring the slight tendency of modality of the one God, but maintaining that God is one God in three modes of being (*Inst.* I.xiii.2), securing the unity of God by distinguishing God's unity from idols and declaring God as the Lord in the encounter with the revelation of Jesus

Christ.² It is also the power and efficacy of the Spirit enabling trinitarian fellowship. Through the reciprocal perichoresis of the triune God, the life-creating spirit becomes the Spirit of Jesus Christ. This Spirit involves itself in a communicative way mediating dynamically the divinity and humanity of the one person Jesus Christ. The *ensarkos/asarkos* dynamic relation can be conceptualized in a dynamic and actual manner. Thus, the filioque addition to the creed is required to be understood not as a monarchical concept of God, rather a concept of attesting to the correspondence between the Son and the Spirit.

For Calvin, every efficacious presence of God in Christ is also to be interpreted in the horizon of the Spirit. Spirit brings Christ's benefits to us as the Spirit of communicator. From the Spirit we expect the gift of eternal life, the rebirth and the new creation of all living things, because the eternal spirit is *auctor resurrectionis Christi*.³ From here occurs our mystical union with Christ, in which we undergo mortification of self and vivification in the bosom of the Spirit. This becomes a new spirituality of *vita Christiana*. Here God is experienced not merely individually, but also interpersonally and socially. Based on the love for one another, human beings discover the image of God in one another, which actually correspond to the social fellowship of image of the Trinity. At this juncture, Calvin's concept of spirituality, which is grounded in the mystical union-experience of Christ, opens up the Christian life for justification, sanctification, and election.

Seeing *pietas* as the essential expression of Calvin's spirituality, Richard takes seriously the relationship between piety and justice as two attitudes constituting the wholeness of life.⁴ He is right in differentiating Calvin's spirituality from that of the *Devotio Moderna*. As he writes, "In Calvin, theology and spirituality found their unity: revelation, faith and doctrine, obedience and piety belong together. Calvin did not admit a mystical theology that exists independently of knowledge and doctrine."⁵ However, his characterization of Calvin's spirituality as "inner-worldly

---

2. Niesel, *Theology of Calvin*, 60.
3. CR 47, 48. Cf. Krusche, *Das Wirken des Heiligen Geistes nach Calvin*, 137ff.
4. Richard, *Spirituality of John Calvin*, 117.
5. Ibid., 129.

Conclusion

asceticism"⁶⁶ seems to me skeptical because he does not see Calvin's spirituality in solidarity with the poor and in favor of social emancipation.

In recent studies of spirituality, a separation is made between a dogmatic approach and an anthropological approach. Sandra Schneiders characterizes a dogmatic position as a definition "from above" and an anthropological position as a "definition from below."⁷ The former equates spirituality with the Christian life under power of the Holy Spirit and revelation. Spirituality is understood as dependence on dogmatic theology. The latter describes spirituality "as a way of engaging anthropological questions and preoccupations in order to arrive at an ever richer and more authentically human life."⁸

However, as far as Christian spirituality is concerned, a dogmatic approach in which human experience of God in Jesus Christ comes about through the power of the Holy Spirit should not be separated from the anthropological approach, integrating the cultural and social dimensions of human existence. In this sense, Calvin's spirituality, which stands not in separation, but distinction from the dogmatic reflection of the Spirit, can offer a good example for the study of spirituality.

When it comes to the relationship between sanctification and justification, the kingly and priestly offices correspond to sanctification (regeneration) and justification (reconciliation, forgiveness) of human beings: Jesus Christ died for our justification and was risen for our sanctification. This saving work of Christ becomes efficacious *pro nobis* and *in nobis* only through the work of the Holy Spirit. The Spirit may not be apart from Christ. Along this line, Calvin is not distracted from good works. Therefore, in his structuring of the *Institutes*, he arranges sanctification prior to justification. Instead of describing justification as the initial point in the process of renewal, Calvin conceives of justification as proceeding throughout the whole course of life. It is necessary to have this blessing not just once, but to keep it through the course of life (*Inst*.III.xiv.11). *Non separatio, sed distinctio* is characteristic of Calvin's thought in matters pertaining to sanctification and justification. As Lewis Rambo delves into

---

6. Ibid., 126.

7. Sandra Schneiders, "Spirituality in the Academy," in Bradley C. Hanson, ed., *Modern Christian Spirituality: Methodological and Historical Essays* (Atlanta: Scholars, 1990) 21.

8. Jean-Claude Breton, "Retrouver les assises anthropologiques de la vie spirituelle." *Studies in Religion/Sciences religiuses* 17 (1988) 101. Cf. Scneiders, "Spirituality in the Academy," 21.

religious conversion as a process, in terms of holistic considerations,[9] our spiritual relationship with God, in Calvin's view, is also considered as a continuous process and progress in a holistic manner.

Additionally, what is striking is Calvin's extraordinary insight of the secret impulse of the Holy Spirit in connection with the ungodly. His controversial concept of predestination is required to be seen from the hidden work of the Spirit: "God guides the heart of a profane man by a secret impulse" (*Comm.* Acts 23:19; cf. *Inst.* I.xvii.2). The ungodly are led by a secret impulse beyond the purpose of their own minds. Articulating the vestiges of the *imago Dei* in all human beings, Calvin refers to *singulares motus, specialis instinctus* and *particulares motus* in terms of works of the Spirit (*Inst.* II.ii.17).

The natural knowledge of God can be opened by, or derives from the secret operation of the Spirit. Reprobates in predestination should not be understood in a fatalistic, deterministic way. Rather the pneumatological aspect paves the way for the elect to bear witness to the ungodly by the proclamation of the Word. An understanding of God's eternal decree in light of the universal work of the Spirit could be a corrective to Calvin's complex of double predestination in supralapsarian sense.

In speaking of the Spirit and the law, there occurs a theological integration of Christian spirituality with social ethics in the pneumatological framework. Calvin is tireless in stressing Jesus Christ as the basis and foundation for Christian ethics. Christ *extra nos* is the norm for human spiritual experience and social concern. From this perspective, any individualistic approach to spirituality or, direct identification between the divine and the human is rejected by Calvin, because it is the Spirit who enables and communicates the spiritual relationship with God in a genuine sense.

In his ethical reflection on the law and discipleship, both the vertical and horizontal dimensions play a key part in the formation of Christian spiritual and social discipleship. His ethical concern for emancipation is a penetrating factor of Christian freedom. Calvin is, in fact, the theologian of freedom in such a way that this freedom means Jesus Christ. His theological reflection on the relation between church and state or political resistance, or economic justice in defense of the poor and the weak, can be seen as a part of his concern for emancipation and freedom. Calvin

---

9. Bieler, *Social Humanism of Calvin*, 68.

Conclusion

as an example for today teaches us to confront and continuously renew political and social realities in this line. When we come to his economic thought, "prosperity becomes general when the benefits of riches are shared among all men, when the means of production are spread among all, and when the work of each person receives an equitable part of collective wealth."[10]

In reflecting on spirituality and social ethics in Calvin's theology of the Spirit, the life of Christian spirituality is located and embodied in the midst of the world's turmoil. In this context, Calvin takes an ethical option for God's justice in solidarity with the poor and the oppressed, which articulates also an expression of our spiritual experience with God in Jesus Christ under the guidance of the Spirit. Basically this integration means "simultaneous commitment to God and to persons."[11]

In a nutshell, spirituality and social justice are for Calvin two sides of the same coin. This integration is primarily initiated from the divine side. However, God's action of God in Christ does not block out our discipleship and deeds; rather it encourages our response to God and our responsibility to neighbors in need, deepening gratitude, humility and hope in expectation of the coming God. Thus, Calvin's spirituality can be seen as one for the transformation of the world in light of the Word of God. Calvin's ethics exemplifies "Christ the Transformer of Culture."[11] Richard Schall refers to this model as the character of liberation in Reformed theology: "The vision of a reformed church always undergoing reformation, an *ecclesia reformata semper refeormanda*, along with the Protestant principle, which undercuts all attempts to sacralize the established order and thus directed the Christian life toward the radical transformation of society."[12]

In light of the gospel and culture in Calvin's thought, *theologia naturalis* is an object not merely transformed, but integrated, deepened and renewed in light of the theology of the Spirit. The Holy Spirit is the preserver of culture and the embracer of people outside the walls of Christianity. Christ in the presence of the Spirit is the mutual Transformer of gospel and culture so that a meaning of gospel could be deepened and actualized

---

10. Brown, *Spirituality and Liberation*, 117.

11. H. Richard Niebuhr, *Christ and Culture* (New York: Harper, 1951) 190–229.

12. Richard Schaull, *The Reformation and Liberation Theology: Insights for the Challenges of Today* (Louisville: Westminster John Knox, 1991) 18.

in an encounter with the hidden presence of the Spirit in other cultures and religions.

A study of the Spirit is constitutive for understanding the mutual relationship between spirituality and social ethics. To put it another way, the theory/practice relation is indispensable and must come into the picture if we understand the totality of human concrete life. At least for Calvin this relation arises from his struggling with his own times. For Calvin, theological reflection on secular matters "does not fall from the skies."[13] Rather it emerges through the social quest for solidarity and emancipation of the poor and oppressed in light of the Word of God. Therefore, the Christian is called as the one in the world witnessing the gospel and serving the poor and the weak. Unfortunately, this prophetic side of Calvin has been neglected and caricatured in subsequent development of Calvinism.

As far as the Spirit and the church are concerned, they are correlated to each other. The church is founded on Christ alone by the preaching of the Word and administration of the sacraments. For this particular task no one is qualified without being endowed with the Spirit. Preaching and the two sacraments are efficacious under the work of the Holy Spirit. It is not the sacraments, but the Spirit who confers the grace of Jesus Christ to us. In understanding the real presence of Christ, the Holy Spirit is at the heart of Calvin's theology. The real presence should not be localized at one place or be in a bodily presence. Rather, it is the Spirit who joins us to Christ, and makes possible a genuine participation in his flesh and blood. The Spirit brings us into the presence of Christ, that is, into spiritual communion with him. Based on this, Calvin opposes the Roman Catholic and Lutheran views of the real presence.

However, the difference between Luther and Calvin is not irreconcilable. In this matter, Calvin was never under the influence of Zwingli, but an ardent reader of Luther. The Zurich concordance between Calvin and Bullinger should not be the basis for Calvin's teaching of the Eucharist. Unfortunately, the debate between Calvin and the defenders of Lutheran orthodoxy was mistakenly overestimated. In the 1536 edition of the *Institutes* Luther's influence is predominant in Calvin's reflection on the Eucharist. From Luther's writings—for example, *De captivitate Babylonica Ecclesiae*, "Sermon upon the True and Sacred Body of Christ" (1519), or "Confession and the Sacrament" (1524)—Calvin showed his agreement

13. Georges Casalis, *Correct Ideas Don't Fall from the Skies: Elements for an "Inductive Theology,"* trans. Jeanne Marie Lyons and Michael John (Maryknoll, NY: Orbis, 1984).

Conclusion

with Luther's theology of the Eucharist. However, from 1536 onward, Calvin was not comfortable with Luther's doctrine of the ubiquity of the body of Christ. Melanchthon, a sympathizer with Calvin, encouraged him to avoid any conflict with Luther. Apart from the idea of ubiquity, Calvin showed his dependence on Luther in the *Institutes*.

However, Calvin's sympathy could not be applied to Zwingli and Oecolampadius. Calvin wrote in the *Second Defense Against Westphal*: "I read in Luther that Oecolampadius and Zwingli had allowed nothing to remain of the sacraments but bare and empty figures (symbols). I was so set against their works, I confess, that for a long while I abstained from reading them."[14]

Against a Zwinglian overemphasis on the subjective side of human faith, Calvin stressed faith as the work of the Holy Spirit. This faith is directed toward the Word and the sacraments. Because they are of divine institution for our salvation, we have no right to reject them. For Calvin, the sacraments are not merely understood in a subjective way, but in a sense necessary for salvation. In opposition to those who recognized nothing but spiritual communion with the spirit of Christ, Calvin reaffirms that in communion Christians enter not only into a relationship with the spirit of Christ, but also to his body and blood.

Although this teaching is very strongly emphasized in the *Confession on the Eucharist* (1537), Westphal saw in Calvin the same spiritualistic attitude as done in Zwingli. Calvin never gave up a realistic concept of the real presence of Christ in the power of the Holy Spirit. Like Luther, Calvin affirms that the Eucharist resides in the promise, i.e., the words of institution. Neither the Roman transubstantiation nor the Lutheran consubstantiation, but also neither the Zwinglian symbolization were in accord with Calvin's notion of the real presence, which includes Christ with his death and resurrection as the content of the Eucharist. In his commentary on 1 Corinthians 11:24, Calvin writes:

> For Christ does not simply present to us the benefit of his death and resurrection, but the very body in which he suffered and rose again. I conclude, that Christ's body is really, that is, truly given to us in the Supper, to be wholesome food for our souls. I use the common form of expression, but my meaning is, that our souls are

---

14. Wendel, *Calvin*, 333.

nourished by the substance of the body, that we may truly be made one with him.[15]

Apart from the particular question regarding the way Christ's body is present, we have no difficulty in this passage discovering an echo of Luther in Calvin's thought. Calvin had no hesitation in putting his agreement with the Confession of Augsburg and the Concord of Wittenberg.

As the church is regarded to be the body of Christ, so Christ is the head of the body. Life in the body of Christ is a binding of its members with each other. This is *communio sanctorum*. The communal life in the body of Christ is also expressed in prayer. Prayer is not meritorious work or achievement, but becomes efficacious through the power of the Spirit. The Spirit takes effect within us through prayer. The church under the power of the Spirit speaks of the correlation between the Spirit and the church.

With the correlation between Christology and pneumatology in mind, I depict Calvin's political ethics as an ethics of freedom in confession, obedience and resistance. This political, ethical orientation basically favors the emancipation of the oppressed from the oppressor. Calvin's conclusions on civil government refer to "modern representative assemblies as the bearers of *ephoral* powers," and as a result, Calvin saw them as "possessing the authority to resist tyrannical kings."[16] In this light Calvin can be regarded as a prime mover encouraging "his followers to look for alleged examples of *ephoral* authorities within the ancients and to the humanist legal scholar, the normative-constitution of France, so prompting them to sustain their revolutionary conclusions with arguments drawn from legal and historical as well as purely theological sources."[17]

This prophetic spirit gained a more democratic form by way of the French Monarchomachs. Finally, this idea can be seen as a forerunner of the development of people's initiative or sovereignty of people in the future, which was later elaborated by Althusius, and finally Jean Jacques Rousseau by moving toward the French Revolution on the one hand, and by Goodman and John Knox on the other hand. Even though Calvin was hesitant about directly granting to individual people the right of open

---

15. Ibid., 340.
16. Skinner, *Foundations of Modern Political Thought*, 2:314.
17. Ibid., 234.

Conclusion

rebellion in Scotland,[18] his appeal to the magistrate's right of resistance can be regarded as a prime mover for democratic development in later history.

From the socio-economic thought of Calvin, he was keenly aware that riches were robbed from the lives of the poor. His socio-economic ethics is really prophetic in its concern for the poor and the weak. His positive attitude about socio-economic matters is not based on "worldly asceticism," but on Christian love for mutual common good. It points toward Christian democracy with social justice. Weber's ideal type, which focused on the relationship between Calvinism and capitalism, missed one important point: the rationalization of life was already in existence in Greek thought as well as scholasticism. The medieval work-prayer connection, medieval spirituality and a positive appraisal of human achievement were a part of the contribution to rationalization. Calvin never approved of the idea of a competitive society based on rivalry and struggle, which is really impossible within the true Christian body. The spirit of capitalism cannot be one-sidedly attributed to Calvin's theology.[19]

Calvin was not a scientist, economist, or political scientist, but a theologian. What he intended programmatically was to shape human life in light of the Word of God under the dynamism of the Spirit, which stands basically in political and economic solidarity with the poor and in *diakonia* for them. This prophetic concern, which is socially oriented, is what Calvin strove to seek in the field of politics and social economy. According to Tawney, the best of the social theory and practice of early Calvinism is that they were consistent. Most tyrannies have satisfied themselves with oppressing the poor. Calvinism had little pity for poverty; however, Calvinism also distrusted wealth, when "it [Calvinism] distrusted all influences that distract the aim or relax the fibers of the soul." "It did its best to make life unbearable for the rich."[20]

---

18. Cf. Hotman's writings to Calvin in December 1558: "Everyone was pleased with your letters in which you openly indicated that you were outraged by the inflammatory writings of Goodman and Knox." Calvin, *Opera Omnia*, ed. Baum et al., 17:396–97. See Skinner, *Foundations of Modern Political Thought*, 2:302.

19. Troeltsch's insistence that "capitalism was able to steal into the Calvinistic ethic, while it was rejected by the Catholic and the Lutheran ethic," does not articulate the point of the problem. Troeltsch, *Social Teaching of the Christian Churches*, 2:643.

20. Tawney, *Religion and the Rise of Capitalism: A Historical Study* (London: Murray, 1926) 132.

It is Calvin who encouraged his followers to question and challenge any kind of political absolutism, standing in favor of the oppressed. This political idea is coupled with his economic thought in which the state ought to intervene in regulating the wealth for the common good and benefits. *Laissez-faire* capitalism of Puritan Calvinism was not his concern. According to Calvin, the church in society is, in terms of the spirit of the gospel, called and committed to social justice and human concern. The business of the church is to proclaim the Word of God, and to bring its spirit actively to the world in concern for transformation.

Unfortunately, in contrast to Calvin, churches in the Reformed tradition and heritage have lost sight of this dynamism through history by overstressing intellectualism and by expressing allegiance and adherence to the status quo of their national, social, racial and economic surroundings, even solidifying false solidarity with those powers and principalities. By uncritical adaptation to the world, individualism and self-seeking spiritual egoism substitute for compassion and concern for the total structure of the society.

It is vital to talk about Calvin as an example concerning spirituality and social justice, because "we accept Calvin as an example or as a model only in the measure in which he has, in an unforgettable way, pointed out to the church of his time the road of obedience: obedience of thought and deeds, social and political obedience. An authentic and true follower of Calvin has only one road to follow: obeying not Calvin himself but the one who was the Master of Calvin."[21]

In the ecumenical dialogue with the Eastern church, which prevents theology from isolating spirituality, there is a tendency running toward integrity between Christian life and the experience of God with the doctrine. According to Vladimir Lossky, spirituality is the expression of a doctrinal attitude: "Mysticism and theology support and complete each other. Moreover, "Theology could not be merely a rational deduction from revealed premises because *theologia* was inseparable from *theoria* or contemplation."[22]

In the history of Western Christianity, a separation has been made between theology and spirituality. Therefore, theological reflection is assigned to formulate and analyze dogmatic statements, while the expe-

21. Bieler, *Social Humanism of Calvin*, 64.
22. Philip Scheldrake, *Spirituality & History: Questions of Interpretation and Method* (New York: Crossroad, 1992) 49.

rience of God remains related to the inner dimension of spiritual life. Out of this a false dichotomy can occur. However, similar to the Eastern tradition, in understanding theology as vital and experiential in character, Calvin integrates spirituality with a theological method, exemplifying the unity of theology and spirituality. This unity between theology and spirituality is required today, as Hans Küng has argues:

> The dogmatist and the mystic, the theologian and the saint were each to go his separate way . . . In the final analysis . . . theological research carried on without reverence and meditation easily degenerates into a speculating or historicizing scholasticism . . . Similarly, pious meditation engaged in without . . . clear theological norms has a way of degenerating into an intellectually inbred or sentimental religiosity.[23]

Furthermore, in the midst of social problems, we should not shrink from our prophetical *diakonia* towards reconciliation of racial antagonism, social justice, preservation of the creation of which our society is most urgently in need: "All the church can do is to let herself be led ever anew and be reformed by this only truth which is the living Christ—the eternal Christ who by his Holy Spirit is active in human history. The church therefore is always in movement, always becoming, always reformable, always in quest of new discoveries concerning the truth about herself,"[24] or, in other words, "*Il est trespasse apres avoir acheve sa course: mais cependant L'Esprit de Dieu est immortel.*"[25]

---

23. Cf. Richard, *Spirituality of John Calvin*, 188.

24. Bieler, *Social Humanism of Calvin*, 71.

25. "He has passed away after finishing the course of his life: Nonetheless, the Spirit of God is immotal." CR 51, 250. Cf. Karl Barth, *The Theology of John Calvin*, trans. Geoffrey W. Bromiley (Grand Rapids: Eerdmans, 1995) 3.

Afterword

The Ecumenical Legacy of John Calvin in Reformed and Neo-Pentecostal Dialogue

THIS IS A RESPONSE to "the Final Report of the International Dialogue between Representatives of the World Alliance of Reformed Churches and Some Classical Pentecostal Churches and Leaders 1996–2000."[1] The final report entails a dialogical effort and a mutual fellowship over the period of five years from 1996 to 2000 and shows a genuine *esprit* for aiming at a confessional ecumenicity between two different traditions that have long been uncomfortable with and even hostile to each other. It reflects how participants of both parties have renewed their misunderstanding and prejudices within the spirit of mutual understanding and respect. Additionally, the significance of this report lies not in theological or professional achievements but in its spiritual effort and practical concern to surmount differences.

The dialogue fosters friendship, and encourages participants to carry out the study performed in the dialogue, and to help them realize the necessity and importance of dialogue between two churches within self-critique and self-transformation in terms of reciprocal investigation and challenge. The concern in this response essay is to help two churches improve future ecumenical fellowship and cooperation in terms of my several suggestions and proposals.

In this report we see Jesus Christ at the center of two churches in that both confess their loyalty to the Nicene-Constantinopolitan Creed. Therefore, the witness to Jesus Christ is the common basis, albeit in different approaches to the person and the work of the Holy Spirit. Generally speaking, the reformed understanding of Jesus Christ is based on a

---

1. *Pneuma: The Journal of the Society for Pentecostal Studies*, 23 (2001) 9–37, 54–60. My article in this text is revised and reprinted here with permission.

AFTERWORD: *The Ecumenical Legacy of John Calvin*

threefold understanding of the person and work of Jesus Christ, so-called Christ's *munus triplex*, which is of pneumatological relevance and even closely related to the anointing of the Holy Spirit. As for Christ's prophetic office, we notice that "Jesus Christ received anointing, not only for himself that he might carry out the office of teaching, but for his whole body that the power of the Spirit might be present in the continuing preaching of the gospel." (*Inst.* II.xv.2)

The kingly office refers to the eternity of Christ's dominion, which inspires us to have hope for blessed eternity and immortality. In addition, the spiritual nature of Christ's kingly office refers to the sovereignty of Christ. "Christ's kingdom lies in the Spirit" (*Inst.* II.xv.5). Christ's kingly office is also related to personal and social sanctification, as long as Christ as King rules us through his Spirit, by leading our struggle with the oppressed world. The priestly office is treated in the context of reconciliation and intercession of the Mediator.

Beginning with Christ's sacrificial death, we are granted the efficacy and benefits of his priesthood. Our justification becomes possible through the priestly office in which Christ offers a sacrifice and is the objective basis of our justification. Given this fact, the report needs to reflect more on the person and work of Christ and the relevance of justification by the Holy Spirit for promoting the purpose of dialogue with the Pentecostal churches.

Addtionally, in the report we see an omission of discussing justification *extra nos* (Reformed understanding of it) and justification of synergism (Pentecostal-Holiness understanding) in a thorougoing way. This aspect underlines a traditional tension between election and human will. Like Luther who sees justification *extra nos* correlated with sanctification and divinization in light of the presence of Christ dwelling in faith, Calvin, in his concept of Christ-union, distinguishes justifying grace from sanctifying grace. This double grace is not merely "spiritless" or legalistic, as some Pentecostalists argue. Rather, Reformation theology of justification, as seen in light of Christ-union, accentuates experiential and transformative relationship with the living Christ in the power of the Spirit. What makes the double grace so vivid, lively, dynamic, and effective lies in our union with Christ.

Although Calvin's view of justification implies the imputation of God's righteousness based on forgiveness of sins (*Inst.* III.xi.4), the righteousness of Christ makes us also partakers in the eternal blessing of the heavenly Father. The effect of our incorporation into Christ, which is dynamically communicated to us through the presence of the Spirit, leads to the double movement of *mortification* of the flesh and *vivification* of the spirit. The aspect of Christ *extra nos* is not separated from the aspect of Christ *pro nobis* and *in nobis* which characterizes the progress of sanctification in light of *semper reformanda*.

According to Wesley, a preliminary divine grace comes first to awaken the natural conscience and empowers human will. The grace of God is experienced objectively as justification and subjectively as regeneration, thus leading the regenerated gradually toward the state of Christian perfection. When compared to Calvin, Wesley's idea of justification and sanctification seems strikingly similar, albeit with different approaches and accents. What has been an obstacle to a fellowship between the Reformed church and Methodist or Holiness churches, however, is the contrast between the Calvinist doctrine of double predestination and human will in cooperation with the grace of God. To the degree that human responsibility in Wesley's thoughts can be understood as an initial expression of prevenient grace, it is important to note that Calvin's idea of election can be seen also as an initial expression of *arcano Spiritus instinctu*.

Calvin was not able to fully develop an inclusive concept of predestination following the consequence of his *universal* concept of the Spirit. This leaves open a possibility of particularism or inclusivism in his teaching of predestination. Calvinist orthodoxy (Beza and Gomarus) affirmed the doctrine of double predestination (*praedestinatio gemina*) in the Canons of Dort in 1618 and in the Leyden Synopsis of 1628. This doctrine proposes that before the creation of the world, God resolved to elect the ones in Christ, but to reject the others because of their sins. In fact, God's eternal decision about salvation and damnation depends provisionally and historically on human faith or disbelief regardless of God's grace in Jesus Christ in eternity for all.

However, Moyse Amyraut at the Huguenot Academy in Saumur in the seventeenth century followed in the footsteps of Calvin's concept of *electio generalis* according to which God "announces salvation to all men indiscrimately (*Inst.* III.xxiv.17)." This aspect refers to the general proclamation of the gospel in the sense of a hypothetical universalism (*universalismus hypotheticus*).[2]

2. Moltmann, *Coming of God: Christian Eschatology*, trans. Margaret Kohl (Minneapolis: Fortress, 1996) 246–48.

AFTERWORD: *The Ecumenical Legacy of John Calvin*

In a similar fashion, Karl Barth's theology of election has little to do with particularism in principle nor with automatic universalism. His Christocentric understandimg of predestination retrieves Luther's *theologia crucis* and radicalizes the concept of election beyond Calvin in favor of God's determination of Godself in eternity. God's eternal resolve is so inclusive that it becomes manifest in Jesus Christ. As Barth states, "God in His free grace determines Himsef for sinful man and sinful man for Himself. He therefore takes upon Himself the rejection of man with all its consequences, and elects man to participation in His own glory" (*CD* II/2 & 33, 94ff.). Luther's profound insight into *theologia crucis* provides a point of departure for Barth to deepen a Christological election in the sense of open universalism. Karl Barth, defender of Calvin, is navigating on the basis of "the irrevocably dialectical reality of God's Revealed Word in Jesus Christ"[3] toward universalism.

Given this fact, it is vital to retrieve Calvin's inspiring idea of the cosmic and hidden work of the Spirit in relation to the double predestination. Calvin's remark on a relation between the secret impulse of the Spirit and the reprobate is worthy of consideration. "The reprobate are sometimes affected by almost the same feeling as the elect, so that even in their own judgment they do not in any way differ from the elect ... But this does not at all hinder that lower working of the Spirit from taking its course even in the reprobate (*Inst.* III.ii.11)." According to Calvin, the truth of predestination does not lie in spiritual egotism of the elect, but in witnessing to the sovereign initiative of God. Although *electio generalis* as such is not identical with the election of salvation, *election specialis*, the actual election can be understood as effective of general election.[4]

In light of God's initiative grace, a human effort in receiving the Holy Spirit—as visible in Pentecostal Holiness churches and sometimes resulting in overemotionalism—needs to take into account Wesley's idea of preveneint grace. Likewise, the Reformed church should take issue with Calvinistic predestination in light of the hidden work of the Spirit.

The report, in the heading of Spirit, Kingdom, and Creation (thesis 88), "recognizes the Spirit's role at the beginning of creation as well as acknowledge the Spirit's role in the sustaining and renewing of creation." If the fulfilled Kingdom means Shalom for the totality of creation (thesis

---

3. David Tracy, *The Analogical Imagination: Christian Theology and the Culture of Pluralism* (New York: Crossroad, 2000) 417.

4. Krusche, *Das Wirken des Heiligen Geistes nach Calvin*, 235.

91), the theology of the Spirit meets a theology of ecology and nature. When it comes to nature, one suggestion is a theological way of integrating and renewing *theologia naturalis* by way of the pneumatology in Calvin's thought. It would be meaningless to talk about an independent natural theology on the ground of nature alone in estrangement from a cosmic work of the Spirit. Natural theology is included and integrated into clear focus within the theology of pneuma. Along this line, it is necessary to consider that *Gratia non tollit naturam sed perficit* (Grace does not destroy but completes it) in light of universal work of the Holy Spirit.

Unlike the medieval theology of the doctrine of grace and sacraments, Calvin takes seriously the Spirit in creation as *creator spritus*, Spirit of God and of the Son. For Calvin the Spirit as life-giver creates, preserves, and quickens all living creatures, continuously working as *continua inspiratio* (Ps 104: 29) from the presence of God's future within that process.[5]

The universality of God is also part of God's revelation and reconciliation in light of the in-breaking reality of the eschatological kingdom. Concepts such as *theatrum gloriae Dei* (John Calvin), the parabolic character of the world in service of God's Word (Karl Barth) or "Christian theology itself as the true natural theology"[6] need to be deepened and expanded by encounter with the wisdom of other religions and natural sciences politically, culturally, and ecologically toward the Future of God.

In fact, Calvin's language of *theatrum gloriae Dei* is of metaphorical and hermeneutical character. Nature in the stage of God's glory would become the indwelling space of the Spirit, becoming a theater in expectation of God. As Bouwsma states, "Calvin's spirituality was suffused with a numinous awe that characteristically found expression in figures drawn from the energies operating in nature."[7]

In this time of global ecological crisis, Judeo-Christian tradition is heavily charged with assuming "nature as a mere backdrop for the human play."[8] Furthermore, in speaking of historical roots of the modern ecological and environmental crisis, Lynn White Jr., accuses the "orthodox

---

5. Pokinghorne's theistic approach seems to be more in similiarity with Calvin's doctine of the Holy Spirit rather than the panentheist thinkers. Cf. John Polkinghorne, *The Faith of a Physicist* (Minneapolis: Fortress, 1996) 152.

6. Moltmann, *Experiences in Theology*, 73.

7. W. Bouswma, "Spirituality of John Calvin," in *Christian Spirituality*, 2:323.

8. H. Paul Santmire, *The Travail of Nature: The Ambiguous Ecological Promise of Christian Theology* (Minneapolis: Fortress, 1985) 1.

Christian arrogance toward nature" "bearing a huge burden of guilt" for the contemporary dying process of nature.[9]

In recent literature about improving a relation between theology and nature, we are aware that a theology of nature, unlike a traditional doctrine of creation, constructs a theological perspective and spectrum influenced and reconceived by natural scientific findings. Given the relationship between theology and natural science, Pannenberg argues that Christian theology has failed to explore a teaching of the Holy Spirit with respect to the phenomena and structures of life as explored in biology.[10]

If the presence of God can be recognized in the process of *creatio continua*, a theological concept of divine interaction within a cosmic process can be consonant with the activity of the Spirit in a universal and cosmic dimension. Nonetheless, the work of the Spirit in continuing creation cannot be identical with unfolding physical process as such, because the experience of God's otherness or sovereign freedom is not compatible with the problem of evil and victimization not only in society and cosmos, but also in an evolutionary optimism. For Calvin the Spirit's work is hidden and concealed within the flow of the very present process. The Triune God loves human beings, the world, and the cosmos in freedom and self-limitation, that is, in a Spirit of transcendence and immanence.[11]

This aspect refers to Calvin's language of hidden-revealed God or comprehensible-incomprehensible God. In this light, Calvin's emphasis on the role of the Spirit in creation needs to be extended and developed to reconstruct an ecological theology of nature. The doctrine of the Spirit and creation cannot be adequately discussed without relation to a theology of nature for today.[12] Calvin's sense of the beauty of nature is marvelously striking: "While we contemplate in all creatures, as in a mirror, those immense riches of his wisdom, justice, goodness, and power, we should not merely run them over cursorily, and, so to speak, with a fleeting glance,

---

9. Ibid., 2

10. Pannenberg, *Jesus—God and Man*, 171.

11. In a discussion of Spirit's immanence and evolutionary process, Polkinghorne takes into consideration the freedom of the Spirit. Cf. Polkinghorne, *Faith of a Physicist*, 150–51.

12. Cf. "The Doctrine of the Spirit and the Task of a Theology of Nature" in Wolfhart Pannenberg, *Toward a Theology of Nature: Essays on Science and Faith* (Louisville: Westminster John Knox, 1993) 123–37.

but we should ponder them at length, turn them over in our mind seriously and faithfully, and recollect them repeatedly" (*Inst.* 1.xiv.21).

Furthermore, Calvin apprehends the living creatures as witness of God to human beings. "The little singing birds are singing of God; the beasts cry unto Him; the elements are in awe of Hm, the mountains echo His name; the waves and fountains cast their glances at Him; grass and flowers laugh out to Him. Nor indeed need we labor to seek Him afar, since each of us may find Him with himself, inasmuch as we are all upheld and preserved by His Power dwelling with us."[13]

A critical realist, Ian Barbour, in analysis of God's relation to the world, presupposes that Calvin's insistence on God's sovereignty along the lines of Jewish thought (God as Lord and King of the universe) and medieval thought (its emphasis on divine omnipotence) is regarded as a systematic development of the monarchical model of God as the absolute monarch ruling over God's kingdom.[14] In a similar fashion, Sallie McFague deals with Calvin's idea of *theatrum gloriae dei* in such a way that nature is only the stage or background for the real action. To overcome a Christian understanding of creation as "merely the backdrop of salvation"[15] she proposes a Cosmic Christ. Another feminist theologian Rosemary Ruether has bolstered a strong critique of Calvin's understanding of human beings in light of the divinely created social order. In the Calvinist tradition, male domination and female subordination has come into a positivist and legal order of creation, in which "domination and subjugation represent the original divinely created order of things."[16]

Nonetheless, Calvin's metaphorical sense in his religious discourse appears to be social and inclusive, so that Calvin has little to do with the ascetic tradition of Western spirituality. Calvin was well aware that God's fatherhood was metaphorical, because God's incomparable love for all living creatures could not be expressed better than that. Calvin, although coupled oftentimes with an image of the most patriarchal type, did not

---

13. Calvin, "Preface to the New Testament," 1535; cf. John T. McNeill, *The History and Character of Calvinism* (Oxford: Oxford University Press, 1967) 232.

14. Ian Barbour, *Myths, Models and Paradigm: A Comparative Study in Science and Religion* (New York: Harper & Row, 1974) 156.

15. Sallie McFague, *The Body of God: An Ecological Theology* (Minneapolis: Fortress, 1993) 181.

16. Rosemary R. Ruether, *Sexism and God-Talk: Toward A Feminist Theology* (Boston: Beacon, 1983) 99.

AFTERWORD: *The Ecumenical Legacy of John Calvin*

discard the biblical language of expressing human experience of God as a mother.

In commentary on Isaiah 42:14 "I will cry out like a woman in labor, I will gasp and pant," Calvin writes: "[God] compares himself to a mother who singularly loves her newborn child, though she brought him forth with extreme pain ... But in no other way than by such figures of speech can his ardent love towards us be expressed."[17] Similarly Calvin describes Christian community as mother. "There is no other way to enter into life unless this mother (the church) conceive us in her womb, give us birth, nourish us at her breast, and lastly, unless she keep us under her care and guidance until, putting off mortal flesh, we become like the angels"(*Inst.* IV.i.4).

A feminist challenge for the discipleship of equals is based on the inclusive, open and multicultural aspirations of early Christian communities. At this juncture, a Reformed–Pentecostal dialogue needs to seek an ecclesiology in affirmation of the difference, diversity, and plurality in the presence of the Spirit.[18]

When Christianity comes to East Asian countries, an inevitable encounter with indigenous culture takes place. If we agree that "the Holy Spirit is present and active, not only in the Christian Church, but also in human history and in various cultures" (Thesis 19), how do we discern and listen attentively to God's strange, even ominous voices outside the walls of Christianity, even from the spirituality of indigenous people? East Asian culture is deeply embedded with religious pluralism. There has been religious tradition in co-existence between Confucianism, Taoism, and Buddhism which are still influential in the life, orientation, and mindset of people living in the East Asian culture. When Christianity comes to such a multi-religious matrix, a discussion of gospel and enculturation poses a serious question and challenge to Western Christianity heavily influenced under Greco-Roman culture. The task of enculturation refers to a new task of *missio Dei* in light of the prevenient work of the Holy Spirit. To what extent do theology and church in a pluralistic context pursue their unique confession of Jesus Christ without doing harm to other religious ways?

17. Calvin, *Comm.* Isa 42:14.

18. For the creative encounter between feminism and Reformation theology, see Serene Jones, *Feminist Theory and Christian Theology: Cartographies of Grace* (Minneapolis: Fortress, 2000) 159.

Christian Spirituality and Ethical Life

Concerning the relationship between gospel and culture, the report emphasizes the Reformed notion of the Spirit universally at work in other cultures and religions as compared to Pentecostal individualistic understanding of the Spirit. The report deals with gospel and culture under the heading of Holy Spirit and *Missio Dei*. In light of *Missio Dei*, participants in the dialogue need to pay more attention to the current debate on theology and religious pluralism, because the cultural and religious issue has become a point of conflict especially in Asian contexts. Western Christianity is oftentimes associated with imperialism in the past. Every culture is unique and regarded as an integral part of the theatre of the glory of God, not merely an object to be transformed. Rather, it can serve as a vehicle for deepening and actualizing the biblical message in its own context.

Western theology and philosophy, based as they are on reason and rationality of Enlightenment, are deeply challenged in present day discussion by postmodern thinkers in view of their collaboration with scientific nihilism, totalization of the other, and ecological devastation.

If the Reformed/Pentecostal dialogue expresses its trust in *Spiritus Creator*, they cannot remain exclusivist but must be dialogical and recognize the other in witnessing to the work of the Spirit outside the walls of Christianity. In this regard, the Reformed church has to take into consideration a theological discussion of religious pluralism.[19]

In response to Calvin's theology of the Spirit in cosmic and universal dimension, Karl Barth deepens this line of thought, actualizing a universal reconciliation in light of death and resurrection of Jesus Christ. Let us introduce his daring insight into the relationship between gospel and culture: "No Prometheanism can be effectively maintained against Jesus Christ. As the One who suffered and conquered on the cross, He has destroyed it once and for all in all its forms. But this means that in the world reconciled by God in Jesus Christ there is no secular sphere abandoned by Him or withdrawn from His control, even where from the human standpoint it seems to approximate most dangerously to the pure and absolute form of utter godlessness... Even from the mouth of Balaam the well-known voice of the Good Shepherd may sound, and it is not to be ignored in spite of its sinister origin."[20]

---

19. John Hick and Paul F. Knitter, eds., *The Myth of Christian Uniqueness: Toward a Pluralistic Theology of Religions* (Mayknoll, NY: Orbis, 1987) x–xi.

20. *CD* IV/3.1:119.

AFTERWORD: *The Ecumenical Legacy of John Calvin*

Concerning the liturgy, the Reformed church in the report has a unilateral understanding of worship. As for the marks of the church, we include two sacraments (i.e., baptism and the Lord's Supper alongside the preaching.) Instead of the twofold understanding of baptism, (i.e., water baptism and spirit baptism), which is dominant in the Pentecostal church, the Reformed church confesses that there is one baptism in water and the Holy Spirit in line with Pauline theology. The sacraments do not confer the grace they promise. Instead, this grace is effective only through the work of the Holy Spirit under whose power the church exists. In the life of worshipping congregations, Word and sacrament have an inseparable and integral relationship in celebrating the death, resurrection, and coming of Jesus Christ.

Fortunately, the report finds it significant that "deep dialogue concerning the role of sacraments or ordinances, and the place of the gifts of the Holy Spirit, may lead to mutual enrichment" (Thesis 41). Calvin understands the sacrament as the visible form of the real presence of Christ through the power of the Sprit, just as preaching is the audible form of the Word. Calvin is consistent and more emphatic in using his favorite image of engrafting to describe what is happening in the Lord's Supper. "Christ descends to us both by the outward symbol and by his Spirit that he may truly quicken our souls by the substance of his flesh and of his blood" (*Inst.* IV.xvii.24). At this point, participants are encouraged, Reformed representatives in particular, to study Lutheran/Reformed dialogue concerning the Lord's Supper.[21]

From an East Asian perspective, the significance of Lord's Supper should be reformulated and restressed in relation to Jesus's descent into hell, which has been long neglected especially in the Korean Protestant Church. Unlike the Korean Presbyterian Church which does not allow for recitation of Jesus's descent to hell in the Apostle's creed, Calvin himself takes seriously Jesus's descent to hell (*Inst.* II.xvi.10). For Calvin, Jesus's descent into hell expresses "the spiritual torment that Christ underwent for us." Calvin makes the point that Christ paid "a greater and more excellent price in suffering in his soul, the terrible torments of a condemned and forsaken man." This is the place where the lowest humiliation of his suffering takes place.[22]

---

21. Cf. William G. Rusch and Daniel F. Martensen, eds., *The Leuenberg Agreement and Lutheran-Reformed Relationships* (Minneapolis: Fortress, 1989).

22. Jan M. Lochman, *An Ecumenical Dogmatics: The Faith We Confess*, trans. David Lewis (Philadelphia: Fortress, 1982) 143–46.

If Christ is fully present and received in the Supper, we need to ask who Jesus Christ coming in the Supper is. This is the cosmic Lord who died, descended into hell, destroyed the power of death, was resurrected, and is coming. Does this Lord have to exclude our departed ancestors who died without having known the gospel of Jesus Christ? The East Asian understanding of the Eucharist can serve as an inspiration in the encounter with the Asian spirituality of filial piety in Confucianism.

As for the spiritual gifts in the Reformed tradition, an understanding of the supernatural gifts has been neglected. Many Reformed scholars prefer to use Calvin's following remark to keep aloof from or to reject charismatic manifestations. In opposition to the Roman Catholic theology of miracle or to Anabaptist fanatics, Calvin insisted that "that gift of healing, like the rest of miracles, which the Lord willed to be brought forth for a time, has vanished away in order to make the new preaching of the gospel marvelous forever" (*Inst.* IV.xix.18).

Following this statement, the Reformed-Presbyterian churches have tended to favor a dispensationalism of spiritual gifts. However, Calvin's understanding of charismatic gifts should be discussed anew in the context of the Christ-union. Calvin takes the mystical urge, which is the last stage of contemplative life prior to purgation and illumination, as his point of departure when considering a mystical union with God (or Christ) from a pneumatological point of view. Calvin explains our union with Christ in emphatic terms, such as the "joining together of Head and members," the "indwelling of Christ in our hearts," or the "mystical union." Hereby "Christ, having been made ours, makes us sharers with him in the gifts with which he has been endowed" (*Inst.* III.xi.10).

In this regard, justification and sanctification, faith and morality, and election and human freedom are seen in light of engrafting into Christ. Calvin's statement in his letter to Peter Martyr Vermigli is worth considering: "I know only this: that through the power of the Holy Spirit the life of heaven flows down to earth, for the flesh of Christ is neither life giving in itself nor can its effect reach us without the immeasurable work of the Spirit. Thus it is the Spirit who makes Christ live in us, who sustains and nourishes us, who accomplishes everything on behalf of the Head."[23]

The mystical union between Christ and human beings in Calvin's teaching presents not only an ethical concern but also a possible similar-

---

23. John Calin, Letter 2266 to Peter Martyr Vermigli, August 8, 1555; *C.O.* 15: 723.

AFTERWORD: *The Ecumenical Legacy of John Calvin*

ity to the Greek Orthodox teaching of theosis (i.e., human participation in the divine nature.) Calvin, reminiscent of Irenaeus and other Geek fathers, stresses that "We trust that we are the sons of God because the Son of God by nature assumed to himself a body of our body, flesh of our flesh, bone of our bones, that he might be one with us, so might be in common with us both Son and Son of Man" (*Inst.* II.xii.2).

Seen in this perspective, Calvin's mystical union is viewed as analogous to the Greek Orthodox teaching of participation, so that the relation between sanctification and divinization can be united dynamically through the power and efficacy of the Spirit. In recent ecumenical dialogue between the Orthodox and Lutheran church, *theologia crucis* becomes a basis for a discussion of the relevance of justification for theosis. Thus Calvin's understanding of mystical union may well be a basis for encouraging the Reformed representatives to engage in a more profound understanding of the power and efficacy of the Spirit in their own tradition. Like Luther's idea of "the real presence of Christ in our faith" (*In ipsa Christus adest*),[24] Calvin's union with Christ is not satisfied with the forensic dimension of justification, but it goes beyond by actualizing the effective, transformative dimension of sanctification. It also implies an idea of participation in the divine life, in which human work and spirituality could be positively appreciated in the sight of God. In fact, the spiritual life for Calvin highlights and culminates in the *visio Dei*.

Calvin's theology is ecumenically relevant and fruitful. His concept of the union with Christ, with its profound meaning for spirituality, should be renewed in our encounter with Pentecostal spirituality. In a sense, the Reformed/Pentecostal dialogue is one of the most stimulating and challenging areas of ecumenical theology, calling for global awareness and sensitivity to the work of the Spirit as *Creator Spiritus* in the church, society, and cosmos. It is my expectation that those who participate in the dialogue will learn from each other and make this spiritual venture more successful through ongoing consultation and publication. Hopefully, the Reformed church can be renewed and transformed by the deep challenge of Pentecostal friends, taking seriously its lost tradition of spirituality and the Holy Spirit.

Calvin's ecumenical legacy is dialogical, in embrace of others, and inclusive. In his time of turbulence he was highly concerned about "pro-

---

24. Cf. Braaten and Jenson, eds., *Union with Christ*.

mote (ing) the consolidation of the churches of the Reformation and even proposing 'a free and universal council' to end the divisions and 'reunite (ing) all Christianity.'"[25] My last word is one of thanks and encouragement to all who participate in a continuing conversation between these two traditions, Reformed and Pentecostal. May the future of the Reformed/Pentecostal friendship reveal the Holy Spirit encouraging us "into a solidarity of destiny and hope with all creation."[26]

---

25. McNeil, *History and Character of Calvinism*, 200.
26. Lochman, *Ecumenical Dogmatics*, 194.

Index

Adiaphora, 104, 105
Arianism, 35
Arcano Dei instinctu, 17, 20, 76, 150
Aristotle, 117
Asarkos, 41–43, 138
Athanasius, 42, 55
Augustine, Saint, 3, 4, 36, 55, 56, 136

Baptism, 115, 157
Barth, Karl, 1, 2, 14, 25, 55, 58, 59, 75, 90, 128, 136, 151, 156
Beza, Theodore, 133, 150
Brunner, Emil, 14, 25, 26
Buber, Martin, 31
Buddhism, 155

Capitalism, 145, 146
Charismata, 1, 53, 54, 57
Christian freedom, 13, 103–8
Christ-union, 14, 46, 51, 53, 59, 70, 77, 79, 81, 109
Communicatio idiomatum, 40
Communio sanctorum, 144
Communion with Christ, 11, 47, 61, 67, 72, 75, 76, 96
Concord of Wittenberg, 144
Confession of Augsburg, 144
Confession of Westminster, 5, 32
Confessions of Dort, 5, 150
Confucianism, 155, 158
Consubstantiation, 143
Continua inspiratio, 22, 23, 152

Creatio continua, 21, 153
Creatio ex nihilo, 16, 21
Creator spiritus, 16, 20, 75, 77, 80, 152, 159

De Condé, Louis I., 130
Decalogue, 81, 91–95
Deification, 54–56
Devotio Moderna, 33, 138
Divinization, 55–57
Du Bourg, Anne, 130
Duplex gratia, 14, 60, 68, 69, 79, 90

Election, 8, 14, 70–80, 110, 113
Ensarkos, 41, 42, 138
Ephor, 125
Ephorial power, 125, 144
Essentia, 23, 137
Eutyches, 41
Extra Calvinisticum, 43

Fidei effectus, 53
Filioque, 37,
French Calvinists, 14, 127, 128
French Revolution, 144

Gaspard de Coligny, 131, 133

Henry IV, 130
Homoousios, 35
Huguenots, 127, 133
Hypostasis, 34, 39

Note: Some entries that appear throughout the book, such as John Calvin, are not listed in the Index.

Index

Hypostatic union, 6, 41
Hypostatic unity, 39, 43

Imago Dei, 24, 64, 76, 89, 91, 100, 110, 135, 136
Imitatio Christi, 101
Inner-worldly asceticism, 138, 139
In ipsa christus adest, 159
Irenaeus, 55

Justification, 7, 8, 13, 14, 47, 48, 49, 55, 60, 61, 64–70, 75, 79, 90, 103, 104, 107, 109, 111, 139, 149, 150, 158

Knox, John, 144
Krusche, Werner, 3, 4, 42, 50, 64, 65

Libertines, 20, 87
Logos ensarkos, 41–43, 138
Lossky, Vladimir, 146
Luther, Martin, 41, 43, 56, 90, 142–44, 151
Lutherans, 142

Martyr, Vermigli Peter, 48, 158
Marx, Karl, 13
Melanchthon, 128, 143
Missio Dei, 155, 156
Modalism, 36
Moltmann, Jűrgen, 1–4
Monarchical Sabellianism, 36
Monarchomachs, 127, 144
Munus triplex,
 of Christ, 6, 43, 44, 65, 68, 79, 149
Mysterium tremendum, 25
Mystical communion, 47
Mystical theology, 49
Mystical union, 11, 12, 47, 52, 54–57, 68, 158, 159

Nestorius, 41
Nicene Creed, 35
Nicodemites, 128, 129

Niesel, Wilhelm, 5, 12
Officium ususque legis, 86
Opera trinitatis ad extra sunt indivisa, 38
Ordinatio Dei, 107, 125
Ordo politicus, 107
Ordo salutis, 68
Osiander, 52, 56

Perichoresis, 35, 36–38, 42, 44
Persona, 33–35
Pneuma, 22
Point of contact, 25
Predestination, 5, 70, 71–77, 103, 140, 150
Prosopon, 34
Puritanism, 5, 144, 146

Real presence, 111, 117, 118, 142
Regeneration, 8, 29, 30, 59–61, 69, 84, 103
Reprobatio, 70, 73–77, 79, 151
Ritschl, Abrecht, 49

Sabellianism, 36
Sacra unitas, 48
Sacraments, 8, 50, 55, 109, 111, 114–16, 118, 119, 142, 143, 152, 157
Sadolet, Jacob, 128
Sanctification, 7, 8, 12–14, 29, 48, 54, 56, 60, 61, 63, 64, 66–70, 79, 88, 91, 103, 104, 109, 139, 149, 150, 158
Seinsweise, 23, 36
Semper reformanda, 63, 141, 150
Sensus divinitatis, 25, 27
Servetus, 34, 41
Signa posteriora, 73
Solus Christus, 104
Spiritus creator, 7, 19–22, 31, 75, 77, 80, 135, 156
Subsistentia, 34, 137
Supralapsarian, 140

Index

Syllogismus practicus, 73, 74, 77

Tamburello, Dennis, E., 11, 12, 25, 27, 49
Taoism, 155
Theosis, 54, 55
Transubstantiation, 117, 143
Trinitas, 2

Ubiquity, 43, 117
Unio cum christo, 11, 50, 68, 118
Unio mystica, 50, 68

Union sacrée, 11
Union with Christ, 7, 11, 12, 49, 56, 71, 75, 97, 118, 158

Vestigia trinitatis, 136
Vivification, 61, 64, 150

Weber, Max, 145
Wendel, Francois, 73

Zwingli, Ulrich, 142, 143

www.ingramcontent.com/pod-product-compliance
Lightning Source LLC
Chambersburg PA
CBHW050815160426
43192CB00010B/1765